Sentiment Analysis in NLP

Sentiment Analysis in NLP

Techniques, Applications, and Future Directions

Shanliang Yang

Shandong University of Technology
China

IEEE*Press*
WILEY

Published by John Wiley & Sons, Inc., Hoboken, New Jersey.

Library of Congress Cataloging-in-Publication Data has been applied for:

Print ISBN: 9781394349111
Epdf ISBN: 9781394349142
Epub ISBN: 9781394349128
OBook ISBN: 9781394349159

Cover Design: Wiley
Cover Image: BlackJack3D/Getty Images

To my family, whose unwavering love and support made this book possible, and to all researchers and practitioners dedicated to advancing the understanding of human emotion through artificial intelligence.

Contents

Acknowledgments

I would like to express my sincere gratitude to the editorial team at Wiley for their professional guidance and continuous support throughout the publication process. This work was supported by the Shandong Provincial Natural Science Foundation (No. ZR2024QF022). I am also thankful to the reviewers and colleagues who provided valuable feedback on the manuscript. Special appreciation goes to the open-source community and researchers whose datasets and tools greatly contributed to this work. Finally, I extend my deepest thanks to my family for their patience, understanding, and encouragement during the long period of writing and revision.

About the Author

Shanliang Yang, PhD, is a faculty member and master's supervisor at the School of Computer Science and Technology, Shandong University of Technology, China, specializing in natural language processing and artificial intelligence (AI) with a strong focus on sentiment analysis, multimodal learning, and ethical AI. He has led one project funded by the Provincial Natural Science Foundation and published 30 academic papers, and this book represents his comprehensive contribution to the field, designed to serve as a bridge between foundational linguistic theories and state-of-the-art deep learning and large language model applications for researchers, practitioners, and graduate students.

About the Companion Website

This book is accompanied by a companion website.

https://www.wiley.com/go/yang/sentimentanalysis1

To access the website materials, click on the link under Related Resources on the book's page on wiley.com. You can also find this by searching www.wiley.com for the ISBN 9781394349111.

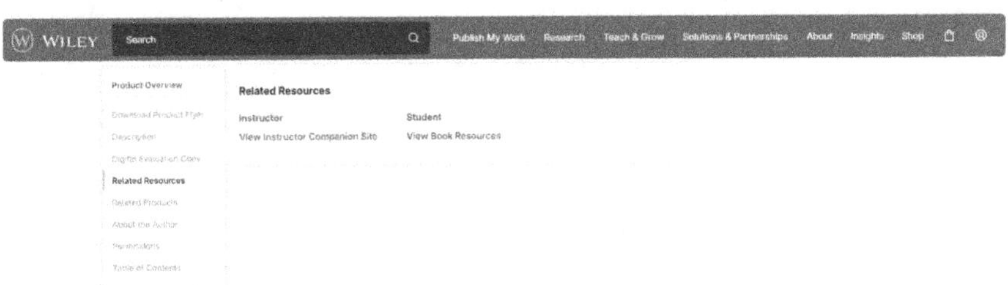

This website includes:

- Complete list of links

1

Introduction

1.1 Overview of Sentiment Analysis

Sentiment analysis, a key subfield within natural language processing (NLP), has gained immense importance in recent years due to its ability to extract and analyze subjective information from large volumes of text, audio, and visual data [1, 2]. As digital content and social media have proliferated, the need to understand public opinion, emotional tone, and consumer sentiment has become crucial for businesses, governments, and organizations. Whether it's assessing customer feedback, monitoring social media conversations, or gauging political sentiment, sentiment analysis provides valuable insights into the collective mood of a population or specific group. This book serves as a comprehensive reference for researchers, practitioners, and graduate students, aiming to bridge the gap between foundational linguistic theories and state-of-the-art deep learning techniques in sentiment analysis.

At its core, sentiment analysis involves identifying emotions, opinions, and sentiments expressed in various forms of communication. These sentiments are typically classified into categories such as positive, negative, or neutral, though more sophisticated models can detect nuanced emotions and subjectivity. As technologies like deep learning and machine learning (ML) have evolved, sentiment analysis has become increasingly accurate, able to handle more complex tasks such as aspect-based analysis, sarcasm detection, and real-time sentiment monitoring. The growing demand for sentiment analysis tools and techniques is driven by its applications in business intelligence, public safety, marketing, healthcare, and beyond.

1.1.1 Definition and Scope of Sentiment Analysis

Sentiment analysis refers to the computational task of identifying and extracting subjective information from natural language data [3]. It involves determining the emotional tone behind a body of text, audio, or visual data, and classifying it into various sentiment categories such as positive, negative, neutral, or even more specific emotions like anger, joy, fear, and surprise. Sentiment analysis, as a key component of opinion mining, focuses on understanding the emotions, attitudes, evaluations, and subjective states expressed by individuals or groups within digital content.

Sentiment analysis is not just about detecting words that indicate sentiment but also about understanding the context and polarity of those words. It considers aspects such as sarcasm, irony, and implicit sentiment, which are essential for accurately interpreting opinions in nuanced communications. Beyond mere categorization, sentiment analysis also involves assessing the intensity or strength of the sentiment, which can vary in degree (e.g., "very happy" vs. "somewhat happy"). Furthermore, it increasingly integrates multimodal data, combining text with audio cues (such as tone or pitch in speech) and visual cues (such as facial expressions) to achieve a more comprehensive understanding of sentiment [4]. These key modalities—textual, audio, and visual data—each contribute unique insights, enabling sentiment analysis systems to capture a fuller spectrum of emotional expression.

To better understand how these modalities and techniques converge into a functional system, Figure 1.1 illustrates the general framework of a sentiment analysis system. The process typically begins with data ingestion from various sources, followed by preprocessing and feature extraction phases where raw data is converted into a machine-readable format. These features are then fed into a sentiment classification model, ranging from lexicon-based approaches to advanced deep learning architectures, which outputs the sentiment polarity, intensity, or specific emotion. Finally, these results are translated into actionable insights for specific domain applications.

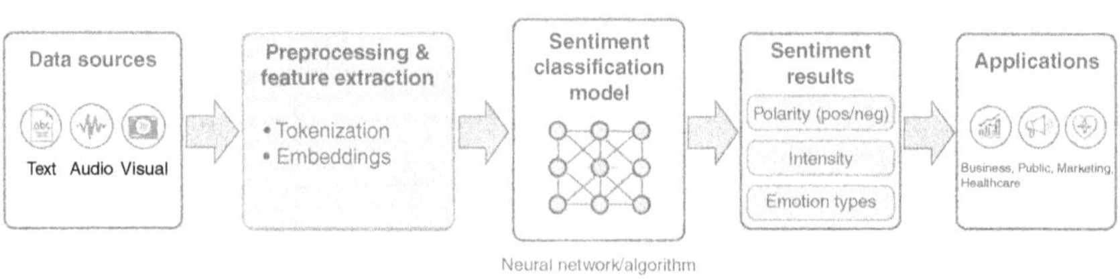

Figure 1.1 A general framework for sentiment analysis.

1.1.1.1 Key Modalities of Sentiment Analysis

- Textual Data: The most common and primary source for sentiment analysis, involving textual content from sources like product reviews, social media posts, blogs, and news articles. Text-based sentiment analysis typically involves techniques such as tokenization, part-of-speech tagging, and dependency parsing to capture the emotional connotations of the words used.
- Audio Data: Sentiment analysis is extended to voice data, where features like intonation, pitch, and speech rate are analyzed to detect the emotional state of the speaker. In customer service applications, for example, analyzing the tone of a caller's voice can help assess frustration or satisfaction levels, even when the words themselves may be neutral.
- Visual Data: With advancements in computer vision, sentiment analysis is now being applied to visual data such as facial expressions and body language. By analyzing how a person expresses emotions through their face or posture, systems can infer whether someone is happy, sad, angry, or neutral.

1.1.1.2 Scope of Sentiment Analysis

The scope of sentiment analysis has expanded considerably in recent years, evolving from its early focus on simple text-based emotion detection to more complex, multimodal, and cross-cultural applications. Initially, sentiment analysis was primarily concerned with analyzing written text—such as product reviews, social media posts, and blogs. Today, however, sentiment analysis spans a wide range of data types and methodologies, reflecting the growing demand for tools that can process vast amounts of subjective data across multiple platforms and domains. As technologies in artificial intelligence (AI), deep learning, and real-time data processing continue to evolve, sentiment analysis is becoming more sophisticated and capable of addressing diverse challenges.

- Multimodal Sentiment Analysis: One of the major developments in sentiment analysis is its ability to integrate multiple modalities—text, speech, and visual data—into a cohesive analysis [5]. For instance, while textual sentiment analysis identifies the words used to express sentiment, speech sentiment analysis adds another layer by evaluating intonation, pitch, and rhythm in spoken language. Similarly, visual sentiment analysis interprets facial expressions and body language, providing a richer, more nuanced understanding of emotional cues. By combining these various data streams, sentiment analysis can offer a more complete and accurate assessment of public or individual sentiment in contexts such as customer service, political debates, and healthcare.

- Industry-specific Applications: While sentiment analysis has broad applications, its scope within specific industries is also growing. In marketing, it is used not just to understand customer opinions but also to influence purchasing decisions through targeted advertising and sentiment-driven strategies. In finance, sentiment analysis has emerged as a tool to predict stock market movements based on public sentiment and market sentiment indicators. Similarly, in political science, sentiment analysis is increasingly used to monitor public opinion during elections or political campaigns, providing insights into voter behavior and preferences.
- Real-time and Large-scale Analysis: With the rise of big data and social media, sentiment analysis is increasingly being used in real-time applications. The ability to analyze massive streams of data as they are generated—such as tweets, news articles, and blog posts—has revolutionized how businesses, governments, and organizations monitor public opinion. Real-time sentiment analysis enables instant feedback loops, allowing for immediate responses to emerging trends, customer concerns, or public sentiment shifts. Whether it's managing a public relations crisis or responding to customer inquiries, the ability to assess sentiment as it happens is a critical advantage in today's fast-paced digital landscape.
- Cross-cultural and Cross-lingual Challenges: As sentiment analysis tools are applied globally, understanding sentiment across different languages and cultures has become a key challenge. Sentiments and expressions of emotion can vary significantly between languages and regions, complicating the task of building universally applicable sentiment analysis models. For example, humor, irony, and sarcasm are often culturally specific and may not be easily understood by algorithms trained on data from one culture. Additionally, linguistic nuances such as idiomatic expressions or regional slang can alter the sentiment conveyed in a message, requiring sophisticated cross-lingual and cross-cultural models. This area of research is particularly important for global businesses and organizations aiming to monitor and understand sentiment in diverse populations.
- Ethical and Privacy Concerns: As sentiment analysis tools become more powerful and pervasive, concerns around ethics and privacy have come to the forefront. The ability to analyze and infer emotions from individuals' digital footprints raises significant issues related to data privacy, consent, and transparency. Ensuring that sentiment analysis is used responsibly—especially when dealing with sensitive data such as personal opinions or mental health information—is a critical aspect of the field's future. Moreover, ethical considerations around the potential for sentiment manipulation (e.g., using sentiment analysis in political campaigns or marketing) highlight the need for strict regulations and guidelines.

The scope of sentiment analysis has expanded beyond simple text-based emotion detection into a more complex, multimodal, and cross-cultural domain. This evolution has been driven by advances in AI, deep learning, and real-time data processing, allowing sentiment analysis to address a wide range of challenges and applications. From integrating multiple data types for more accurate analysis to handling real-time, large-scale data in applications like social media monitoring and customer feedback, sentiment analysis continues to grow in its capacity to provide actionable insights. However, challenges remain, particularly in terms of cross-cultural and cross-lingual sentiment understanding, ethical concerns, and domain-specific adaptation. As sentiment analysis evolves, its scope will likely continue to broaden, further embedding it into industries ranging from marketing to healthcare, politics, and beyond.

1.1.2 The Growing Importance of Sentiment Analysis

Sentiment analysis has rapidly gained significance in recent years, driven by the explosive growth of digital content and the increasing complexity of data analysis. As organizations collect vast amounts of data from social media, customer feedback, surveys, and online forums, sentiment analysis has become an indispensable tool for extracting valuable insights from unstructured, subjective data.

With the rise of big data technologies, the volume of data generated daily has reached unprecedented levels. Traditional data analysis methods, which are typically structured and quantitative, fall short when it comes to processing the vast amount of unstructured, emotional, and opinion-driven content found in social media posts, product reviews, and other digital interactions. As a result, sentiment analysis has become a critical component of big data analytics, allowing organizations to process, categorize, and analyze subjective information at scale. By doing so, businesses can uncover hidden insights from their data, such as customer sentiments, emerging trends, and social attitudes, enabling them to make data-driven decisions with greater accuracy.

The ability to analyze sentiment in real time is particularly crucial in the era of big data [6]. Sentiment analysis allows for immediate understanding of public opinion on topics like political events, product launches, or marketing campaigns, making it possible to respond swiftly to emerging trends or concerns. For instance, companies can use sentiment analysis to track brand health, measure the success of new products, or manage public relations crises by identifying shifts in sentiment early on.

Sentiment analysis plays a pivotal role in decision-making across various industries by offering actionable insights into public perception, consumer behavior, and social trends [7]. In the realm of business intelligence, sentiment analysis helps companies understand customer feedback, detect patterns in consumer preferences, and improve product offerings. By analyzing customer sentiment, businesses can identify pain points, gauge satisfaction, and fine-tune their strategies to better meet the needs of their target audience.

In public safety, sentiment analysis is increasingly used by governments, law enforcement, and emergency management agencies to monitor public opinion and manage crises [8]. Social media platforms are often the first place where people express their thoughts during emergencies, protests, or public safety events. By analyzing the sentiment in these communications, authorities can gain a better understanding of public concerns, mood, and potential risks. This allows for more effective crisis management, such as mobilizing resources to areas of heightened concern, addressing public fears, and preventing the spread of misinformation.

In the healthcare sector, sentiment analysis provides crucial insights into public attitudes toward health policies, medical treatments, and public health campaigns [9]. By tracking health sentiment, organizations can gauge how the public feels about specific health issues, identify trends in mental health, and evaluate the effectiveness of health interventions. Moreover, sentiment analysis can support mental health monitoring by identifying signs of emotional distress or depression in online conversations, offering early warnings for mental health professionals to intervene.

Sentiment analysis directly contributes to enhancing customer experience by providing businesses with a deeper understanding of customer emotions and preferences [10]. By examining the sentiment in customer reviews, service interactions, and social media posts, companies can tailor their products, services, and communications to align with customer expectations. This, in turn, leads to greater customer loyalty, improved satisfaction, and better overall brand perception. Real-time sentiment analysis also enables businesses to address customer complaints or issues as they arise, further strengthening the customer relationship.

Moreover, sentiment analysis can contribute to community well-being by identifying the emotional needs and concerns of specific populations. Governments and organizations can use sentiment analysis to track sentiment trends around issues like social inequality, mental health, or environmental concerns. This information can inform public policies, social initiatives, and community outreach programs aimed at improving the quality of life and addressing the emotional well-being of citizens.

As sentiment analysis continues to evolve, its importance in decision-making and real-time insights will only increase, helping organizations, governments, and institutions navigate the complexities of the digital age while improving the experiences and well-being of individuals and communities.

1.1.3 Applications Across Various Domains

The growing capabilities of sentiment analysis have led to its widespread application across numerous domains. As businesses, governments, healthcare providers, and other institutions seek to understand public opinion, consumer sentiment, and emotional trends, sentiment analysis has become an invaluable tool in shaping decision-making and strategies. Table 1.1 provides an overview of key domains where sentiment analysis is applied, highlighting specific use cases and utilizing techniques ranging from traditional support vector machines (SVMs) to advanced deep learning models such as long short-term memory (LSTM) networks, graph neural networks (GNNs), and transformers like BERT (bidirectional encoder representations from transformers) and GPT (generative pretrained transformers). It also outlines data sources and the value these approaches bring to various industries.

1.1.3.1 Business Intelligence and Marketing

- Brand Monitoring: In today's digital age, a company's brand reputation is heavily influenced by what customers say online. Sentiment analysis enables businesses to continuously monitor online discussions, reviews, and social media mentions about their brand, helping them understand how their brand is perceived in the market [11]. By assessing the overall sentiment toward their brand, companies can quickly identify any negative trends or emerging issues and take proactive steps to manage their public image.
- Customer Sentiment: Beyond general brand perception, sentiment analysis can help companies assess customer sentiment toward specific products, services, or features. By analyzing customer feedback, businesses can identify areas of satisfaction and dissatisfaction [12]. For example, if a new product feature receives overwhelmingly negative feedback, businesses can use this information to make necessary improvements or address customer concerns directly.

1.1.3.2 Public Safety and Social Media Monitoring

- Crisis Management: During times of crisis—such as natural disasters, political unrest, or public health emergencies—real-time sentiment analysis of social media posts, news reports, and online discussions provides invaluable insights into public sentiment and reactions [13]. Monitoring emotional cues in online content can help government agencies, emergency responders, and organizations better understand public concerns, address misinformation, and prioritize responses. For example, sentiment analysis can track the level of panic, fear, or frustration during a natural disaster and guide the deployment of emergency services.

Table 1.1 Applications of sentiment analysis across various domains.

Domain	Specific Use Cases	Key Techniques	Data Sources	Value & Impact	Typical Examples
Business intelligence & marketing	Brand monitoring, customer sentiment analysis, and product reviews	Lexicon-based methods, ML (SVM and RF), and deep learning (BERT and GPT)	Social media, customer reviews, and e-commerce platforms	Improve brand reputation, enhance customer satisfaction, and optimize marketing strategies	Amazon product review analysis and social media brand monitoring
Public safety & social media monitoring	Crisis management, public opinion analysis, and fake news detection	Rule-based + sentiment lexicon, LSTM, Transformer, and GNNs	Twitter, news, and forums	Improve emergency response, manage crises effectively, and optimize information dissemination	Social media sentiment analysis during the 2020 US election, COVID-19 public response monitoring
Public health & mental health monitoring	Public sentiment on health policies and mental health monitoring	NLP-based sentiment analysis and speech emotion recognition	Social media, health forums, and user feedback	Improve public health communication and enhance mental health intervention strategies	COVID-19 public sentiment tracking and psychological state monitoring via social media
Financial & stock market analysis	Investment sentiment analysis, market trend prediction, and financial news monitoring	Topic modeling (LDA), sentiment scoring, and time-series analysis (LSTM and GRU)	Financial news, social media, and online forums	Provide investment insights, predict market fluctuations, and assess policy impact	Stock market sentiment analysis and financial sentiment indices

Politics & public governance	Voter sentiment analysis, policy feedback, and election monitoring	Word embeddings (Word2Vec), Transformer models, and large-scale sentiment data mining	Election debates, social media, and news comments	Optimize policies, adjust election strategies, and analyze social concerns	Social media sentiment analysis during election campaigns, policy feedback tracking
E-commerce & customer service	Customer review analysis, automated customer support sentiment detection	Keyword extraction, chatbots (GPT), and multimodal sentiment analysis (text, audio, and video)	Customer support logs, user reviews, and online comments	Enhance customer experience, optimize product recommendations, and boost brand loyalty	Automated customer support systems, e-commerce sentiment analysis

- Public Opinion: Sentiment analysis is increasingly used to gauge public opinion on political events, policies, or social movements [14]. Governments and political organizations leverage sentiment analysis to understand how the public is reacting to specific issues, candidates, or policies. For instance, analyzing social media posts during election campaigns or after the introduction of new legislation can provide insights into voter sentiment, allowing politicians to fine-tune their strategies, messaging, and outreach efforts.
- Social Media Trend Analysis: Social media platforms like Twitter, Facebook, and Instagram are rich sources of real-time sentiment data. By analyzing social media posts, sentiment analysis helps identify trends, emerging topics, and viral content. Businesses and political organizations use this analysis to monitor consumer or voter reactions to advertisements, campaigns, and public statements. Additionally, social media monitoring can help detect the early signs of negative sentiment, enabling brands to manage potential PR crises before they escalate.

1.1.3.3 Public Health and Mental Health Monitoring

- Sentiment on Health Issues: Sentiment analysis plays an important role in understanding public attitudes toward health policies, medical treatments, and public health campaigns. For instance, during a health crisis like the COVID-19 pandemic, sentiment analysis was used to track how people felt about quarantine measures, mask mandates, vaccination efforts, and other government actions [15]. By understanding public sentiment, health organizations can adjust communication strategies, address concerns, and ensure that critical health messages are effectively reaching the public.
- Mental Health Diagnostics: Sentiment analysis is also becoming a tool in the field of mental health, especially for early diagnosis and monitoring of emotional well-being. By analyzing individuals' language in social media posts, blogs, or even speech patterns, sentiment analysis can help detect early signs of mental health issues such as depression, anxiety, or stress. This enables mental health professionals to intervene early and offer appropriate support. Moreover, sentiment analysis can be used to track the emotional state of individuals over time, providing valuable data for therapy and ongoing mental health care.

1.1.3.4 Financial & Stock Market Analysis

- Investment Sentiment Analysis: Sentiment analysis helps investors assess market sentiment by analyzing discussions on financial news platforms, social media, and online forums. By detecting public perception toward specific stocks or industries, businesses can anticipate investment trends and market movements [16].

- Market Trend Prediction: By using time-series analysis (LSTM and GRU) and sentiment scoring, financial analysts can track sentiment fluctuations over time, identifying potential bullish or bearish trends in the stock market. Sentiment-driven insights contribute to more informed trading strategies and risk management.
- Financial News Monitoring: Automated sentiment analysis tools process vast amounts of financial news articles, extracting key insights about economic events, corporate earnings reports, and policy changes. This helps financial institutions respond to market developments in real time.

1.1.3.5 Politics & Public Governance

- Voter Sentiment Analysis: Political campaigns and government agencies leverage sentiment analysis to understand public opinion on candidates, policies, and election outcomes. By analyzing debates, social media discussions, and news articles, politicians can adjust their messaging to align with voter concerns.
- Policy Feedback: Sentiment analysis enables governments to track public reactions to newly implemented policies. By monitoring sentiment trends across social media and public forums, policymakers can refine strategies and improve public engagement.
- Election Monitoring: During elections, real-time sentiment tracking provides insights into public support for different candidates and political parties. Analyzing election-related discussions using word embeddings (Word2Vec) and Transformer-based models helps gauge shifts in voter sentiment and predict possible election outcomes.

1.1.3.6 E-commerce & Customer Service

- Customer Review Analysis: Businesses utilize sentiment analysis to process customer reviews from platforms like Amazon, Yelp, and e-commerce websites. By extracting sentiment from product feedback, companies can identify strengths and areas for improvement in their offerings.
- Automated Customer Support Sentiment Detection: AI-powered chatbots and customer service platforms analyze customer queries and detect emotional tone in real time. Sentiment-aware support systems help prioritize urgent cases and deliver personalized responses, improving customer satisfaction.
- Personalized Shopping Experience: By analyzing user sentiment and engagement patterns, e-commerce platforms optimize product recommendations and tailor shopping experiences. Sentiment-driven personalization helps enhance customer loyalty and sales performance.

Sentiment analysis is increasingly being integrated into a wide variety of domains, providing actionable insights and supporting decision-making in business intelligence, public safety, public health, and emerging applications such as politics, customer support, and e-commerce. By leveraging sentiment data from diverse sources like social media, reviews, and customer feedback, organizations can better understand and respond to public opinion, customer emotions, and societal trends. As sentiment analysis technology continues to improve, its applications are expected to grow even further, offering even more nuanced and real-time insights to guide strategic decisions across various sectors.

1.1.4 Research Significance, Challenges, and Future Directions

The field of sentiment analysis has not only emerged as a critical component of NLP but has also made significant contributions to Data Science and AI. As sentiment analysis continues to evolve, its theoretical and practical significance grows, opening new avenues for research and application. However, as with any rapidly advancing field, there are several challenges that need to be addressed, along with exciting directions for future development.

Sentiment analysis has had a profound impact on the evolution of NLP by pushing the boundaries of how machines understand human language. While early NLP techniques focused on simple tasks like part-of-speech tagging and named entity recognition, sentiment analysis has encouraged a deeper exploration of the semantic and pragmatic layers of language. Understanding sentiment requires machines to go beyond basic text parsing and instead engage in complex tasks like contextual interpretation, emotion detection, and irony recognition—skills that are foundational to advanced NLP models.

In the broader context of Data Science, sentiment analysis plays a crucial role in the analysis of unstructured data. Traditionally, structured data (such as numerical or categorical data) dominated data analytics, but sentiment analysis enables the processing of unstructured data, such as customer reviews, social media content, or audio and video signals. This shift allows data scientists to integrate both quantitative and qualitative data, providing a more holistic understanding of trends, patterns, and behaviors. As a result, sentiment analysis not only enhances decision-making processes but also opens up new possibilities for data-driven research and business strategy.

From an AI perspective, sentiment analysis contributes to the broader challenge of teaching machines to recognize and interpret human emotions. The ability to assess sentiment adds an emotional intelligence layer to AI systems, enabling more natural and effective human-computer interactions. Whether it's chatbots, virtual assistants, or automated customer service agents, sentiment analysis allows AI to understand not just what users are saying but how they feel—an essential step toward building empathetic and intelligent AI systems.

Despite significant advancements, sentiment analysis faces several limitations that need to be overcome to improve its accuracy and applicability.

- Sarcasm: One of the biggest challenges in sentiment analysis is the identification of sarcasm. A sentence like "Oh, great, another meeting!" is ostensibly positive in its words but negative in sentiment. Sarcasm detection remains difficult because it often relies on context, tone, and cultural understanding that current sentiment analysis models struggle to capture. Even with the rise of deep learning models, detecting sarcasm remains a significant hurdle, especially in text-based sentiment analysis.
- Sentiment Ambiguity: Sentiment is inherently subjective and can be ambiguous. A single statement can carry mixed emotions depending on the context or the individual's perspective. For example, a statement like "I'm not sure if I should be excited or scared" conveys both positive and negative sentiment. Current models, particularly those using binary or ternary classification (positive, neutral, and negative), often fail to account for such nuanced sentiment. Fine-grained sentiment analysis, which detects and classifies multiple emotions in a single text, is still in its early stages and requires more advanced models to achieve high accuracy.
- Cross-lingual Challenges: Another significant limitation is the cross-lingual challenge. Sentiment analysis tools are often optimized for a single language, and applying these tools to languages with different syntactic structures, cultural contexts, and idiomatic expressions can result in inaccurate predictions. This is particularly problematic when dealing with low-resource languages where labeled data is scarce, making it difficult to train robust sentiment analysis models. Additionally, sentiment expressions vary across languages and cultures, which means that a model trained on English data might not perform well on other languages like Mandarin, Arabic, or Hindi.

As sentiment analysis continues to evolve, several key trends are expected to shape its future:

- Real-time Analysis: One of the most exciting future directions for sentiment analysis is its application in real-time analysis. As social media, online forums, and news platforms generate large volumes of data at a rapid pace, the ability to process and analyze sentiment in real time becomes increasingly valuable. Real-time sentiment analysis can be used to track breaking news, public opinion on political events, or consumer reactions to product launches. For instance, political campaigns can analyze the shifting sentiment around candidates or policies during debates or speeches, allowing them to adjust messaging immediately.
- Ethical Concerns: As sentiment analysis becomes more pervasive, ethical issues related to privacy, data security, and bias are gaining attention. For

example, sentiment analysis systems that process personal data (e.g., social media content or health-related discussions) may raise privacy concerns if users are not fully informed about how their data is being used. Additionally, there is the risk that sentiment analysis models could be manipulated or used for misleading purposes—such as influencing political campaigns or exploiting vulnerable populations. Future research will need to focus on creating ethical guidelines and safeguards to ensure that sentiment analysis is used responsibly and transparently.

- Cross-cultural Models: The need for cross-cultural models is a critical direction for the future of sentiment analysis. As the world becomes increasingly interconnected, businesses and organizations will need to understand sentiment across diverse cultural contexts. This includes not only detecting sentiment but also interpreting it accurately across languages, regions, and cultural nuances. Future models should be capable of cross-lingual sentiment analysis, leveraging techniques like transfer learning to apply sentiment analysis models across languages with limited training data.
- Sentiment Synthesis: Another frontier in sentiment analysis is sentiment synthesis, where AI models not only detect sentiment but also generate it. This could be applied in areas like creative writing, content generation, or customer service. For instance, sentiment synthesis could enable chatbots to create emotionally appropriate responses, making interactions with AI more empathetic and human-like. Additionally, sentiment synthesis could be used to generate content (e.g., product reviews or social media posts) that matches a desired emotional tone.

The future of sentiment analysis holds immense promise, from addressing current limitations like sarcasm and cross-lingual challenges to embracing new technologies for real-time analysis and sentiment synthesis. As sentiment analysis becomes increasingly integral to decision-making processes in business, public safety, healthcare, and beyond, its theoretical and practical significance will only continue to grow. The road ahead will involve overcoming several obstacles, including improving model accuracy, tackling ethical concerns, and expanding the scope of sentiment analysis to more languages and cultures. By addressing these challenges, the field of sentiment analysis can pave the way for more intelligent, empathetic, and globally applicable AI systems.

1.2 Fundamentals of Sentiment Analysis

Sentiment analysis involves a range of techniques and methodologies designed to extract and classify subjective information from text, audio, or visual data. The primary goal is to determine the emotional tone—whether positive, negative, or neutral—behind various forms of communication. This process includes tasks such as sentiment classification, where the goal is to categorize emotions or opinions expressed in the data, as well as more complex functions like detecting sentiment intensity and addressing ambiguities. The challenges of sentiment analysis are compounded by the intricacies of language, including context-dependent meanings, sarcasm, and subtle shifts in sentiment. In this section, we will explore the fundamental principles and tasks of sentiment analysis, laying the groundwork for understanding the methods used to tackle these challenges and provide actionable insights from subjective data.

1.2.1 Core Principles and Tasks

Sentiment analysis is grounded in fundamental emotional theories and principles while encompassing a variety of technical tasks to extract, classify, and interpret subjective data. The following sections outline the core principles that underpin sentiment analysis and the key tasks that operationalize these principles, as shown in Figure 1.2.

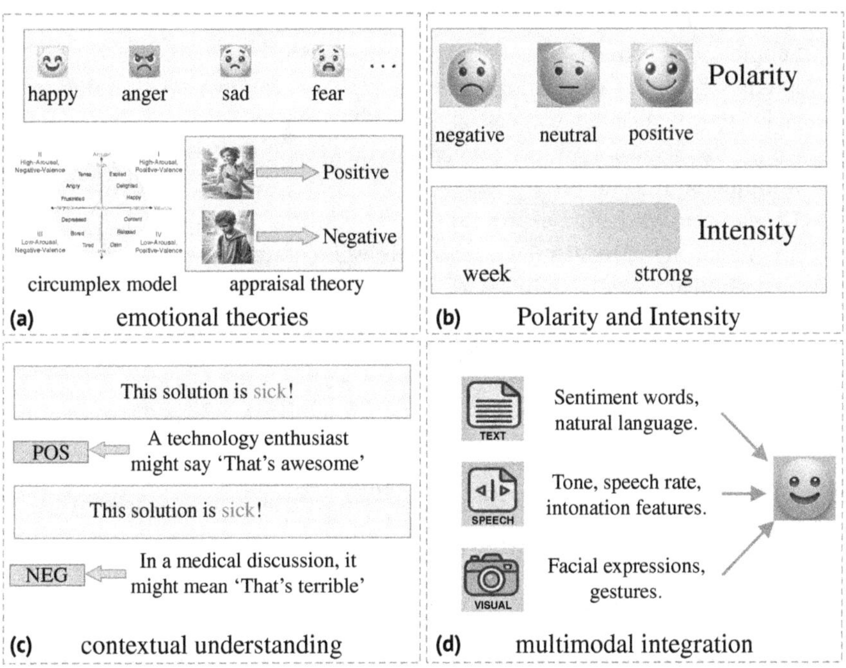

Figure 1.2 Core principles of sentiment analysis.

1.2.1.1 Core Principles of Sentiment Analysis

1. Emotional Theories
   Sentiment analysis draws from established psychological and linguistic theories to interpret emotions and sentiments.
   - Basic Emotion Theory: This theory posits that humans have universal, discrete emotions (e.g., happiness, sadness, anger, and fear) that can be detected across languages and cultures. Sentiment analysis often uses these categories to classify sentiments [17].
   - Dimensional Emotion Theory: Emotions are represented along dimensions such as valence (positive to negative) and arousal (calm to excited) [18]. This allows sentiment analysis to quantify emotions on a continuous scale.
   - Appraisal Theory: Emotions arise from evaluations or appraisals of events [19]. Sentiment analysis leverages this theory to associate emotions with specific aspects or contexts within text.
2. Polarity and Intensity
   Sentiments are categorized based on their polarity (positive, negative, and neutral) and their intensity (e.g., weak, moderate, and strong) [20]. These concepts are central to sentiment classification and enable more granular analysis.
3. Contextual Understanding
   Sentiment is context-dependent; the same word or phrase can carry different sentiments depending on its usage. For example, "This solution is sick!" may be positive in a casual context but negative in a medical context. Context-awareness is crucial for accurate sentiment analysis.
4. Multimodal Integration
   Human sentiments are expressed through multiple modalities: text, speech, and visual cues. Modern sentiment analysis integrates these data types to provide a holistic understanding of emotions.

1.2.1.2 Key Tasks of Sentiment Analysis

1. Feature Extraction
   Extracting meaningful features from raw data is the foundation of sentiment analysis. These features can be:
   - Textual Features: Words, phrases, or syntactic structures extracted using techniques like tokenization, n-grams, and part-of-speech tagging.
   - Semantic Features: Word embeddings (e.g., Word2Vec and GloVe) and sentiment lexicons (e.g., SentiWordNet) capture deeper meanings and relationships between words.
   - Multimodal Features: Non-textual data, such as intonation in speech or facial expressions in video, are extracted for comprehensive sentiment analysis.

2. Sentiment Classification
   The task of categorizing text into predefined sentiment labels, such as positive, negative, or neutral. Models trained on labeled datasets using algorithms like SVMs, Naive Bayes, and deep learning models (e.g., CNNs and RNNs).
3. Sentiment Entity Recognition
   Identifying entities (e.g., products, people, and places) in text that are associated with specific sentiments. For example, in "I love my iPhone but hate the battery life," the entities "iPhone" and "battery life" have contrasting sentiments.
4. Aspect-based Sentiment Analysis (ABSA)
   Focusing on specific aspects or attributes of an entity to determine sentiment. For instance, in "The camera is excellent, but the screen is too dim," sentiment is classified for the aspects "camera" and "screen" separately.
5. Sentiment Relation Extraction
   Identifying relationships between entities and sentiments. For example, in "The customer praised the product's design but criticized its durability," the system detects the sentiment relations "praised → design" and "criticized → durability."
6. Sentiment Intensity Detection
   Quantifying the strength of sentiment expressed. This task goes beyond polarity classification to assign a sentiment score (e.g., −1 to +1) or intensity category (e.g., mild, moderate, and strong).
7. Multimodal Sentiment Analysis
   Combining textual, audio, and visual data to assess sentiment comprehensively. For example, analyzing a customer's words, tone, and facial expressions during a service interaction.

1.2.2 Typical Methods in Sentiment Analysis

Sentiment analysis employs a variety of methods that break down and interpret subjective information from subjective data. These methods differ in granularity, complexity, and the types of data they analyze. The following sections detail the most common methods used in sentiment analysis, showing how they categorize and interpret sentiment at different levels, from document-wide assessments to finer, multimodal analyses.

1. Document-level Sentiment Analysis
   Document-level sentiment analysis focuses on determining the overall sentiment expressed in a document, such as a product review, news article, or social media post [21]. The goal is to classify the entire document as positive, negative, or neutral based on the general tone and content. This approach is best suited for cases where sentiment is consistent throughout the text, without significant conflicting sentiments.

Document-level analysis is commonly applied in product reviews, where the overall sentiment toward a product or service needs to be assessed. For example, a review that says, "This phone has great features, but it drains battery too quickly," may be classified as negative if the overall tone leans toward dissatisfaction, despite mentioning some positive aspects.

Document-level sentiment analysis often relies on bag-of-words (BoW) models, TF-IDF (term frequency-inverse document frequency), and deep learning techniques like convolutional neural networks (CNNs) and recurrent neural networks (RNNs) to capture sentiment across the entire document, aggregating the sentiments expressed in different parts into one sentiment label.

2. Sentence-level Sentiment Analysis

   Sentence-level sentiment analysis involves detecting sentiment at the level of individual sentences [22]. This method is more detailed than document-level analysis and is useful in cases where different sentences within a document express different sentiments. It helps to understand the sentiment behind specific statements in a piece of text.

   This approach is particularly valuable in customer service or dialogue systems, where each sentence or query needs to be classified individually. For example, the sentence "The product is fantastic!" would be classified as positive, while "The shipping was slow, though" would be classified as negative.

   Techniques such as SVMs and deep learning models (e.g., LSTMs) are commonly used for sentence-level sentiment analysis. These models are trained to classify sentiment based on the specific structure and context of each sentence, considering its words, phrases, and overall meaning.

3. ABSA

   ABSA goes beyond document or sentence-level analysis by identifying and evaluating sentiment associated with specific aspects or features of an entity [23]. For instance, it can assess how people feel about a product's price, quality, or customer service, providing a more granular understanding of sentiment.

   ABSA is widely used in e-commerce and product feedback to analyze sentiment regarding various product features. For example, in a review like "The phone is very fast, but the battery life is terrible," ABSA would separately assess the positive sentiment toward the speed and the negative sentiment toward the battery life.

   ABSA typically involves dependency parsing and attention mechanisms in deep learning models (e.g., BERT or Transformer-based architectures) to capture relationships between aspect terms (e.g., "battery," "speed," and "design") and their corresponding sentiments.

4. Fine-grained Sentiment Analysis
Fine-grained sentiment analysis focuses on detecting more specific emotions and sentiment intensity, capturing nuanced sentiments like joy, anger, fear, sadness, and intensity levels (e.g., very happy vs. somewhat happy). This allows for a more detailed emotional understanding of the text.

   Fine-grained sentiment analysis is useful in applications such as mental health monitoring, where it is essential to detect and analyze subtle emotional changes or the intensity of feelings expressed in written text.

   This method often uses multi-class classification or regression models to detect emotions and classify sentiments on a continuous scale, going beyond simple positive, negative, or neutral labels.
5. Multimodal Sentiment Analysis
Multimodal sentiment analysis integrates multiple sources of data, such as text, audio, and visual information, to create a more comprehensive sentiment understanding [24]. This approach assumes that sentiment is conveyed not only through words but also through voice tone, facial expressions, and body language.

   Multimodal sentiment analysis is especially useful in customer service, social media monitoring, and virtual assistants. For example, in a video review, a customer may express positive sentiment through words but show negative emotions through facial expressions, and multimodal systems can detect and analyze both to provide a more accurate sentiment assessment.

   This approach combines text-based sentiment analysis with speech emotion recognition (to analyze tone, pitch, and rhythm in audio) and computer vision (to analyze facial expressions and body language in videos). Techniques like deep neural networks and multitask learning are commonly used to process and integrate data from these various modalities.

Sentiment analysis employs a diverse set of classification methods, each suited to different types of data and analysis needs. Document-level sentiment analysis provides an overall sentiment classification for a piece of content, while sentence-level analysis offers more granular insights into individual statements. Aspect-based sentiment analysis allows organizations to analyze sentiment toward specific features or attributes, providing deeper insights into consumer opinions. Fine-grained sentiment analysis captures nuanced emotions and intensity, while multimodal sentiment analysis combines multiple data types for a more comprehensive understanding of sentiment in dynamic, real-world contexts. These methods reflect the growing sophistication of sentiment analysis, enabling more accurate, context-aware models that can be applied across a wide range of industries and applications.

1.3 Historical Evolution of Sentiment Analysis

Sentiment analysis has undergone significant evolution since its inception, with advances in techniques and technologies that have shaped its capabilities today. From rule-based systems to the advent of ML, and the recent breakthroughs in deep learning, each stage of development has contributed to improving the accuracy and application of sentiment analysis models. This section will explore the historical progression of sentiment analysis, beginning with its early approaches and moving through the rise of ML, the development of deep learning, and the current challenges faced by the field.

1.3.1 Early Approaches: Rule-based and Lexicon-based

The earliest methods of sentiment analysis were rule-based and lexicon-based, both of which relied on predefined structures and dictionaries to interpret and classify sentiment. These approaches laid the foundation for sentiment analysis, focusing on extracting emotions and opinions from text by using simple patterns, word associations, and sentiment lexicons. While these methods were a significant breakthrough at the time, they also presented several limitations, particularly in understanding the subtleties and complexities of human language.

Rule-based sentiment analysis systems worked by applying a set of predefined rules to identify sentiment in a given text [25]. These rules were often created by domain experts and linguists who manually constructed them to match specific linguistic patterns, such as the presence of certain words or phrases associated with positive or negative emotions. For example, a rule might state that if a sentence contains the word "love" or "great," it should be classified as positive, while words like "hate" or "terrible" would indicate negative sentiment. Rule-based systems could be relatively simple, yet effective for analyzing short, clear expressions of sentiment.

Complementing rule-based methods, lexicon-based approaches relied on sentiment dictionaries (also called sentiment lexicons) that assigned predefined sentiment scores to individual words. These lexicons contained lists of words and their associated sentiments, typically ranging from positive to negative. One example is SentiWordNet [26], which provides sentiment scores for words based on their meanings and usage contexts. Lexicon-based systems classified sentiment by matching words in a given text to entries in these dictionaries. For instance, a system might classify a text with words like "joy," "fantastic," and "love" as positive, based on their associations in the lexicon.

These approaches were valuable for their simplicity and efficiency, especially in the early stages of sentiment analysis. However, their reliance on predefined rules and dictionaries also limited their ability to handle complex or nuanced language.

One of the most glaring limitations of early sentiment analysis models was their inability to detect sarcasm. Sentiment analysis systems based on lexicons or rules could easily misinterpret sarcastic statements because they focus on the literal meaning of words, not the intended sentiment behind them. For example, the sentence "Oh great, another meeting!" would likely be flagged as positive due to the presence of the word "great," even though the speaker is clearly expressing frustration. Detecting sarcasm requires a deeper understanding of context, tone, and the speaker's intent, which rule-based systems were not equipped to handle.

Early sentiment analysis systems also struggled with understanding the context in which words appeared. In natural language, words can have different meanings based on their surrounding text. For example, the word "good" can express a positive sentiment in "It's a good day" but may have a more neutral or even negative connotation in "He's a good liar." Rule-based and lexicon-based systems could not effectively differentiate between these varying meanings, leading to inaccurate sentiment classification.

Another significant challenge was the inability of early sentiment analysis systems to handle domain-specific terms. Words that may have a neutral or positive sentiment in one domain could have a different sentiment in another. For instance, in the medical domain, the word "sick" generally carries a negative sentiment, while in the sports domain, "sick" might be used to describe something impressive or exciting ("That was a sick play!"). Lexicon-based systems, with their reliance on general-purpose dictionaries, struggled to adapt to these domain-specific variations, leading to misclassifications when applied to specialized fields like finance, healthcare, or technology.

These challenges highlighted the need for more sophisticated techniques that could move beyond simple keyword matching and incorporate deeper understanding of language, leading to the development of more advanced methods such as ML and deep learning in subsequent years.

1.3.2 The Rise of ML and Statistical Methods

With the limitations of rule-based and lexicon-based approaches becoming apparent, sentiment analysis began to evolve toward ML and statistical methods, marking a significant shift in how sentiment was analyzed and classified. The advent of these techniques brought greater flexibility and scalability to sentiment analysis, allowing systems to learn from data and adapt to a broader range of contexts. ML models were able to capture complex patterns in large datasets and improve sentiment prediction accuracy, especially when dealing with ambiguous, contextual, or domain-specific language.

ML techniques revolutionized sentiment analysis by introducing models that could automatically learn patterns from labeled data and make predictions without the need for manually predefined rules [27].

A decision tree is a flowchart-like model used for classification tasks. It splits the data into branches based on feature values (e.g., specific words or phrases), and each branch leads to a final sentiment classification. Decision trees were one of the earliest ML algorithms applied to sentiment analysis because they are easy to interpret and can handle both categorical and numerical features. However, decision trees could suffer from overfitting, where they model noise in the data instead of generalizable patterns.

The Naive Bayes classifier is based on Bayes' theorem, which calculates the probability of a class (e.g., positive, negative, or neutral) given certain features (typically words or phrases). It assumes that features are independent, which is a simplification but it works surprisingly well for text classification tasks like sentiment analysis [28]. In sentiment analysis, Naive Bayes models analyze the frequency of specific words in a document and compute the likelihood of those words corresponding to a particular sentiment class. This approach was widely used in early sentiment analysis because of its simplicity, speed, and efficiency, especially when dealing with large datasets.

SVMs became a popular choice for sentiment analysis because of their ability to handle high-dimensional data (such as text) and separate data into distinct classes by finding the optimal hyperplane that maximizes the margin between different sentiment classes [29]. SVMs are particularly effective in binary classification tasks, such as distinguishing positive sentiment from negative sentiment. While SVMs were computationally more expensive than Naive Bayes, they generally offered higher accuracy, especially in more complex or high-dimensional sentiment analysis problems.

In addition to ML techniques, statistical models were essential in transforming raw text data into structured inputs for sentiment analysis algorithms. These models focused on extracting meaningful features from the text that could be fed into ML classifiers.

The BoW model is one of the simplest and most widely used statistical techniques for representing text. In this model, the text is broken down into individual words, and the frequency of each word is counted. The position and order of the words are ignored, which is why it is called BoW. The resulting feature vector represents the presence and frequency of words in the document. For sentiment analysis, the BoW model allows algorithms to identify common sentiment-related terms (e.g., "love," "hate," "good," and "bad") and use them as features for classification.

TF-IDF refines word frequency counts by considering how common or rare a word is across a corpus of documents. TF measures how often a word appears in a document, while IDF reduces the weight of common words that appear in many documents, emphasizing words that are unique to specific documents. This adjustment helps improve sentiment classification by focusing on more informative terms that carry greater meaning in distinguishing sentiment.

These advances laid the groundwork for the next wave of innovation in sentiment analysis, which would involve the application of deep learning models that could further capture the complexities of human language and sentiment.

1.3.3 Deep Learning and Modern Methods

With the growing complexity of language and the limitations of traditional ML methods, deep learning emerged as a powerful tool for sentiment analysis. Deep learning models, especially neural networks, have significantly improved the ability to understand nuanced and contextual sentiment in text, capturing intricate patterns that earlier models struggled with Tang et al. [30]. The development of these advanced methods has enabled systems to process and analyze language in more sophisticated ways, resulting in better performance across a wide range of tasks, including sentiment analysis. This section discusses the rise of deep learning, the advent of Transformer models, and the breakthrough innovation of transfer learning in NLP.

Early neural networks, sometimes referred to as shallow networks, consisted of one or two layers of neurons. While they were a step forward from traditional ML models, their capacity to capture complex patterns in language was still limited. Shallow networks could process simple text representations, such as one-hot encoding or word embeddings, but they often failed to grasp the deeper, contextual relationships within the text. For example, a shallow neural network might struggle to differentiate between "I'm not happy" and "I'm happy" because these two sentences differ by a single word that, in isolation, seems insignificant.

The true breakthrough in sentiment analysis came with the development of deep neural networks, which use multiple layers of neurons to capture hierarchical relationships in data. Deep learning models, such as CNNs and RNNs, introduced the ability to analyze more complex structures in language. RNNs, particularly LSTM networks, were well-suited for sentiment analysis tasks because they could process sequences of words and retain information about earlier words to understand context. LSTMs and their variant, gated recurrent units (GRUs), were particularly powerful for tasks involving sequential data, such as text. These models could preserve long-range dependencies between words, which helped in understanding context and sentiment in sentences where word order and relationships mattered, such as detecting sarcasm or capturing sentiment intensity.

The introduction of the Transformer architecture was a game-changer in NLP. Transformer models, such as BERT [31] and GPT [32], revolutionized the way machines process text and understand language at scale. Unlike earlier models that processed text sequentially (word by word), Transformers process the entire text in parallel, allowing them to capture more complex dependencies between words.

BERT's key innovation lies in its bidirectional nature—meaning it looks at both the left and right context of a word simultaneously. This bidirectionality enables BERT to better understand the meaning of words based on their surrounding context. For sentiment analysis, this is particularly valuable because it allows the model to identify subtle nuances in sentiment that depend on the full context of the sentence. For instance, in the sentence "I don't like this movie, but the soundtrack is amazing," BERT can understand the contrast in sentiment between the negative opinion about the movie and the positive sentiment about the soundtrack. BERT has set a new standard in NLP, achieving state-of-the-art results in numerous tasks, including sentiment analysis.

GPT is primarily designed for text generation, but its generative pretraining on large, unlabeled text corpora allows it to learn complex linguistic patterns and contextual relationships. This makes GPT effective for tasks like sentiment analysis when fine-tuned on task-specific labeled data. By leveraging the knowledge gained during pretraining, GPT can classify sentiment in text without requiring significant changes to the model architecture. This approach—generative pretraining followed by discriminative fine-tuning—enables GPT to achieve strong performance on sentiment analysis and other NLP tasks, outperforming traditional models that rely solely on task-specific training.

A key factor behind GPT's success is the concept of transfer learning, one of the most transformative innovations in NLP. In traditional ML, models are trained from scratch for each task, often requiring large amounts of labeled data. In contrast, transfer learning allows models to be pretrained on large, general datasets and then fine-tuned on smaller, task-specific datasets. This dramatically reduces the need for vast amounts of labeled data and speeds up the training process, making it an efficient and powerful approach for a wide range of tasks, including sentiment analysis.

These advancements have brought sentiment analysis to the forefront of NLP, making it an essential tool for a wide range of applications, from customer feedback analysis to social media monitoring and beyond.

1.3.4 Current Challenges and Limitations

Despite the remarkable advancements in sentiment analysis, several challenges persist that continue to hinder the full potential of these models. These challenges arise from the inherent complexities of language, cultural differences, and the specialized nature of certain fields [33]. As sentiment analysis continues to evolve, addressing these limitations will be crucial for improving the accuracy, reliability, and applicability of sentiment analysis models in diverse real-world scenarios.

One of the most persistent challenges in sentiment analysis is understanding contextual ambiguities. The meaning of words can vary significantly depending on the context in which they are used. For instance, the word "good" might convey a positive sentiment in "This is a good movie," but it could take on a negative connotation in "He's a good liar." Similarly, words like "fast" can be seen as positive in "The internet speed is fast" but might have a negative meaning in "He made a fast decision without thinking." Even deep learning models, which are more advanced than traditional approaches, often struggle with disambiguating such cases, especially when subtle contextual cues or irony are involved. These ambiguities can lead to misclassifications, underscoring the difficulty of capturing the true sentiment in complex, real-world language.

Another significant challenge in sentiment analysis is handling cross-lingual and cross-cultural differences in sentiment expression. Most sentiment analysis models are trained on large text corpora in specific languages, often focusing on English. However, sentiment analysis is increasingly being applied to global datasets that include text in a variety of languages. Models trained on English data may not perform well on languages with different syntactic structures, idiomatic expressions, or cultural references.

Many languages have different ways of expressing sentiment, making it difficult to transfer sentiment analysis models from one language to another. For example, the sentiment of a word or phrase might not map directly between languages. Additionally, some languages may lack rich sentiment lexicons or have different emotional connotations for the same words. As a result, sentiment analysis models trained on English data may struggle with languages like Arabic, Chinese, or Hindi. Transfer learning and multilingual models like M-BERT (multilingual BERT) [34] are emerging solutions that aim to address these issues by training models on multiple languages, but challenges remain in achieving consistent accuracy across languages.

In addition to linguistic challenges, cultural differences play a significant role in how sentiment is expressed and interpreted. What is considered a positive sentiment in one culture may be viewed as negative or neutral in another. For example, expressions of politeness or indirectness, which are common in some Asian cultures, may be misunderstood by models trained primarily on Western text. Similarly, humor, sarcasm, and emotional expressions vary widely across cultures, complicating sentiment analysis in global contexts. To address these issues, sentiment analysis systems need to be culturally aware, adapting to the norms and idioms specific to each culture or region.

Sentiment analysis models trained on general-purpose corpora often struggle to perform well in specialized domains where domain-specific language and terminology are used. In fields such as finance, healthcare, legal, or technology, words and phrases may have different meanings or connotations compared to their everyday usage.

In the finance domain, for instance, words like "bullish" or "bearish" carry specific meanings related to market trends, which may not be captured by general-purpose sentiment analysis models. Similarly, in the medical domain, words like "sick" or "symptoms" are associated with a specific context of health but may be classified inaccurately if the model is not trained on medical data. Without sufficient domain-specific training data or domain adaptation techniques, sentiment analysis systems may misinterpret important terms, leading to inaccurate sentiment predictions.

While transfer learning and fine-tuning methods (e.g., fine-tuning BERT or other Transformer models on domain-specific data) have made it easier to adapt general-purpose models to specific domains, the quality and availability of labeled data remain a significant hurdle. In many specialized fields, acquiring enough labeled data to train or fine-tune models can be challenging, leading to lower accuracy and performance in niche applications.

The current challenges in sentiment analysis highlight the complexities of understanding human language in all its nuance and diversity. Contextual ambiguities and sarcasm continue to be difficult for models to handle, requiring more sophisticated methods for interpretation. Cross-lingual and cross-cultural issues further complicate sentiment analysis in global and multilingual contexts, where cultural differences and linguistic structures play a significant role in sentiment expression. Finally, domain-specific adaptation challenges show that models trained on general text may not perform adequately in specialized fields unless they are fine-tuned on domain-specific data. Overcoming these challenges will require continued research into more robust, context-aware, and culturally sensitive sentiment analysis models, with a focus on improving transferability across languages and domains.

1.4 Book Structure

This book is designed to provide a comprehensive exploration of sentiment analysis in the context of NLP, offering readers both foundational knowledge and advanced insights into the techniques, challenges, and applications of sentiment analysis. The structure of the book is organized to guide researchers and practitioners through the core principles, historical developments, and modern techniques of sentiment analysis. By balancing theoretical rigor with practical applications, the book aims to provide a robust foundation for understanding both traditional methodologies and the latest advancements in sentiment analysis. Each chapter builds upon the concepts introduced in previous sections, gradually progressing from introductory material to more specialized, advanced topics.

1.4.1 Overview of Chapter Structure

The book begins with Chapter 1: Introduction, which sets the stage for understanding sentiment analysis by introducing its importance and broad applications, especially in business intelligence, public safety, and social media monitoring. It also provides an overview of the history of sentiment analysis, covering early methods and their evolution into modern techniques.

Chapter 2: Basic Concepts and Techniques in Sentiment Analysis delves into the foundational elements of sentiment analysis, covering key technologies in NLP, data preprocessing, sentiment annotation methods, and introduces the unique challenges of non-text data, such as speech and visual sentiment analysis. The chapter also explores sentiment classification approaches and addresses issues like detecting fake opinions.

As the book progresses, Chapter 3: Text-based Sentiment Analysis explores traditional methods of sentiment detection through rule-based and lexicon-based approaches, along with ML and deep learning methods such as SVMs and CNNs. The chapter also discusses aspect-based sentiment analysis, where sentiment is tied to specific features within a text.

Chapter 4: Implicit Sentiment Analysis tackles the complexities of analyzing sentiment that is not explicitly stated but implied in the text, such as sarcasm or subtle emotional tones, and explores solutions to these challenges.

The book then shifts to more complex and integrated techniques, starting with Chapter 5: Multimodal Sentiment Analysis, which introduces the fusion of different data types—text, audio, and visual data—to create a more complete picture of sentiment. The chapter covers deep learning methods used in multimodal settings and includes real-world case studies.

Chapter 6: Application of Attention Mechanisms in Sentiment Analysis brings attention mechanisms into the spotlight, explaining their role in enhancing sentiment analysis models, particularly in handling complex data interactions. The chapter also introduces graph attention networks (GATs) and their application in sentiment recognition.

Chapter 7: Advanced Technologies and Future Trends takes the reader through cutting-edge developments in sentiment analysis, such as large language models (LLMs) like BERT and GPT, as well as the emerging use of Generative AI in sentiment analysis. It explores the challenges of cross-lingual and cross-cultural sentiment analysis and speculates on the future directions of sentiment analysis, including real-time analysis and ethical considerations.

Chapter 8: Practical Applications of Sentiment Analysis shifts focus to practical uses of sentiment analysis in real-world contexts, such as business intelligence, public safety, public health, and social media monitoring. The chapter also reviews various sentiment analysis tools and their effectiveness in different applications.

Finally, Chapter 9: Conclusion and Outlook summarizes the major insights from the book, reflecting on the key techniques and applications discussed. It also delves into the ethical implications of sentiment analysis and offers suggestions for future research, especially regarding the integration of multimodal data and more accurate implicit sentiment analysis.

1.4.2 Integration of Chapters

The chapters are seamlessly connected, with each one building on the knowledge established in earlier sections. The book starts with foundational concepts and techniques, moving through challenges such as implicit sentiment detection, sarcasm, and domain adaptation, and culminating in more complex applications and future trends. By addressing both the technical and practical aspects of sentiment analysis, the chapters provide a holistic view of the field, connecting theoretical methods with real-world applications.

As the book progresses, readers will see how various sentiment analysis techniques—from supervised learning methods to deep learning models—are applied to increasingly complex challenges, such as multimodal sentiment analysis and the integration of cross-lingual or cross-cultural considerations. Each chapter incorporates practical examples, case studies, and real-world scenarios, ensuring that the reader can connect the underlying theories to practical applications.

The structure of the book is designed to guide readers through a natural progression of complexity. Starting with the basics of sentiment classification in text-based analysis, the chapters then lead into more specialized areas such as multimodal sentiment analysis and deep learning techniques that handle complex datasets, including audio and visual inputs.

By the time readers reach Chapter 7: Advanced Technologies and Future Trends, they will have acquired a deep understanding of how sentiment analysis has evolved and where it is headed, including the integration of generative AI and real-time sentiment detection. The journey through these chapters will equip readers with both the theoretical insights and practical skills necessary to tackle current and emerging challenges in sentiment analysis.

The structure of the book ensures a logical progression from foundational knowledge to advanced techniques and practical applications. Each chapter is carefully designed, taking readers through the evolution of sentiment analysis from simple methods to cutting-edge models like Transformers and multimodal analysis. The integration of challenges, techniques, and applications throughout the book provides a comprehensive view of sentiment analysis, preparing readers to tackle both theoretical and real-world problems in this dynamic field.

References

1 Rodríguez-Ibánez, M., Casánez-Ventura, A., Castejón-Mateos, F., & Cuenca-Jiménez, P. M. (2023). A review on sentiment analysis from social media platforms. *Expert Systems with Applications*, 223, 119862.
2 Das, R., & Singh, T. D. (2023). Multimodal sentiment analysis: A survey of methods, trends, and challenges. *ACM Computing Surveys*, 55(13s), 1–38.
3 Birjali, M., Kasri, M., & Beni-Hssane, A. (2021). A comprehensive survey on sentiment analysis: Approaches, challenges and trends. *Knowledge-Based Systems*, 226, 107134.
4 Hazarika, D., Zimmermann, R., & Poria, S. (2020). Misa: Modality-invariant and -specific representations for multimodal sentiment analysis. In Proceedings of the 28th ACM International Conference on Multimedia, Seattle, WA, USA, 1122–1131.
5 Zhu, L., Zhu, Z., Zhang, C., Xu, Y., & Kong, X. (2023). Multimodal sentiment analysis based on fusion methods: A survey. *Information Fusion*, 95, 306–325.
6 El Barachi, M., AlKhatib, M., Mathew, S., & Oroumchian, F. (2021). A novel sentiment analysis framework for monitoring the evolving public opinion in real-time: Case study on climate change. *Journal of Cleaner Production*, 312, 127820.
7 Trillo, J. R., Herrera-Viedma, E., Morente-Molinera, J. A., & Cabrerizo, F. J. (2023). A large scale group decision making system based on sentiment analysis cluster. *Information Fusion*, 91, 633–643.
8 Suhaimin, M. S. M., Hijazi, M. H. A., Moung, E. G., Nohuddin, P. N. E., Chua, S., & Coenen, F. (2023). Social media sentiment analysis and opinion mining in public security: Taxonomy, trend analysis, issues and future directions. *Journal of King Saud University - Computer and Information Sciences*, 35(9), 101776.
9 Gohil, S., Vuik, S., & Darzi, A. (2018). Sentiment analysis of health care tweets: review of the methods used. *JMIR Public Health and Surveillance*, 4(2), e5789.
10 Park, S., Cho, J., Park, K., & Shin, H. (2021). Customer sentiment analysis with more sensibility. *Engineering Applications of Artificial Intelligence*, 104, 104356.
11 Ingole, A., Khude, P., Kittad, S., Parmar, V., & Ghotkar, A. (2024). Competitive sentiment analysis for brand reputation monitoring. In 2024 2nd International Conference on Emerging Trends in Information Technology and Engineering (ICETITE), Vellore, India, (pp. 1–7). IEEE.
12 Alsemaree, O., Alam, A. S., Gill, S. S., & Uhlig, S. (2024). An analysis of customer perception using lexicon-based sentiment analysis of Arabic Texts framework. *Heliyon*, 10(11), e30320.

13 Myint, P. Y. W., Lo, S. L., & Zhang, Y. (2024). Unveiling the dynamics of crisis events: Sentiment and emotion analysis via multi-task learning with attention mechanism and subject-based intent prediction. *Information Processing & Management*, 61(4), 103695.

14 Wan, B., Wu, P., Yeo, C. K., & Li, G. (2024). Emotion-cognitive reasoning integrated BERT for sentiment analysis of online public opinions on emergencies. *Information Processing & Management*, 61(2), 103609.

15 Storey, V. C., & O'Leary, D. E. (2024). Text analysis of evolving emotions and sentiments in COVID-19 Twitter communication. *Cognitive Computation*, 16(4), 1834–1857.

16 Gu, W., Zhong, Y., Li, S., Wei, C., Dong, L., Wang, Z., & Yan, C. (2024). Predicting stock prices with FinBERT-LSTM: Integrating news sentiment analysis. In Proceedings of the 2024 8th International Conference on Cloud and Big Data Computing, Dali, China, (pp. 67–72).

17 Yadollahi, A., Shahraki, A. G., & Zaiane, O. R. (2017). Current state of text sentiment analysis from opinion to emotion mining. *ACM Computing Surveys (CSUR)*, 50(2), 1–33.

18 Russell, J. A. (1980). A circumplex model of affect. *Journal of Personality and Social Psychology*, 39(6), 1161.

19 Soo-Guan Khoo, C., Nourbakhsh, A., & Na, J. C. (2012). Sentiment analysis of online news text: A case study of appraisal theory. *Online Information Review*, 36(6), 858–878.

20 Tian, L., Lai, C., & Moore, J. D. (2018). Polarity and intensity: The two aspects of sentiment analysis. arXiv preprint arXiv:1807.01466.

21 Zhu, W., Qiu, J., Yu, Z., & Luo, W. (2024). A survey on personalized document-level sentiment analysis. *Neurocomputing*, 609, 128449.

22 Phan, H. T., & Nguyen, N. T. (2024). A fuzzy graph convolutional network model for sentence-level sentiment analysis. *IEEE Transactions on Fuzzy Systems*, 32(5), 2953–2965.

23 Shang, W., Chai, J., Cao, J., Lei, X., Zhu, H., Fan, Y., & Ding, W. (2024). Aspect-level sentiment analysis based on aspect-sentence graph convolution network. *Information Fusion*, 104, 102143.

24 Liu, Z., Zhou, B., Chu, D., Sun, Y., & Meng, L. (2024). Modality translation-based multimodal sentiment analysis under uncertain missing modalities. *Information Fusion*, 101, 101973.

25 Hutto, C., & Gilbert, E. (2014). VADER: A parsimonious rule-based model for sentiment analysis of social media text. *Proceedings of the International AAAI Conference on Web and Social Media*, 8(1), 216–225.

26 Esuli, A., & Sebastiani, F. (2007). SentiWordNet: A high-coverage lexical resource for opinion mining. *Evaluation*, 17(1), 26.

27 Agarwal, B., & Mittal, N. (Eds.). (2016). Machine learning approach for sentiment analysis. In Prominent feature extraction for sentiment analysis, Cham, Switzerland, (pp. 21–45). Springer.

28 Narayanan, V., Arora, I., & Bhatia, A. (2013). Fast and accurate sentiment classification using an enhanced Naive Bayes model. In 14th International Conference on Intelligent Data Engineering and Automated Learning (IDEAL 2013), Hefei, China, (pp. 194–201). Springer.

29 Ahmad, M., Aftab, S., Bashir, M. S., Hameed, N., Ali, I., & Nawaz, Z. (2018). SVM optimization for sentiment analysis. *International Journal of Advanced Computer Science and Applications*, 9(4), 393–398.

30 Tang, D., Qin, B., & Liu, T. (2015). Deep learning for sentiment analysis: Successful approaches and future challenges. *Wiley Interdisciplinary Reviews: Data Mining and Knowledge Discovery*, 5(6), 292–303.

31 Devlin, J. (2018). Bert: Pre-training of deep bidirectional transformers for language understanding. arXiv preprint arXiv:1810.04805.

32 Radford, A., Narasimhan, K., Salimans, T., & Sutskever, I. (2018). Improving language understanding by generative pre-training. OpenAI. https://cdn.openai.com/research-covers/language-unsupervised/language_understanding_paper.pdf

33 Islam, M. S., Kabir, M. N., Ghani, N. A., Zamli, K. Z., Zulkifli, N. S. A., Rahman, M. M., & Moni, M. A. (2024). Challenges and future in deep learning for sentiment analysis: A comprehensive review and a proposed novel hybrid approach. *Artificial Intelligence Review*, 57(3), 62.

34 Pires, T., Schlinger, E., & Garrette, D. (2019). How multilingual is multilingual BERT? In Proceedings of the 57th Annual Meeting of the Association for Computational Linguistics (pp. 4996–5001). Association for Computational Linguistics. https://doi.org/10.18653/v1/P19-1493

2

Basic Concepts and Techniques in Sentiment Analysis

2.1 Basic Concepts of Sentiment Analysis

2.1.1 Definition of Sentiment

Sentiment is a fundamental concept in the field of sentiment analysis, which aims to automatically identify and extract subjective information from text or other media. The term "sentiment" generally refers to human emotional responses, such as happiness, anger, sadness, and so on. In the context of sentiment analysis, sentiment is often seen as the subjective attitude or emotion expressed in text [1].

2.1.1.1 Various Definitions of Sentiment

1. Sentiment as Emotional Tone
   Sentiment analysis is a method within natural language processing (NLP) that evaluates and identifies the emotional tone or mood conveyed in textual data. This involves scrutinizing words and phrases to categorize them into positive, negative, or neutral sentiments [2].
2. Sentiment as Opinion Mining
   Sentiment analysis, also known as opinion mining, is the field of study that analyzes people's opinions, sentiments, appraisals, attitudes, and emotions toward entities and their attributes expressed in written text [3]. Entities can include products, services, organizations, individuals, events, issues, or topics.
3. Sentiment as Subjective Response
   Sentiment refers to the subjective response of organisms to external stimuli. In the context of sentiment analysis, it involves the examination of sentiment polarity using available information.

4. Sentiment as Text Classification
   Sentiment analysis is a specific subtask within the broad area of opinion mining, focusing on the classification of texts according to the emotion that the text appears to convey. It typically classifies texts into positive, negative, and neutral categories.
   In this book, we define sentiment as the subjective attitude or emotion expressed in text, speech, or visual content, which can be categorized into positive, negative, or neutral. This definition aligns with the widely accepted view in the field of sentiment analysis, emphasizing the emotional tone conveyed through various forms of communication, including written language, spoken words, and visual cues. Sentiment is not limited to text alone, as humans express emotions and opinions through multiple modalities, making sentiment analysis a broader interdisciplinary field that encompasses various types of data.

2.1.2 Types of Sentiment

Sentiment analysis requires a systematic categorization of emotions to enable computational modeling. The granularity of sentiment classification varies depending on application requirements and theoretical frameworks. This section introduces three primary classification paradigms adopted in research and industry.

1. Basic Sentiment Classification
   The ternary classification system (positive, negative, and neutral) serves as the foundation for most sentiment analysis tasks due to its simplicity and broad applicability. For example, in customer reviews, a positive sentiment might indicate satisfaction with a product or service, while a negative sentiment could signal dissatisfaction.
   - Positive Sentiment: Expresses approval, satisfaction, or optimism (e.g., "This smartphone's camera performance is outstanding!").
   - Negative Sentiment: Indicates disapproval, dissatisfaction, or criticism (e.g., "The battery life of this laptop is disappointingly short.").
   - Neutral Sentiment: Lacks explicit emotional polarity, often presenting factual statements (e.g., "The conference will be held in Paris next month.").
2. Fine-grained Sentiment Classification
   Fine-grained sentiment analysis extends beyond the rudimentary categorization of sentiments into positive, negative, and neutral by identifying more nuanced emotions and sentiments. This advanced approach allows for a more detailed understanding of human emotions in various contexts. Two

prominent frameworks used in fine-grained sentiment analysis are Ekman's basic emotions and Plutchik's emotion wheel.

Ekman's basic emotions framework identifies six fundamental emotions: anger, disgust, fear, happiness, sadness, and surprise [4]. These emotions are universally recognized and can be applied across diverse contexts. For instance, in movie reviews, fine-grained sentiment analysis can track emotional arcs by identifying specific emotions evoked by different scenes.

Plutchik's emotion wheel is a psychological model that arranges eight basic emotions in a wheel format. This structure not only illustrates the intensity variations and combinations of emotions but also provides a structured framework for understanding complex emotions [5]. Additionally, the model includes intensity gradations, allowing for a more granular analysis of emotions. It has been effectively applied in mental health chatbots to detect suicidal ideation by identifying and monitoring the intensity of emotions expressed by users.

The linguistic manifestations and practical application scenarios corresponding to Ekman's six basic emotions are summarized in Table 2.1.

3. Aspect-based Sentiment Analysis

Aspect-based sentiment analysis (ABSA) focuses on evaluating sentiments related to specific aspects or features of a product or service. For instance, a single review might contain positive sentiment about a product's design but negative sentiment about its battery life. ABSA involves identifying these specific aspects and then classifying the sentiment associated with each one. This type of analysis is highly valuable in industries such as retail, technology, and automotive, where understanding customer opinions on individual product features can inform product development and improvement.

Table 2.1 Fine-grained sentiment classification based on Ekman's basic emotions theory.

Emotion	Linguistic Markers	Application Context
Happiness	"Delighted," "ecstatic,"	Customer satisfaction analysis
Sadness	"Devastated," "grieving,"	Mental health monitoring
Anger	"Outraged," "infuriating,"	Crisis management systems
Surprise	"Astonishing," "unexpected,"	News event impact assessment
Fear	"Terrified," "apprehensive,"	Public safety monitoring
Disgust	"Repulsive," "nauseating,"	Product defect detection

2.1.3 Sentiment Versus Opinion

Sentiment and opinion are two closely related but distinct concepts in the field of NLP and text analysis. Sentiment refers to the emotional or subjective stance conveyed in a piece of text. It often involves personal emotions, feelings, or subjective judgments. For example, the statement "This restaurant is great" expresses a positive sentiment. Sentiment analysis aims to identify whether the expressed emotion is positive, negative, or neutral. Sentiment is inherently subjective and can vary from person to person.

Opinion, on the other hand, refers to a viewpoint or evaluation of something, usually without clear emotional coloring. Opinions may carry sentiment, but they are often more rational or objective assessments. For example, "The restaurant has a good location" is an opinion that can be considered positive but is less emotionally charged than a sentiment. Opinions are typically more fact-based and less emotionally driven. They often aim to provide a more balanced or reasoned evaluation.

In summary, sentiment is more about the emotional tone and subjective feelings, while opinion is about the rational evaluation and viewpoint. Both are crucial for understanding human expressions and are widely studied in the field of sentiment analysis and opinion mining. In this book, we will use the term "sentiment" uniformly and will not make a strict distinction between the two.

2.2 Data Sources for Sentiment Analysis

2.2.1 Social Media Platforms

Social media platforms such as Twitter, Facebook, and Instagram are treasure troves of user-generated content, offering a vast and dynamic dataset for sentiment analysis. These platforms enable millions of users worldwide to express their opinions, emotions, and experiences in real time through posts, comments, likes, and shares. By applying sentiment analysis to this content, researchers, businesses, and policymakers can uncover valuable insights into public sentiment regarding specific topics, brands, or events, ranging from consumer preferences to societal reactions to global crises.

The data generated on social media platforms has distinct features that make it particularly suited for sentiment analysis, while also posing unique challenges. Platforms like Twitter provide instantaneous updates, allowing sentiment analysis to capture public reactions as events unfold. This is invaluable for tracking time-sensitive phenomena such as breaking news or product launches. Beyond text, social media includes images, videos, GIFs, and emojis. For instance, a smiling emoji or a celebratory video can enhance or alter the sentiment expressed in accompanying text. Features like retweets, comments, and hashtags create a web of interactions that amplify or contextualize sentiment. Hashtags, for example, link individual posts to broader discussions, aiding in topic-specific sentiment analysis. Social media content often features slang, abbreviations (e.g., “tbh” for “to be honest”), and casual phrasing, reflecting the natural voice of users but complicating automated analysis.

Sentiment analysis leverages social media data for a variety of practical purposes. Companies analyze posts mentioning their products or services to gauge customer satisfaction. For example, a spike in negative tweets about a new smartphone could prompt a company to address design flaws. Social media serves as a pulse for societal views on issues like climate change or healthcare policies. Researchers can analyze sentiment around hashtags like #BlackLivesMatter to understand public attitudes. During elections, sentiment analysis of social media posts can reveal voter preferences or reactions to campaign events, helping political strategists refine their approaches.

2.2.2 Customer Reviews

Customer reviews, abundantly available on e-commerce platforms (e.g., Amazon and Taobao), restaurant websites (e.g., Yelp and Tripadvisor), and movie review sites (e.g., IMDb and Rotten Tomatoes), serve as a rich source of user-generated content. These reviews are packed with sentiment-laden feedback from customers about their experiences with products, services, or entertainment, making them an ideal dataset for sentiment analysis.

Customer reviews stand out due to their explicit expression of opinions, often detailing what users liked or disliked about a product or service. Sentiment analysis of customer reviews has a wide range of practical applications, enabling businesses to make data-driven decisions. Companies can gauge overall customer satisfaction with their offerings. For instance, a smartphone brand might analyze reviews to assess how users perceive a new model, identifying whether sentiment is predominantly positive, negative, or mixed. Reviews often highlight specific strengths and weaknesses, allowing companies to refine their products. For example, a laptop manufacturer might learn from reviews that users praise the keyboard but criticize the battery life, guiding future design improvements. Service-based businesses, such as restaurants or hotels, can monitor customer experiences through reviews. A restaurant might use sentiment analysis to identify recurring complaints about slow service or praise for tasty dishes, prompting targeted enhancements.

2.2.3 News Articles

News websites serve as a rich and dynamic source of data, delivering vast amounts of content on current events, reports, and analyses daily. Unlike other text-based sources such as social media or reviews, news articles often combine factual reporting with subjective commentary, making them an invaluable resource for sentiment analysis. By examining the sentiment expressed in news content, it becomes possible to gauge public sentiment regarding major events, offering insights into how the media shapes or reflects societal views.

News articles provide a unique lens through which to understand public sentiment. They capture real-time reactions to unfolding events, such as elections, natural disasters, or policy changes. Articles often include detailed context, stakeholder quotes, and analysis, enriching the emotional narrative. As authoritative sources, news outlets can both reflect and influence public opinion, making their sentiment a key indicator of societal trends.

Sentiment analysis of news content has several practical and impactful applications. News articles often mirror or shape how the public perceives major events. By analyzing the sentiment in news coverage, one can infer how people might feel about specific occurrences. For example, sentiment analysis of articles about a corporate scandal could reveal whether the public leans toward outrage or indifference, helping organizations respond effectively. Policymakers can leverage sentiment analysis to understand how proposed or enacted policies are received. For instance, analyzing news articles about a new healthcare reform can highlight public support or opposition, enabling governments to refine their strategies or communication efforts to better align with societal sentiment.

2.2.4 Forums and Blogs

Forums and blogs serve as platforms for long-form discussions, distinguishing them from the concise exchanges typical of social media. These online spaces—forums as discussion boards where users post messages and engage in conversations and blogs as personal or thematic websites featuring articles with reader comments—host rich emotional content. This depth and expressiveness make them prime candidates for sentiment analysis, a process that examines text to uncover underlying social emotions or public opinions. By analyzing the sentiments expressed in these platforms, insights into collective attitudes, individual feelings, and societal trends can be revealed.

Unlike brief social media posts, forums, and blogs allow users to elaborate on their thoughts, providing detailed narratives laden with emotion and context. Platforms like Reddit or niche discussion boards host threads where users debate topics, share experiences, or troubleshoot issues, often revealing frustration, enthusiasm, or curiosity. Writers publish opinion pieces or personal stories, while comment sections spark further dialogue, amplifying the emotional range from agreement to dissent.

This long-form content offers sentiment analysis more material to work with, enabling a deeper understanding of user perspectives compared to the limited scope of a tweet or review. Companies analyze forums to understand customer satisfaction. For instance, Tesla might study Reddit's r/TeslaMotors to identify praise for a new feature or complaints about battery life. Sentiment in political blogs can signal public reactions to legislation, helping campaigns refine their strategies. During the COVID-19 pandemic, health forums could have highlighted fears or misinformation, guiding public health responses.

2.2.5 Customer Service Interactions

Customer service call logs and chat transcripts serve as a critical source of data for sentiment analysis, enabling businesses to evaluate customer satisfaction, pinpoint potential issues, and enhance the overall customer service experience. These direct interactions between customers and company representatives provide a wealth of raw, unfiltered feedback that offers deeper insights into customer sentiment compared to more public-facing channels like reviews or social media posts.

Customer service interactions are valuable because they capture detailed, real-time feedback straight from the source. When customers reach out via phone calls or chats, they often express specific concerns, frustrations, or appreciation, providing businesses with a clear view of their experiences. Unlike brief online reviews, these interactions offer more context—revealing not just what customers feel, but why they feel that way and how their issues were addressed. This makes them an essential tool for understanding and improving customer satisfaction.

A telecom company might analyze call logs to find widespread frustration with confusing bills, prompting a redesign for clarity. An online retailer could use chat transcripts to discover that fast shipping earns consistent praise, reinforcing it as a competitive edge. A tech firm might spot confusion about a product feature in support calls, leading to better user guides or tutorials. Call logs and chats often contain sensitive details, so businesses must ensure compliance with privacy laws through careful data handling. A customer's sentiment might shift multiple times in one interaction, and accurately interpreting these dynamics demands nuanced analysis.

2.3 Core Techniques in Text Sentiment Analysis

Text sentiment analysis aims to determine the emotional tone of a given text. The flowchart in Figure 2.1 depicts the core techniques involved in this process. Initially, text data is the starting point. It then proceeds to the preprocessing stage, which encompasses tokenization, stop-word removal, and lemmatization. After preprocessing, feature extraction takes place. Three main pathways emerge. The first is lexical-based approaches, such as sentiment lexicon matching. The other two involve traditional machine-learning models using techniques like bag-of-words (BoW) and TF-IDF, and deep-learning models relying on word embeddings. Ultimately, each of these distinct techniques independently generates either a sentiment category or a measure of sentiment intensity, quantifying the degree of sentiment within the text.

2.3.1 Lexical-based Approaches

Lexical-based approaches are straightforward yet powerful techniques in sentiment analysis and represent an effective method that has been utilized in the early stages of sentiment analysis research. These methods determine the emotional tone of a text by relying on sentiment lexicons, which are precompiled lists of

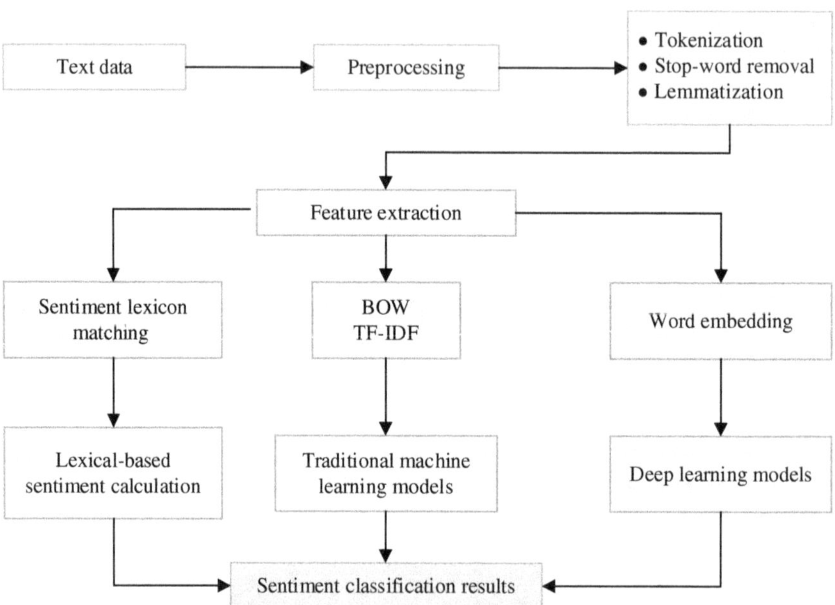

Figure 2.1 Schematic diagram of text sentiment analysis.

words or phrases annotated with sentiment scores that indicate their polarity. Due to their simplicity, computational efficiency, and ease of interpretation, lexical methods are particularly valuable for applications requiring rapid analysis of large datasets, such as social media monitoring or customer feedback evaluation. This section provides a detailed exploration of lexical-based approaches, focusing on their key techniques: the construction and application of sentiment lexicons, text preprocessing, and sentiment strength calculation.

1. Sentiment Lexicons: Building and Matching
   In lexicon-based sentiment analysis, sentiment lexicons are essential tools that map words or phrases to sentiment values, enabling the evaluation of a text's emotional tone. These lexicons can be developed through various approaches, including manual annotation, semiautomated methods, and fully automated techniques. Below is an overview of five widely used sentiment lexicons: SentiWordNet, AFINN, VADER, NRC EmoLex, and LIWC.
   SentiWordNet [6]**:** SentiWordNet is built upon WordNet [7], a lexical database that groups words into synonym sets. Each synset in SentiWordNet is assigned three numerical scores: Obj(s) (objectivity), Pos(s) (positivity), and Neg(s) (negativity), ranging from 0 to 1, with the sum equaling 1. These scores reflect the emotional orientation of the words within the synset. By leveraging synsets, SentiWordNet captures a word's sentiment across different contextual meanings, making it ideal for fine-grained sentiment analysis.
   AFINN [8]**:** AFINN is a manually curated lexicon created by experts. Each word is assigned an integer sentiment score between −5 (strongly negative) and +5 (strongly positive). For instance, "excellent" might score +4, while "awful" scores −4. Its straightforward scoring system makes AFINN efficient for rapid sentiment calculations, particularly in concise texts like social media posts.
   VADER [9]**:** VADER is tailored for social media text, combining expert annotations with a rule-based system. It includes approximately 7,500 terms, each assigned a sentiment intensity score from −4 to +4, and accounts for informal elements like emojis, slang, and intensifiers. VADER excels at analyzing short, informal texts, making it a popular choice for sentiment detection on platforms like Twitter and Facebook.
   NRC EmoLex [10]**:** Developed through crowdsourcing, NRC EmoLex contains about 10,000 English words. Each word is labeled with one or more of the eight basic emotions (joy, sadness, anger, fear, trust, disgust, anticipation, and surprise) and a positive or negative polarity. The lexicon ensures high-quality annotations through rigorous quality control measures during the crowdsourcing process.

LIWC [11]: LIWC can perform computerized text analysis by counting psychologically meaningful word categories, revealing information on attentional focus, emotion, social relationships, thinking styles, and individual differences in texts. Content words convey the core message, while style words reflect communication methods and are more closely linked to social and psychological aspects.

In practice, sentiment analysis using lexicons involves matching words or phrases in a text to their corresponding lexicon entries and aggregating the sentiment scores to determine the overall emotional tone. For example, in the sentence "The product is great," the word "great" might match a +3 score in AFINN, suggesting a positive sentiment. In real-world scenarios, such as evaluating a brand's reputation on Twitter, thousands of posts can be scanned using a lexicon like SentiWordNet or VADER. The matched scores are summed or averaged to reveal whether the sentiment trend is positive or negative.

2. Text Preprocessing: Preparing the Data

   Text preprocessing is essential for accurate sentiment analysis, transforming raw text into a structured format by eliminating noise and standardizing vocabulary. Key techniques include tokenization, stop-word removal, and lemmatization, which enhance the reliability of lexicon-based sentiment evaluation.

   Tokenization segments text into tokens. In sentiment analysis, preserving multi-word expressions like "not good" as single units is critical to retain their emotional meaning, as splitting them risks misinterpreting sentiment. Advanced methods ensure emotionally significant phrases are accurately captured.

   Stop-word removal eliminates common words that carry minimal emotional weight, reducing noise. For example, in "The movie is fantastic," removing "the" and "is" focuses analysis on "movie" and "fantastic." Context-specific stop-word lists are crucial to avoid discarding meaningful terms.

   Lemmatization reduces words to their base form for consistency. This ensures a sentiment lexicon matches all morphological variants, improving coverage and accuracy compared to stemming, which may produce invalid roots.

   Tokenization, stop-word removal, and lemmatization refine text by removing irrelevant elements and standardizing vocabulary, ensuring accurate sentiment scoring. Without these steps, noise or inconsistent word forms may compromise analysis quality, making preprocessing indispensable for reliable results.

3. Calculating Sentiment Strength

   After text preprocessing, lexical-based sentiment analysis calculates the overall sentiment strength of a text by aggregating scores from a sentiment lexicon. This process typically involves adjusting scores for linguistic modifiers like negation and intensifiers.

The foundational step is to sum the sentiment scores of individual words found in the lexicon. For a document D, with matched sentiment words w_i, and $\text{Score}_{\text{lex}}(w_i)$ being the lexicon score for word w_i, a basic sentiment score can be:

$$\text{Sentiment}_{\text{base}}(D) = \sum \text{Score}_{\text{lex}}(w_i) \tag{2.1}$$

However, this simple sum is often insufficient. Linguistic context significantly impacts sentiment:

① **Negation**

Words like "not" or "never" typically invert the sentiment of an adjacent sentiment word w_s. The effective score, $\text{Score}_{\text{eff}}(w_s)$, is often calculated by multiplying its lexicon score by a negation factor V_{neg} (commonly −1):

$$\text{Score}_{\text{eff}}(w_s) = \text{Score}_{\text{lex}}(w_s) \cdot V_{\text{neg}} \tag{2.2}$$

② **Intensifiers and Diminishers**

Intensifiers (e.g., "very," "extremely") amplify sentiment, while diminishers (e.g., "slightly," "somewhat") reduce it. This is usually handled by multiplying the word's lexicon score by a specific factor V_{mod} (where $V_{\text{mod}} > 1$ for intensifiers and $0 < V_{\text{mod}} < 1$ for diminishers):

$$\text{Score}_{\text{eff}}(w_s) = \text{Score}_{\text{lex}}(w_s) \cdot V_{\text{mod}} \tag{2.3}$$

These rules are applied to determine the $\text{Score}_{\text{eff}}(w_i)$ for each sentiment-bearing word w_i in its local context. The final sentiment score for the document D, $\text{Sentiment}(D)$, is then computed by summing these effective scores:

$$\text{Sentiment}(D) = \sum \text{Score}_{\text{eff}}(w_i) \tag{2.4}$$

Alternatively, an average of these effective scores can be used to normalize for document length.

Finally, this continuous $\text{Sentiment}(D)$ score is often mapped to discrete categories by comparing it against predefined thresholds (e.g., θ_{pos} and θ_{neg}). The precise implementation of these rules, the values of modification factors, and the thresholds can vary among different sentiment analysis tools and lexicons.

4. Advantages and Practical Considerations

Lexical-based approaches offer distinct advantages in sentiment analysis, primarily rooted in their simplicity and efficiency. By relying on pre-compiled sentiment lexicons and relatively straightforward scoring rules, these methods bypass the need for complex model training and intensive feature engineering. This translates into minimal computational resource requirements, making them exceptionally suitable for tasks involving large volumes of data or demanding real-time processing, such as monitoring social media streams or analyzing extensive customer feedback databases. Another significant benefit is their interpretability: the final sentiment assessment can often be readily explained by tracing the scores back to individual words or phrases within the text and their corresponding lexicon entries. This transparency is valuable for understanding and validating the results.

However, these strengths are counterbalanced by notable limitations. Lexical methods fundamentally struggle with the context-dependency of word meanings. A word assigned a fixed polarity in a lexicon might convey the opposite sentiment in specific contexts. Furthermore, they are generally ill-equipped to decipher more complex linguistic constructs requiring deeper understanding, such as sarcasm, irony, or nuanced figurative language, where the literal sentiment of words contradicts the intended meaning. When coupled with effective text preprocessing techniques, including tokenization that preserves meaningful phrases, careful stop-word removal, and lemmatization for word normalization, lexical methods provide a foundational and accessible technique for gauging sentiment, offering a solid starting point for understanding textual emotions even if they cannot capture the full spectrum of subjective expression.

2.3.2 Machine Learning Methods

Machine learning offers a data-driven alternative to lexical approaches, enabling models to learn sentiment patterns directly from annotated text data. Sentiment analysis is typically framed as a supervised classification problem, where algorithms learn a mapping from textual features to predefined sentiment labels (e.g., positive, negative, and neutral). This process fundamentally relies on effective feature engineering to convert text into numerical representations and rigorous model training and validation. Below, we discuss four prominent traditional machine learning algorithms frequently employed for sentiment analysis.

1. Naive Bayes

   Naive Bayes classifiers are probabilistic models based on Bayes' theorem. These models make a naive assumption that features are conditionally independent given the class label. Despite this simplification, NB models, particularly Multinomial Naive Bayes, are often effective and efficient for text classification.

   Naive Bayes calculates the probability of a document belonging to each sentiment class based on the presence or frequency of words (using BoW or

TF-IDF features). The class with the highest posterior probability is chosen. The core calculation involves estimating P(class|document) using the formula:

$$P(c|d) \propto P(c) \prod_{i=1}^{n} P(w_i|c) \tag{2.5}$$

where $P(c)$ is the class prior probability and $P(w_i|c)$ is the likelihood of feature w_i given class c.

Naive Bayes is computationally inexpensive and requires relatively little training data, making it an excellent baseline method. Its performance can be surprisingly strong, although the independence assumption limits its ability to model complex word interactions. It remains a common benchmark in comparative studies of sentiment analysis techniques [12, 13].

2. Logistic Regression
Logistic regression is a statistical model used for classification that models the probability of a class outcome using the logistic function applied to a linear combination of input features. Logistic regression predicts the probability of a text belonging to a particular sentiment category based on input features. It's widely used for binary and multi-class sentiment classification.

   Logistic regression is computationally efficient, relatively simple to implement, and provides interpretable results. Feature coefficients indicate importance. It often serves as a strong baseline and performs well, particularly when the relationship between features and sentiment is roughly linear. Its performance is frequently reported in sentiment analysis benchmarks [14].

3. Random Forest
Random forest is an ensemble learning method that constructs multiple decision trees during training and outputs the class that is the mode of the classes output by individual trees. It introduces randomness by building each tree on a different bootstrap sample of the data and considering only a random subset of features at each split.

   Random forest is applied to classify sentiment based on learned decision rules derived from text features. By aggregating the results from many diverse trees, random forest typically achieves higher accuracy and robustness than single decision trees.

   Random forest is powerful, handles high-dimensional data well, is less prone to overfitting than single decision trees, and can capture complex feature interactions. They are frequently used in sentiment analysis tasks and often yield competitive results compared to other traditional methods [15]. Their main drawback is reduced interpretability compared to single trees or linear models.

4. Support Vector Machine
   Support vector machine (SVM) aims to find an optimal hyperplane that best separates data points belonging to different classes in a high-dimensional feature space. The goal is to maximize the margin between the hyperplane and the nearest data points of any class, leading to good generalization.
   SVMs have proven highly effective for text classification tasks, including sentiment analysis, particularly due to their ability to handle high-dimensional and sparse feature spaces generated by TF-IDF or N-gram representations. Linear SVMs are often sufficient and efficient for text, though nonlinear kernels can be explored.
   SVMs frequently achieve high accuracy in sentiment classification tasks and are robust to high dimensionality. They remain a strong contender and benchmark algorithm in the field, often used in comparative analyses even alongside newer deep learning models [12, 16]. Training can be computationally intensive on very large datasets.

2.3.3 Deep Learning Techniques

Deep learning has revolutionized the field of NLP, including sentiment analysis, primarily due to its ability to automatically learn hierarchical feature representations directly from raw text. This end-to-end learning capability often obviates the need for extensive manual feature engineering, a hallmark of traditional machine learning approaches. Deep learning models, particularly neural networks, can capture complex patterns, long-range dependencies, and subtle contextual nuances in text, leading to significant performance improvement.

1. Convolutional Neural Network
   While initially acclaimed for image processing, the convolutional neural networks (CNNs) are effectively adapted for text classification, including sentiment analysis [17]. In this context, word embeddings are dense vector representations of words and are treated as a 1D image. Convolutional filters of varying window sizes slide over these embedding sequences to detect local patterns or salient features, similar to n-grams but with learned representations. These local features are then typically passed through a pooling layer, for example, max-pooling over time, to select the most important features, which are then fed into a fully connected layer for sentiment classification.
   CNN is adept at capturing short, discriminative phrases or keywords that strongly indicate sentiment, irrespective of their position in the text. For instance, a filter might learn to recognize patterns like "absolutely fantastic" or "horrible experience." They are efficient and can be particularly effective for sentence-level sentiment classification where key local cues are often sufficient.

2. Recurrent Neural Network

Recurrent neural networks (RNNs) are specifically designed for sequential data, making them inherently suitable for processing text, which is a sequence of words. Unlike feedforward networks, RNNs have recurrent connections, allowing them to maintain a memory or hidden state that summarizes information from previous tokens in the sequence. This hidden state is updated at each time step as the network processes the sequence word by word.

RNN can model the contextual flow of information in a sentence or document, theoretically capturing how the meaning and sentiment accumulate or change as the text unfolds [18]. For example, the model can learn how negations earlier in a sentence might affect the interpretation of later words. However, simple RNNs suffer from the vanishing or exploding gradient problem, making it difficult for them to learn long-range dependencies effectively.

3. Long Short-term Memory Network

Long short-term memory network (LSTM) is a sophisticated type of RNN designed specifically to address the vanishing gradient problem and effectively learn long-range dependencies. They achieve this through a more complex repeating module that includes a memory cell and three gates: an input gate, a forget gate, and an output gate. These gates regulate the flow of information, controlling what to store in, read from, or erase from the cell's memory. Bidirectional LSTMs (BiLSTMs) process the input sequence in both forward and backward directions, concatenating the hidden states to provide richer context from both past and future tokens.

LSTM is highly effective for sentiment analysis tasks where understanding the entire context of a sentence or document is crucial. The model can capture how sentiment is expressed over longer stretches of text, handle complex sentence structures, and better model the impact of distant words on overall sentiment. BiLSTMs are particularly popular, as they allow the model to consider the full context around each word [19].

4. Gated Recurrent Unit

Gated recurrent unit (GRU) is another type of gated RNN, introduced as a simpler alternative to LSTM. They combine the forget and input gates into a single update gate and also merge the cell state and hidden state. This results in a model with fewer parameters than an LSTM, which can make it computationally more efficient and sometimes less prone to overfitting on smaller datasets, while often achieving comparable performance.

GRU serves a similar purpose to LSTM in sentiment analysis, modeling sequential text data to capture contextual information and long-range dependencies. They are frequently used as a drop-in replacement for LSTMs, particularly when faster training or a slightly simpler architecture is desired. Bidirectional GRUs (BiGRUs) are also commonly employed [20].

5. Attention Mechanism
   Attention mechanism enhances sequence-to-sequence models by allowing the model to dynamically focus on different parts of the input sequence when producing an output or a representation. Instead of relying on a single fixed-length context vector to summarize the entire input, attention computes a weighted sum of input representations, where the weights indicate the relevance of each input part to the current task.

   In sentiment analysis, attention can help the model identify which words or phrases in a text are most crucial for determining its overall sentiment [21]. For example, in a long review, attention can pinpoint the specific sentences or keywords that carry the strongest sentiment. This not only improves performance, particularly on longer texts or in ABSA but also offers a degree of interpretability by visualizing the attention weights.
6. Transformer Network
   The Transformer architecture, introduced by Vaswani et al. [22], revolutionized sequence modeling by relying entirely on self-attention mechanisms instead of recurrence. Self-attention allows the model to weigh the importance of all other words in a sequence when encoding a particular word, capturing complex dependencies regardless of distance. This design also facilitates parallel computation, making it efficient for training on large datasets. Pretrained language models (PLMs) like BERT (bidirectional encoder representations from transformers) leverage the Transformer architecture. They are pretrained on massive unlabeled text corpora using self-supervised learning objectives, enabling them to learn rich, contextualized language representations.

   For sentiment analysis, a pretrained Transformer model like BERT is typically fine-tuned on a task-specific labeled dataset [23]. A classification layer is added on top of the Transformer's output, such as the representation of a special [CLS] token, and the entire model is trained for a few epochs. This approach transfers the vast linguistic knowledge learned during pretraining to the sentiment task, leading to state-of-the-art performance. Transformers excel at understanding context, disambiguating word senses, and handling complex linguistic phenomena like negation and sarcasm.
7. Large Language Model
   Large language models (LLMs), such as GPT-3/4, PaLM, and LLaMA, represent a significant scaling up of Transformer-based architectures, often featuring hundreds of billions or even trillions of parameters and trained on exceptionally vast and diverse text corpora. Their sheer scale leads to emergent capabilities, including the ability to perform a wide range of

tasks with minimal or no task-specific fine-tuning, through prompting and in-context learning. Many modern LLMs are also instruction-tuned, further enhancing their ability to follow natural language instructions for specific tasks.

LLM can be applied to sentiment analysis in several ways without requiring traditional fine-tuning on large labeled datasets. These methods leverage the inherent capabilities of LLMs to understand and generate text based on prompts.

- Zero-shot prompting
  By crafting a prompt that frames sentiment analysis as a question or completion task, LLM can often directly predict the sentiment. For example, "Classify the sentiment of the following review as positive, negative, or neutral: '[review text]' Sentiment:." This approach relies on the model's pre-trained knowledge and ability to infer the task from the prompt structure.
- Few-shot prompting
  Providing a few examples of the sentiment analysis task directly within the prompt allows the LLM to learn the task pattern on the fly and apply it to a new, unseen text. For example, by including two or three input texts with their corresponding sentiment labels. This method enhances the model's understanding by giving it a small set of context-specific examples.
- Chain-of-thought prompting
  For more complex sentiment scenarios, prompting the LLM to think step-by-step can elicit more reasoned sentiment judgments. This approach encourages the model to break down the task into smaller, more manageable steps, leading to more accurate and nuanced sentiment analysis.

  In addition to these prompting methods, LLMs can also provide explanations for their sentiment predictions, identify sentiment towards multiple aspects, or even generate text with a specified sentiment. These capabilities offer a high degree of flexibility and adaptability, making LLM a powerful tool for sentiment analysis tasks without the need for extensive fine-tuning on large labeled datasets.

2.4 Speech Sentiment Analysis

2.4.1 Overview of SSA

While text-based sentiment analysis focuses on the linguistic content of written communication, a significant portion of human emotional expression is conveyed through the paralinguistic cues present in speech. Speech sentiment analysis (SSA), also commonly referred to as speech emotion recognition (SER), is the field dedicated to automatically identifying and categorizing the emotional states of speakers directly from their vocal utterances below [24]. This discipline moves beyond what is said to how it is said, leveraging acoustic features such as tone, pitch, rhythm, intensity, and speech rate to infer underlying emotions.

Unlike text-based analysis, which primarily deals with symbolic representations, SSA operates directly on audio signals, a continuous and complex data modality. The human voice is a rich carrier of affective information. Subtle variations in vocal parameters can significantly alter the perceived meaning and emotional intent of spoken words, even when the lexical content remains identical. For instance, the phrase "That's great" can express genuine enthusiasm, sarcasm, or indifference, depending entirely on the prosody and voice quality. Therefore, SSA necessitates specialized techniques for audio signal processing, feature extraction, and modeling that can capture these dynamic and often subtle vocal cues. As depicted in Figure 2.2, SSA begins with a speech signal, which undergoes audio preprocessing before various features like prosodic, spectral, and voice quality features are extracted and fused, feeding into machine learning and deep learning models to yield sentiment classification results.

The goal of SSA is typically to classify speech segments into discrete emotional categories (e.g., happiness, sadness, anger, fear, surprise, and neutral) or to map them onto continuous affective dimensions (e.g., valence, arousal, and dominance). This capability has profound implications for enhancing human-computer

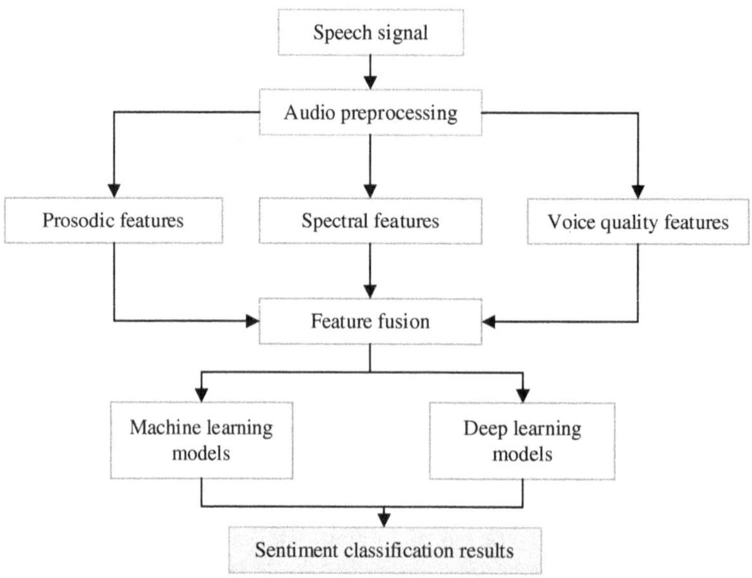

Figure 2.2 Schematic diagram of SSA.

interaction (HCI), understanding human behavior in various contexts, and developing more empathetic and responsive systems. As such, SSA is an interdisciplinary field drawing upon signal processing, acoustics, machine learning, psychology, and linguistics.

2.4.2 Techniques in SSA

1. Acoustic Feature Extraction
   Acoustic features aim to capture the characteristics of the speech signal that are correlated with emotional expression. These features can be broadly categorized into several types, often extracted from short frames of the audio signal and then aggregated over longer segments using statistical functionals (e.g., mean, standard deviation, min, max, and range).
   - Prosodic Features
     Prosodic features relate to the suprasegmental aspects of speech, such as melody, rhythm, and stress, which are highly indicative of sentiment.

     Pitch, or fundamental frequency (F_0), represents the perceived highness or lowness of the voice. Statistics of F_0 (e.g., mean, median, standard deviation, and contour shape) are crucial. For example, a high mean F_0 and a large F_0 range are often associated with excitement or anger, while a flat F_0 contour can indicate sadness.

     Energy or intensity corresponds to the loudness or amplitude of the speech signal. Features such as mean energy, energy contours, and shimmer (perturbations in amplitude) are used. High energy can signal anger or joy, while low energy might denote sadness.

     Duration and speech rate include measures such as the duration of voiced and unvoiced segments, pauses, and the overall rate of speech, expressed in syllables per second. A fast speech rate might indicate excitement or nervousness, while a slow rate can be linked to sadness or boredom.
   - Spectral Features
     Spectral features describe the frequency content of the speech signal, reflecting the vocal tract configuration and articulation.

     Mel-frequency cepstral coefficients (MFCCs) are arguably the most widely used spectral features in speech processing. MFCCs represent the short-term power spectrum of a sound on a nonlinear mel scale of frequency, which approximates human auditory perception. Typically, 12 to 20 MFCCs and their first and second derivatives, which are known as delta and delta-delta coefficients, are used to capture dynamic spectral changes.

     Linear predictive coding (LPC) coefficients model the speech signal as the output of an all-pole filter, representing the vocal tract.

Formants are the resonant frequencies of the vocal tract and are particularly important for vowel articulation. Their values and bandwidths can shift with emotional states.

Log-mel filterbank energies (LFBE/Fbank) are similar to MFCCs but without the final discrete cosine transform step. These are often preferred as input to deep learning models.

- Voice Quality Features

  Voice quality features describe characteristics related to the glottal source and vocal fold vibration.

  Jitter refers to cycle-to-cycle variations in fundamental frequency.

  Shimmer refers to cycle-to-cycle variations in amplitude.

  Harmonics-to-noise ratio (HNR) measures the degree of periodicity in the voice, indicating breathiness or harshness, which can be associated with different sentiments.

2. Modeling Techniques for SSA

   Once features are extracted, various modeling techniques are employed to learn the mapping from these acoustic representations to sentimental labels.

   - Traditional Machine Learning Approaches

     SVMs have been widely used for SSA due to their effectiveness in handling high-dimensional feature spaces and finding optimal separating hyperplanes between emotional classes. Various kernels, including linear, polynomial, and radial basis function (RBF), can be employed.

     Hidden Markov models (HMMs) are well-suited for modeling temporal sequences, making them applicable for capturing the dynamic evolution of acoustic features over time within an utterance.

     Gaussian mixture models (GMMs) can model the distribution of acoustic features for each emotional class. Often, GMM-supervectors are used as features for an SVM classifier.

     Other classifiers such as K-nearest neighbors (KNN), Decision Trees, and ensemble methods like Random Forests have also been applied. However, SVMs and GMMs have often shown more robust performance for this task.

   - Deep Learning Approaches

     Deep learning has brought significant advancements to SER, primarily due to its ability to automatically learn hierarchical feature representations directly from raw or minimally processed audio, such as spectrograms or filterbank energies, and to model complex temporal dynamics.

     CNNs are often applied to speech, taking spectrograms or sequences of spectral features as input. 1D CNNs can convolve along the time axis of frame-level features, while 2D CNNs can treat spectrograms as images, learning spectro-temporal patterns indicative of emotion. They are effective at capturing local acoustic events.

RNNs, especially LSTMs and GRUs, are highly effective for modeling the temporal dependencies in acoustic features, given the sequential nature of speech. They can capture how emotional cues evolve over an utterance. Bidirectional LSTMs/GRUs (BiLSTMs/BiGRUs) are commonly used to leverage both past and future context.

Hybrid CNN-RNN models combine the strengths of CNNs and RNNs. CNN layers first extract local, salient features from spectrograms or feature sequences, and the output of the CNN is then fed into an RNN (LSTM/GRU) layer to model longer-term temporal context and dependencies among these learned features.

Attention mechanisms can be integrated with RNNs or Transformer models to allow the system to dynamically focus on the most emotionally salient segments or frames within an utterance when making a prediction. This can improve performance and offer some interpretability.

Transformer-based models, inspired by their success in NLP, are increasingly being adapted for speech processing tasks, including SER. Models like wav2vec 2.0, HuBERT, and their variants can be pretrained on large amounts of unlabeled speech and then fine-tuned for emotion recognition, often learning robust representations directly from the raw waveform or spectrograms.

End-to-end approaches aim to map raw audio directly to emotional labels, minimizing manual feature engineering. While promising, these systems require substantial datasets to achieve robust performance, as they learn complex mappings without predefined feature constraints.

2.4.3 Applications of SSA

The capacity to automatically discern emotional states from human speech has fostered a diverse array of practical applications across various domains. These applications leverage SSA technology to enhance user experiences, improve operational efficiencies, and gain deeper insights into human affective behavior.

One of the most prominent application areas is in customer service and call centers [25, 26]. By analyzing the vocal expressions of both customers and agents during interactions, SSA systems can provide real-time feedback on customer satisfaction levels. For instance, detecting rising frustration or anger in a customer's voice can trigger alerts for supervisors or prompt recommendations for de-escalation strategies for the agent. Conversely, identifying positive sentiment can help recognize effective agent behaviors. Post-call analysis of aggregated sentiment data allows businesses to identify systemic issues, assess agent performance more holistically, and understand key drivers of customer dissatisfaction or delight, thereby informing training programs and service improvements. This moves beyond simple keyword spotting to a more nuanced understanding of the customer's affective journey.

SSA is also integral to the development of more sophisticated and empathetic HCI systems, particularly in voice assistants and social robotics. Current voice assistants (e.g., Siri, Alexa, and Google Assistant) primarily respond to the literal content of spoken commands. Integrating SSA would enable these systems to perceive the user's emotional state and tailor their responses accordingly, leading to more natural, engaging, and supportive interactions. For example, a voice assistant could detect stress in a user's voice and respond with a more calming tone or offer relevant assistance. In social robotics, particularly in fields like elder care or education, robots equipped with SSA can better understand and adapt to the emotional needs of individuals, fostering stronger human-robot rapport.

The entertainment and media industries also benefit from SSA. Analyzing character emotions in movies, television shows, or video games can provide valuable insights for content creators, aid in automated content tagging and recommendation systems, or even enable interactive narratives that adapt to the player's or viewer's perceived emotional responses. For instance, understanding the emotional arc of characters across a film can assist in script analysis or audience engagement studies. Similarly, in user-generated content platforms, SSA can help moderate content or identify highly engaging emotional moments in audio or video streams.

Beyond these, SSA finds applications in healthcare, such as monitoring the emotional well-being of patients through vocal biomarkers, potentially aiding in the early detection or tracking of conditions like depression or stress. In driver state monitoring, analyzing a driver's speech for signs of anger, drowsiness, or distraction can contribute to road safety systems. Educational applications include assessing student engagement or frustration levels in e-learning environments based on their vocal cues during interactions. As the accuracy and robustness of SSA techniques continue to improve, the range of impactful applications is expected to expand further, driving innovation across numerous sectors that rely on understanding human affective states.

2.5 Visual Sentiment Analysis

2.5.1 Overview of VSA

The conveyance and perception of sentiment extend beyond linguistic and paralinguistic modalities to encompass the rich, multifaceted domain of visual information. Visual sentiment analysis (VSA) has emerged as a significant research area within affective computing and artificial intelligence, dedicated to the automated interpretation and categorization of affective states elicited or expressed by visual stimuli, including static imagery and dynamic video content [27]. This field endeavors to computationally emulate the human proficiency in discerning emotional undertones from a complex interplay of visual cues. These cues range from explicit indicators such as facial expressions and bodily gestures to more implicit, contextual elements including scene composition, object semantics, and aesthetic attributes such as color palettes and illumination patterns.

VSA introduces a critical dimension to the broader study of sentiment by engaging with a modality that frequently offers a more immediate and potent conduit for emotional communication. The human visage, for instance, serves as a primary canvas for affective display, capable of articulating a wide spectrum of emotions with considerable nuance. Beyond facial semiotics, kinesics, the study of body motion, reveals that posture, gait, and gestural patterns are also deeply intertwined with emotional expression. Moreover, VSA grapples with the concept of evoked sentiment, wherein the visual characteristics of a scene itself, independent of human subjects, can induce affective responses in an observer. A tranquil natural vista, for example, might elicit positive sentiment, whereas a depiction of urban decay could evoke negativity.

VSA refers to identifying emotions through facial expressions, body language, and other visual cues in images or videos. It expands sentiment analysis by providing a more direct emotional insight through visual content. The overarching objective of VSA is the assignment of discrete sentiment polarities or more granular emotion categories to visual inputs. As conceptualized in Figure 2.3, a generalized VSA framework involves the transformation of raw visual data into a feature space amenable to machine learning, followed by a classification or regression stage to predict the affective content. The sophistication of this process lies in the development of robust feature representations that can encapsulate the diverse visual indicators of sentiment and in the design of models capable of learning the complex mapping between these features and human affective judgments.

2.5.2 Techniques in VSA

To address the computational challenges of VSA, a diverse array of techniques, primarily drawn from the fields of computer vision and machine learning, is required. These methods aim to extract and interpret affective cues from the multifaceted nature of visual data, ranging from explicit human expressions to more subtle contextual and compositional elements. The evolution of these techniques reflects a progression from hand-crafted feature engineering coupled with traditional classifiers to sophisticated end-to-end deep learning architectures.

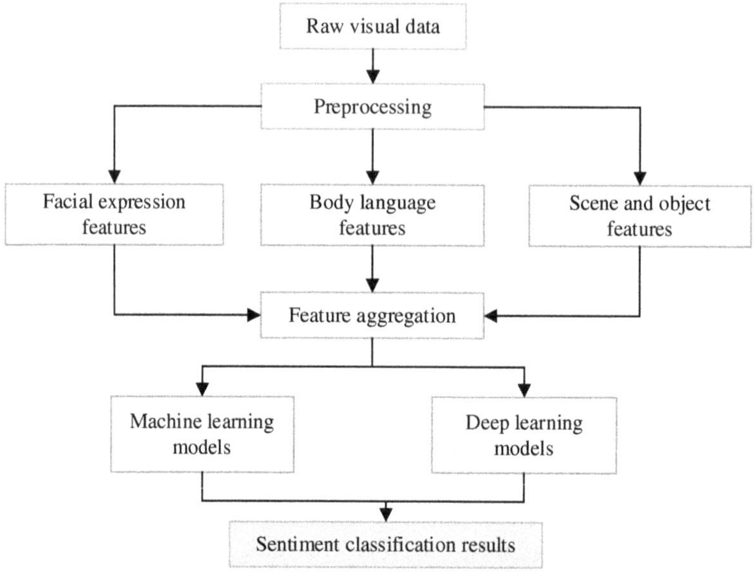

Figure 2.3 Schematic diagram of VSA.

1. FER as a Core Component
Given the primacy of the human face in conveying emotion, facial expression recognition (FER) constitutes a foundational technique within VSA. Early FER systems often relied on geometric approaches, meticulously measuring distances and angles between facial landmarks (e.g., corners of eyes, mouth, and tip of nose) to define feature vectors, or appearance-based methods using texture descriptors like local binary patterns (LBPs) or Gabor wavelets from specific facial regions. These features were then fed into conventional classifiers such as SVMs or AdaBoost.
The advent of deep learning, particularly CNN, has profoundly reshaped FER. CNN can learn discriminative features directly from raw pixel data of facial images, alleviating the need for manual feature design. Architectures like VGGNet, ResNet, or custom-designed CNN are trained on large-scale datasets of faces labeled with discrete emotion categories or continuous affective dimensions like valence and arousal. The challenge in FER for VSA extends beyond recognizing prototypical expressions to handling in-the-wild images characterized by variations in pose, illumination, occlusion, and the subtlety of micro-expressions. Consequently, robust face detection, landmark localization, and alignment are critical preprocessing steps.
2. Body Language and Posture Analysis for Broader Affective Cues
While faces have the potential for emotion recognition, sentiment is also communicated through body language, posture, and gestures. Kinesic analysis

within VSA seeks to interpret these non-facial bodily cues. This process typically involves three stages: human pose estimation, pose feature extraction, and sentiment inference.

Human pose estimation identifies the 2D or 3D spatial configuration of body joints (e.g., shoulders, elbows, hips, and knees). Deep learning models such as OpenPose or HRNet have achieved remarkable accuracy in this area. From the estimated pose, features like joint angles, distances between body parts, overall body posture, and dynamic movement patterns can be derived. These pose-derived features are then used to train models, often LSTMs or GRUs for video data to capture temporal dynamics, or simpler classifiers for static images, to infer emotional states. For instance, an open and expansive posture might correlate with positive sentiment or confidence, while a closed, contractive posture could indicate negative sentiment or submissiveness. However, the interpretation is highly context-dependent and relies on individual postural habits.

3. Scene-level and Contextual Sentiment Understanding
The sentiment conveyed or evoked by an image often transcends individual human subjects, residing in the overall scene composition, contained objects, and aesthetic qualities. Analyzing these elements requires techniques that effectively capture global image semantics. Early approaches relied on handcrafted features like GIST or SIFT, which were aggregated over the image to represent its content. A more dominant method leverages deep features from a pretrained CNN trained on large-scale datasets like ImageNet. Activations from intermediate or later layers of networks, such as ResNet or Inception, provide powerful, high-level feature representations. These representations encode semantic information about objects and scenes. They enable deep features to be used for training sentiment classifiers. Additionally, object detection and attribute recognition are crucial. Identifying objects like flowers or dilapidated buildings, along with attributes like beautiful or gloomy, offers strong sentiment cues. Approaches like Visual Sentiment Ontology (VSO) and adjective-noun pair (ANP) detection connect visual content to sentiment-laden concepts. Furthermore, aesthetic quality assessment contributes significantly. Visual elements like color harmony, lighting conditions, composition based on the rule of thirds, and texture influence an image's aesthetic appeal. This appeal often correlates with evoked sentiment. Models are trained to predict aesthetic scores or directly link these visual qualities to sentiment outcomes.

The development of these techniques is an ongoing process, with significant research focusing on improving robustness to real-world complexities, handling cultural variations in emotional expression and perception, ensuring fairness and mitigating biases, and enhancing the interpretability of VSA models.

2.5.3 Applications of VSA

The capacity to computationally discern sentiment and emotion from visual media has precipitated a growing array of applications across diverse sectors, where understanding human affective responses to visual stimuli is paramount. In the domains of marketing, advertising, and brand management, VSA offers powerful tools for assessing and shaping visual communication strategies [28]. Marketers can leverage VSA to pretest the predicted emotional impact of visual advertisements, thereby optimizing campaigns for enhanced resonance with target audiences before widespread dissemination. Furthermore, VSA facilitates the real-time analysis of user-generated visual content on social media platforms, enabling brands to monitor public sentiment as expressed through images and videos related to their products or services. This continuous feedback loop allows for agile brand reputation management and the refinement of visual branding to align more closely with consumer affective preferences, ultimately fostering deeper engagement.

Beyond commercial applications, VSA plays a crucial role in social media analytics and the broader understanding of public opinion [29]. The proliferation of visual content online necessitates automated methods for interpreting its collective emotional tenor. VSA can be deployed to track societal sentiment concerning unfolding events, prevalent social issues, or public figures by analyzing the affective content of images and videos shared across various platforms. This provides a rich, visually grounded complement to text-based sentiment analyses, offering a more holistic and often more immediate insight into public discourse and collective emotional responses. Such analyses can inform public policy, crisis communication, and sociological research, although the ethical implications of monitoring and interpreting visual sentiment on a large scale, particularly concerning privacy and potential misinterpretation, require careful consideration and robust methodological safeguards.

The advancement of HCI and the design of user-centric systems also significantly benefit from VSA [30]. Integrating the ability to perceive user emotion from visual cues, such as facial expressions captured via webcams or ambient sensors, allows for the development of more adaptive and empathetic interactive experiences. For instance, in educational technology, VSA could enable e-learning platforms to detect a student's frustration or engagement and adjust teaching strategies or visual content accordingly. In entertainment, particularly within immersive environments like virtual reality or gaming, VSA can contribute to dynamic narratives or responsive environments that react to the player's inferred emotional state, thereby enhancing engagement and personalization. While still evolving, applications are also emerging in areas like mental well-being, where visual cues might offer supplementary insights, and in advanced content retrieval systems that allow users to search for visual media based on desired affective qualities. The responsible development and deployment of VSA, balancing technological capability with ethical awareness, will be key to unlocking its full potential across these varied fields.

2.6 Evaluation and Selection of Sentiment Analysis

The development and deployment of effective sentiment analysis systems necessitate rigorous evaluation to quantify performance and deep consideration of various factors to select the most appropriate techniques for a given task or application. This section first details common metrics for evaluating sentiment analysis models and then discusses key considerations for selecting and tailoring approaches based on these evaluations and specific contextual requirements.

2.6.1 Evaluation Metrics for Sentiment Analysis

Rigorous evaluation is essential to quantify the performance of sentiment analysis models. The choice of metrics depends on the specific task formulation, such as classification or regression. These metrics provide objective measures for model comparison and selection.

1. Metrics for Sentiment Classification
   Sentiment analysis is often framed as a classification task. Common metrics assess how well a model assigns predefined sentiment labels. Let TP, TN, FP, and FN denote True Positives, True Negatives, False Positives, and False Negatives, respectively, for a given sentiment class.

   Accuracy measures the proportion of all instances correctly classified. However, accuracy can be misleading for imbalanced datasets.

   $$\text{Accuracy} = \frac{\text{TP} + \text{TN}}{\text{TP} + \text{TN} + \text{FP} + \text{FN}} \tag{2.6}$$

   Precision indicates the proportion of instances predicted as positive that are truly positive. It reflects the exactness of positive predictions. High precision is vital when false positives are costly.

   $$\text{Precision} = \frac{\text{TP}}{\text{TP} + \text{FP}} \tag{2.7}$$

   Recall measures the proportion of actual positive instances correctly identified by the model. It reflects the completeness of positive predictions. High recall is crucial when false negatives are costly.

$$\text{Recall} = \frac{\text{TP}}{\text{TP} + \text{FN}} \tag{2.8}$$

F1-score is the harmonic mean of Precision and Recall. It offers a balanced measure, especially for imbalanced class distributions.

$$\text{F1-score} = 2 \cdot \frac{\text{Precision} \cdot \text{Recall}}{\text{Precision} + \text{Recall}} = \frac{2\text{TP}}{2\text{TP} + \text{FP} + \text{FN}} \tag{2.9}$$

A confusion matrix is an N by N table that visualizes classification performance. Rows typically represent actual classes; columns represent predicted classes. It details the counts of TP, TN, FP, and FN for each class.

The receiver operating characteristic (ROC) curve plots the True Positive Rate (Recall) against the False Positive Rate (FPR = FP / (FP + TN)) at various classification thresholds. The area under the ROC curve (AUC-ROC) quantifies the overall ability of a model to discriminate between classes. An AUC of 1.0 signifies perfect discrimination. An AUC of 0.5 indicates random performance.

For tasks with more than two sentiment classes, metrics like Precision, Recall, and F1-score can be aggregated:

- Macro-averaging: Computes the metric independently for each class and then averages them. This treats all classes equally.
- Micro-averaging: Aggregates the contributions of all classes to compute the average metric globally. This gives more weight to more populous classes.
- Weighted-averaging: Computes the metric for each class and averages them, weighted by the number of true instances for each class.

2. Metrics for Sentiment Intensity and Regression

When sentiment is quantified on a continuous scale, regression metrics are employed.

Mean absolute error (MAE) measures the average magnitude of errors between predicted and actual sentiment scores.

$$\text{MAE} = \frac{1}{n} \sum_{i=1}^{n} |y_i - \hat{y}_i| \tag{2.10}$$

Here, y_i is the actual score, and $\hat{y}_i$ is the predicted score for instance i.

Mean squared error (MSE) measures the average of the squares of the errors. It penalizes larger errors more significantly than MAE.

$$\text{MSE} = \frac{1}{n} \sum_{i=1}^{n} (y_i - \hat{y}_i)^2 \tag{2.11}$$

Root mean squared error (RMSE) is the square root of MSE. It is in the same units as the original sentiment score, making it more interpretable.

$$\text{RMSE} = \sqrt{\frac{1}{n}\sum_{i=1}^{n}(y_i - \hat{y}_i)^2} \tag{2.12}$$

2.6.2 Considerations for Selecting and Tailoring Sentiment Analysis Approaches

Effective sentiment analysis requires more than just model training; it demands careful selection and tailoring of techniques. This selection process is guided by evaluations using metrics and the specific requirements of the task. Several key considerations influence this decision-making.

1. Performance Versus Interpretability
   A fundamental trade-off exists between model performance and interpretability. High-performance models, such as deep learning architectures and large PLMs, often achieve state-of-the-art accuracy, but their internal workings can be opaque, making it difficult to understand their decision rationale, as they function like black boxes. In contrast, interpretable models, including lexical-based methods or simpler machine learning algorithms like Naive Bayes and Decision Trees, may deliver lower raw performance while offering greater transparency, allowing predictions to be traced back to specific words, rules, or features. The choice depends on the application's primary goal, where high-stakes decisions or systems requiring user trust may prioritize interpretability over marginal gains in accuracy.
2. Data Availability, Quality, and Characteristics
   The nature of the available data significantly influences methodological choices. When labeled data is abundant, traditional machine learning and deep learning models trained from scratch typically perform well, but when labeled data is scarce, lexical approaches, few-shot learning with LLMs, or transfer learning through fine-tuning PLMs become more practical. Data quality also plays a critical role, as noise, inconsistencies, and irrelevant information can reduce model performance, making robust preprocessing essential. Additionally, sentiment expression varies across domains, such as product reviews versus financial news, so general models may require domain adaptation to perform effectively. Furthermore, class imbalance, where sentiment classes are unevenly distributed, can bias models, necessitating techniques like resampling, cost-sensitive learning, or the use of appropriate metrics, such as F1-score or AUC-ROC, to address the issue.
3. Computational Resources and Deployment Environment
   Practical constraints significantly influence the feasibility of different approaches. Training large deep learning models requires substantial computational power, such as GPUs or TPUs, and considerable time. For real-time

applications like live social media monitoring, low-latency models are essential, as complex models often incur high inference costs. Additionally, the available hardware and software infrastructure can restrict model choices. In contrast, lexical methods and simpler machine learning models typically demand fewer resources, making them more practical in resource-constrained environments.

4. Task Granularity and Objectives
   The specific sentiment analysis task determines the required model sophistication. For document-level polarity, where the goal is to classify the overall sentiment of a document as positive, negative, or neutral, simpler models may suffice. In contrast, fine-grained emotion classification, which involves identifying specific emotions like joy, anger, or sadness, demands more nuanced models capable of detecting subtle cues. Similarly, ABSA, which focuses on determining sentiment toward specific entities or attributes within a text, requires specialized architectures, such as those using attention mechanisms or targeted fine-tuning, to effectively link sentiment to its target.
5. Multilingual and Multimodal Contexts
   Applications often involve diverse data types. For multilingual sentiment analysis, which entails evaluating sentiment across multiple languages, multilingual models like mBERT or robust cross-lingual transfer learning techniques are necessary, especially since language-specific resources such as lexicons or annotated data are frequently limited. In contrast, multimodal sentiment analysis, which integrates information from text, speech, and vision, requires sophisticated fusion strategies to effectively combine cues from different modalities, potentially weighing them dynamically based on their reliability or relevance. Selecting an appropriate sentiment analysis approach is an iterative process that involves defining clear objectives, understanding data characteristics, rigorously evaluating candidate models, and considering practical deployment trade-offs. Hybrid systems, which combine the strengths of different methods, often provide robust solutions for complex real-world scenarios.

2.7 Summary

This chapter has laid a comprehensive foundation for understanding sentiment analysis, beginning with the core definition of sentiment as subjective emotional expression and exploring its various classifications, from basic polarity to fine-grained emotions and aspect-based evaluations. A critical examination of diverse data sources—ranging from dynamic social media and customer reviews to news articles, forums, and direct customer interactions—highlighted their unique characteristics and utility in capturing public and individual sentiment. The chapter then delved into the primary techniques employed in the field: initial lexical-based approaches leveraging sentiment lexicons and rule-based systems; progressing to data-driven machine learning methods reliant on feature engineering and algorithms like Naive Bayes and SVMs; and culminating in advanced deep learning techniques, including convolutional and recurrent neural networks (CNNs and LSTMs/GRUs), attention mechanisms, and the transformative impact of PLMs and LLMs, which excel in contextual understanding. Recognizing sentiment's multimodal nature, the chapter also introduced the principles and techniques underpinning SSA, focusing on acoustic feature extraction and VSA, which interprets affective cues from images and videos. Finally, the discussion turned to the crucial aspects of evaluating sentiment analysis models through appropriate metrics for both classification and intensity, and the multifaceted considerations for selecting and tailoring these diverse techniques based on performance, interpretability, data availability, computational resources, and specific task requirements, thereby preparing the reader for more advanced explorations in subsequent chapters.

References

1 Saju, B., Jose, S., & Antony, A. (2020). Comprehensive study on sentiment analysis: Types, approaches, recent applications, tools and APIs. In 2020 Advanced Computing and Communication Technologies for High Performance Applications (ACCTHPA), Cochin, India, (pp. 186–193). IEEE.

2 Jim, J. R., Talukder, M. A. R., Malakar, P., Kabir, M. M., Nur, K., & Mridha, M. F. (2024). Recent advancements and challenges of NLP-based sentiment analysis: A state-of-the-art review. *Natural Language Processing Journal*, 6, 100059.

3 Liu, B. (Ed.). (2020). Introduction. In *Sentiment analysis: Mining opinions, sentiments, and emotions* (pp. 1–17). Cambridge University Press.

4 Ekman, P. (1992). An argument for basic emotions. *Cognition and Emotion*, 6(3–4), 169–200.

5 Plutchik, R. (2001). The nature of emotions: Human emotions have deep evolutionary roots, a fact that may explain their complexity and provide tools for clinical practice. *American Scientist*, 89(4), 344–350.

6 Baccianella, S., Esuli, A., & Sebastiani, F. (2010). SentiWordNet 3.0: An enhanced lexical resource for sentiment analysis and opinion mining. In Proceedings of the 7th International Conference on Language Resources and Evaluation (LREC'10), Valletta, Malta, (pp. 665–670).

7 Fellbaum, C. (2005). WordNet and wordnets. In K. Brown (Ed.), *Encyclopedia of language and linguistics* (2nd ed., pp. 665–670). Elsevier.

8 Nielsen, F. A. (2011). A new ANEW: Evaluation of a word list for sentiment analysis in microblogs. In 1st Workshop on Making Sense of Microposts: Big Things Come in Small Packages, Heraklion, Crete, Greece, (pp. 93–98).

9 Hutto, C., & Gilbert, E. (2014). Vader: A parsimonious rule-based model for sentiment analysis of social media text. *Proceedings of the International AAAI Conference on Web and Social Media*, 8(1), 216–225.

10 Mohammad, S. M., & Turney, P. D. (2013). Crowdsourcing a word–emotion association lexicon. *Computational Intelligence*, 29(3), 436–465.

11 Tausczik, Y. R., & Pennebaker, J. W. (2010). The psychological meaning of words: LIWC and computerized text analysis methods. *Journal of Language and Social Psychology*, 29(1), 24–54.

12 Medhat, W., Hassan, A., & Korashy, H. (2014). Sentiment analysis algorithms and applications: A survey. *Ain Shams Engineering Journal*, 5(4), 1093–1113.

13 Ravi, K., & Ravi, V. (2015). A survey on opinion mining and sentiment analysis: Tasks, approaches and applications. *Knowledge-Based Systems*, 89, 14–46.

14 Go, A., Bhayani, R., & Huang, L. (2009). Twitter sentiment classification using distant supervision. *CS224N Project Report, Stanford*, 1(12), 2009.

15 Ahuja, R., Chug, A., Gupta, S., Ahuja, P., & Kohli, S. (2019). Applications of ensemble machine learning in sentiment analysis: A review. *Materials Today: Proceedings*, 18, 28–35.

16 Tripathy, A., Agrawal, A., & Rath, S. K. (2016). Classification of sentiment reviews using n-gram machine learning approach. *Expert Systems with Applications*, 57, 117–126.

17 Kim, H., & Jeong, Y. S. (2019). Sentiment classification using convolutional neural networks. *Applied Sciences*, 9(11), 2347.

18 Tang, D., Qin, B., & Liu, T. (2015). Document modeling with gated recurrent neural network for sentiment classification. In Proceedings of the 2015 Conference on Empirical Methods in Natural Language Processing, Lisbon, Portugal, (pp. 1422–1432).

19 Xu, G., Meng, Y., Qiu, X., Yu, Z., & Wu, X. (2019). Sentiment analysis of comment texts based on BiLSTM. *IEEE Access*, 7, 51522–51532.

20 Gao, Z., Li, Z., Luo, J., & Li, X. (2022). Short text aspect-based sentiment analysis based on CNN+ BiGRU. *Applied Sciences*, 12(5), 2707.

21 Wang, Y., Huang, M., Zhu, X., & Zhao, L. (2016). Attention-based LSTM for aspect-level sentiment classification. In Proceedings of the 2016 Conference on Empirical Methods in Natural Language Processing, Austin, USA, (pp. 606–615).

22 Vaswani, A., Shazeer, N., Parmar, N., Uszkoreit, J., Jones, L., Gomez, A. N., Kaiser, Ł. & Polosukhin, I. (2017). Attention is all you need. In I. Guyon, U. Von Luxburg, S. Bengio, H. Wallach, R. Fergus, S. Vishwanathan, & R. Garnett (Eds.), *Advances in neural information processing systems* (Vol. 30, pp. 1–15). Curran Associates, Inc.

23 Hoang, M., Bihorac, O. A., & Rouces, J. (2019). Aspect-based sentiment analysis using Bert. In Proceedings of the 22nd Nordic Conference on Computational Linguistics, Turku, Finland, (pp. 187–196).

24 Atmaja, B. T., & Sasou, A. (2022). Sentiment analysis and emotion recognition from speech using universal speech representations. *Sensors*, 22(17), 6369.

25 Li, B., Dimitriadis, D., & Stolcke, A. (2019). Acoustic and lexical sentiment analysis for customer service calls. In 2019 IEEE International Conference on Acoustics, Speech and Signal Processing (ICASSP), Brighton, UK, (pp. 5876–5880).

26 Guo, Y., Li, Y., Liu, D., & Xu, S. X. (2024). Measuring service quality based on customer emotion: An explainable AI approach. *Decision Support Systems*, 176, 114051.

27 Cen, J., Qing, C., Ou, H., Xu, X., & Tan, J. (2024). MASANet: Multi-aspect semantic auxiliary network for visual sentiment analysis. *IEEE Transactions on Affective Computing*, 15(3), 1439–1450.

28 César, I., Pereira, I., Rodrigues, F., Miguéis, V., Nicola, S., Madureira, A., Reis, J. L., Dos Santos, J. P. M. & De Oliveira, D. A. (2024). A systematic review on responsible multimodal sentiment analysis in marketing applications. *IEEE Access*, 12, 111943–111961.

29 Al-Tameemi, I. K. S., Feizi-Derakhshi, M. R., Pashazadeh, S., & Asadpour, M. (2024). A comprehensive review of visual–textual sentiment analysis from social media networks. *Journal of Computational Social Science*, 7(3), 2767–2838.

30 Yang, J., Li, Z., & Du, X. (2024). Analyzing audiovisual data for understanding user's emotion in human–computer interaction environment. *Data Technologies and Applications*, 58(2), 318–343.

3

Text-based Sentiment Analysis

The proliferation of digital communication has firmly established text as the predominant modality through which individuals articulate and disseminate their opinions, emotions, and subjective experiences. From concise social media posts and extensive product reviews to news articles, blogs, and customer service transcripts, the sheer volume and rich diversity of textual data present an unparalleled opportunity for computational sentiment analysis. This chapter delves specifically into the methodologies and intricacies of extracting and interpreting sentiment from written language, building upon the foundational concepts introduced previously to explore the unique characteristics and challenges posed by the textual domain. While sentiment can be conveyed through various channels, the explicit nature of language, coupled with its structured form, has made text-based analysis a central and highly developed area.

Understanding sentiment embedded in text requires more than simply identifying positive or negative keywords; it necessitates a deep appreciation for the nuances of linguistic expression. Sentiment in text can be explicit or implicit, conveyed through specific lexical choices, amplified or negated by syntactic constructions, and heavily influenced by discourse context and pragmatic understanding. The representation of this textual sentiment itself can range from simple polarity classifications to fine-grained emotional states and detailed aspect-level evaluations. Consequently, the techniques developed for text-based sentiment analysis are diverse, reflecting a continuous evolution from rule-based lexical systems to sophisticated machine learning (ML) and, more recently, powerful deep learning architectures. This chapter will systematically explore these approaches, highlighting their theoretical underpinnings, practical implementations, and the ongoing quest to develop models that can navigate the complexities of human language to accurately discern its affective content.

3.1 Introduction to Text-based Sentiment Analysis

3.1.1 The Primacy and Pervasiveness of Textual Data for Sentiment Analysis

Textual data holds a position of primacy in the field of sentiment analysis, serving as its foundational bedrock due to an unparalleled combination of volume, accessibility, and inherent structural properties. The digital transformation has catalyzed the creation of a vast and continuously expanding repository of public and private opinion expressed in written form. From the ephemeral micro-opinions broadcast on social media platforms like Twitter and Facebook to the detailed narratives found in product reviews, personal blogs, and professional news forums, this pervasiveness makes text the most abundant and diverse raw material for sentiment mining.

Furthermore, when compared to other modalities such as speech or video, text is often more accessible and computationally tractable. The processes of collecting, storing, and archiving text are typically less resource-intensive. More importantly, the discrete and structured nature of written language, governed by grammar and syntax, lends itself exceptionally well to the established techniques of computational linguistics and natural language processing (NLP). While non-textual data requires complex signal processing to extract meaningful features, text can be directly tokenized and analyzed. Finally, the archival quality of text provides a durable and searchable record of sentiment. This enables powerful longitudinal analysis, allowing researchers and organizations to track shifts in public opinion, brand perception, or societal mood over extended periods, offering historical context that is difficult to replicate with other data types. This unique confluence of scale, accessibility, and historical value solidifies text as the cornerstone modality for the majority of research and application in sentiment analysis.

3.1.2 Defining Sentiment in the Textual Modality

Sentiment within the textual modality manifests in complex and varied ways, extending far beyond a simple dichotomy of positive or negative terminology. A crucial initial distinction lies between explicit and implicit sentiment. Explicit sentiment is articulated directly through affective or opinionated words, such as "This phone has an excellent camera" or "I hate the new software update." In contrast, implicit sentiment is conveyed indirectly, often through factual-sounding descriptions that require contextual or commonsense knowledge to interpret. For instance, the statement, "I had to charge the phone twice in

1 day," implies a negative sentiment regarding its battery life without using any overtly negative words.

The expression of this sentiment occurs at multiple, interwoven linguistic levels:

- Lexical Level
  This is the most direct manifestation, involving individual words or phrases. It includes sentiment-laden adjectives, verbs, and nouns. In modern digital communication, this level is enriched by nonstandard lexical items like emojis and emoticons, which serve as potent and often unambiguous sentiment indicators.
- Syntactic Level
  The grammatical arrangement of words can fundamentally create, amplify, or reverse sentiment. Syntactic structures such as negation, intensification, and comparison are fundamental to accurate sentiment interpretation. The scope of these structures is critical; for example, identifying precisely which part of the sentence is being negated is an important task.
- Discourse Level
  Across multiple sentences or an entire document, the flow of narrative and argumentation can establish an overall sentiment that may not be apparent from any single sentence in isolation. Correctly attributing sentiment often relies on understanding inter-sentential relationships, such as co-reference resolution (e.g., in "I bought the new laptop. It is terrible," the system must link "It" back to "laptop" to assign the negative sentiment correctly).

  Consequently, the computational representation of sentiment in text must accommodate this complexity. This leads to outputs of varying granularity, from simple polarity classification and intensity scaling to more fine-grained sentiment classification and, critically, aspect-based sentiment analysis, which links specific sentiments to particular features or aspects of an entity.

3.1.3 Key Challenges Inherent in Textual Sentiment Analysis

The task of automatically and accurately analyzing sentiment in text is fraught with challenges that stem directly from the inherent complexity, ambiguity, and dynamism of human language. These challenges necessitate the development of sophisticated models that can look beyond surface-level cues and grasp deeper contextual meaning. The most significant hurdles include the following points.

- Context-dependency and Ambiguity
  The sentiment of a word is rarely fixed. It is overwhelmingly determined by its surrounding context. The word "fine" can denote acceptability

("The quality is fine"), excellence ("a fine wine"), or a penalty ("a parking fine"). Similarly, the adjective "unpredictable" could be a highly positive attribute for a movie plot but a dangerously negative one for a car's braking system.

- Sarcasm, Irony, and Figurative Language
  Sarcasm, irony, and figurative language present a major obstacle because the literal sentiment of the words used is often the exact opposite of the intended sentiment. A statement like, "I just love waiting an hour for a cold coffee," uses positive lexical items ("love") to express strong negative sentiment. Detecting such inversions requires a sophisticated understanding of context and pragmatics that most models struggle with.
- Complex Negation
  Handling negation extends far beyond simple markers like "not" or "no." The scope of negation can be intricate, and subtle valence shifters like "hardly," "scarcely," "few," or phrases like "lack of" can invert sentiment in nonobvious ways that are easily missed by simple keyword-matching.
- Domain-specific Language
  As noted, sentiment expression is highly domain-dependent. A model trained on movie reviews, where "thrilling" is positive, will likely perform poorly on financial news analysis. The vocabulary, sentiment indicators, and even the baseline polarity of words can shift dramatically between domains, requiring domain adaptation.
- Implicit Sentiment
  As previously defined, inferring sentiment from objective-sounding statements requires a level of world knowledge or commonsense reasoning that is notoriously difficult to encode in computational models. Understanding that "The phone's screen shattered after a minor drop" is negative requires knowing that fragility is an undesirable quality in a phone.
- Dynamic Nature of Language
  Language, particularly in the online sphere, is in a constant state of flux. New slang, memes, acronyms, and novel uses of emojis emerge continuously. A sentiment analysis system built today may become less effective over time as linguistic conventions evolve, meaning that models require ongoing monitoring and adaptation to remain effective.

These challenges collectively underscore the difficulty of text-based sentiment analysis. They serve as the primary motivation for the field's progression from simple, rigid lexicon-based methods toward the more flexible, context-aware, and powerful ML and deep learning approaches that will be detailed in the subsequent sections of this chapter.

3.2 Lexical-based Approaches for Text Sentiment Analysis

Before the dominance of ML, the earliest and most intuitive approaches to computational sentiment analysis were based on lexicons and handcrafted rules. These methods operate on a simple yet powerful principle: the overall sentiment of a piece of text is a function of the sentiment of the words and phrases it contains. At the heart of these systems lies a sentiment lexicon and other linguistic units pre-annotated with their sentiment polarity and often their intensity. By identifying these sentiment-bearing units in a text and applying a set of rules to account for linguistic structures like negation and intensification, these systems can compute an aggregate sentiment score.

Despite the rise of more sophisticated data-driven models, lexical-based approaches remain valuable due to their transparency, predictability, and independence from large labeled training datasets. This section delves into the construction and application of these foundational methods, exploring how sentiment lexicons are built and refined, how rule-based systems handle linguistic nuances, and the contexts in which these techniques continue to provide significant value.

3.2.1 Sentiment Lexicon Construction and Refinement

The quality and coverage of the sentiment lexicon are paramount to the success of any lexical-based system. The process of creating this core resource can be approached in three primary ways.

1. Manual Method
   This is the most straightforward but labor-intensive approach. Human annotators, typically with linguistic expertise, meticulously compile lists of words and assign sentiment scores to them. They use their intuition and understanding of language to rate terms for polarity and strength. This method yields high-quality, accurate lexicons, as annotators can handle ambiguity and nuance. However, it is extremely time-consuming, expensive, and difficult to scale, often resulting in lexicons with limited coverage. Well-known examples include the MPQA subjectivity lexicon [1] and the Linguistic Inquiry and Word Count (LIWC) dictionary [2].
2. Dictionary-based Method
   This semiautomatic approach begins with a small set of manually defined seed words with clear sentiment polarity. The lexicon is then expanded by leveraging a lexical resource like WordNet or a thesaurus. The system automatically gathers synonyms and antonyms of the seed words, assigning them

corresponding sentiment polarities. For instance, a synonym of a positive seed word is assumed to be positive, while an antonym is assumed to be negative. This process can be iterated to grow the lexicon rapidly. While more scalable than the manual method, it is prone to errors, as a word's synonym may have a different sentiment orientation in a different context.

3. Corpus-based Method
   This data-driven, statistical approach derives sentiment values from a large corpus of text. The underlying assumption is that words with similar sentiment polarity tend to co-occur in similar contexts. One common technique involves using the seed-based method to find words that have a high co-occurrence frequency or pointwise mutual information (PMI) with the initial seed words within the corpus. For example, a word that frequently appears in sentences with "excellent" but rarely with "terrible" is likely to be positive. This method has the distinct advantage of being able to learn domain-specific sentiment, but its effectiveness is highly dependent on the size and nature of the corpus used.

A significant limitation of general-purpose lexicons is their poor performance in specialized domains. A word's sentiment can be highly context-dependent. For example, "small" might be positive for a mobile phone ("a small, compact device") but negative for a hotel room ("a small, cramped room"). Similarly, "unpredictable" is a desired trait in a thriller novel but a critical flaw in a vehicle's steering system.

To address this, domain-specific lexicon adaptation is crucial. This can be achieved through the following steps.

- Rescoring
  Taking a general-purpose lexicon and adjusting the sentiment scores of its words using a corpus from the target domain.
- Extending
  Using corpus-based methods on domain-specific text to identify new, relevant sentiment terms not present in the general lexicon (e.g., financial terms like bullish or bearish).
- Building from scratch
  Creating a new lexicon entirely from the target domain's corpus, which is resource-intensive but often yields the best performance.

Modern textual communication, especially on social media, is rich with informal and nonstandard language. A comprehensive lexicon must therefore account for these informal terms.

- Slang and Acronyms
  Terms like lit, GOAT (Greatest Of All Time), or SMH (shaking my head) are powerful sentiment indicators. These must be manually or semiautomatically added to lexicons with their corresponding polarities.

- Emojis and Emoticons
  These graphical symbols often serve as explicit and unambiguous sentiment markers. A smiling face is a strong positive signal, while an angry face is strongly negative. Modern lexicons, such as VADER (Valence Aware Dictionary and sEntiment Reasoner) [3], incorporate extensive lists of emojis and emoticons with preassigned sentiment scores, making them highly effective for analyzing social media text.

3.2.2 Advanced Rule-based Systems for Text Sentiment

A simple bag-of-words (BoW) approach, where sentiment scores are merely summed, is naive and often inaccurate. To handle linguistic complexity, these scores must be modified by a set of heuristic rules that account for syntax and context.

Negation is the most critical linguistic phenomenon that can completely reverse the polarity of a sentiment. A robust system must do more than just detect words like not, no, or never. It needs to identify the scope of negation, which is the part of the sentence affected by the negator. In the sentence, "I would not say the movie was brilliant," the negation applies to "brilliant," inverting its strong positive sentiment. Advanced systems use syntactic parsing or pattern-based rules to determine this scope. Furthermore, they must handle more subtle negators such as hardly, scarcely, without, and the prefix "un-."

The intensity of a sentiment expression is frequently modified by surrounding words, as commonly illustrated below.

- Intensifier
  These words increase the magnitude of the sentiment. Adverbs like very, extremely, incredibly, and deeply amplify the polarity of the word they modify. A rule would be to multiply the sentiment score of the modified word by a factor greater than 1.
- Diminisher
  These words decrease the magnitude of the sentiment. Terms like slightly, a bit, somewhat, and mildly reduce the intensity. The rule here would be to multiply the score by a factor less than 1.
- Valence Shifter
  This is a broader category that includes negators and intensifiers, but also conjunctions like but, which signal a shift in sentiment. In a sentence like, "The acting was great, but the plot was predictable," the rule-based system should give more weight to the sentiment expressed in the clause following but.

Sarcasm, where the intended meaning is the opposite of the literal meaning, is one of the most difficult challenges in sentiment analysis. While a perfect solution is elusive, rule-based systems can employ heuristics to detect potential sarcasm, as shown in the following examples.

- Polarity Conflict
  Identifying the co-occurrence of a strong positive sentiment expression with a clearly negative situation (e.g., "Wonderful. I just spilled coffee all over my new shirt.").
- Pragmatic Cues
  Using punctuation like exclamation marks or ellipses, or specific emoticons in a context that suggests a nonliteral meaning.
- Hyperbole
  Detecting the use of extreme intensifiers with commonplace events (e.g., "I am ecstatically happy to be stuck in traffic.").

These rules are brittle and not universally applicable, but they can help flag potential instances of sarcasm for more nuanced handling.

3.2.3 Advantages and Limitations for Textual Lexical Methods

Lexicon- and rule-based methods possess a distinct profile of strengths and weaknesses that defines their modern-day utility.

1. Advantages
   Interpretability and transparency are the greatest strengths of lexicon-based sentiment analysis systems. The reason for a sentiment classification is entirely transparent and can be traced back to specific words and rules. This interpretable nature is highly valued in business contexts where decisions must be explainable. Additionally, lexicon-based approaches do not require large, labeled datasets for training, making them quick to deploy and useful in scenarios where labeled data is scarce or expensive to obtain. These systems are typically lightweight and computationally fast, as they involve dictionary lookups and rule application rather than complex model inference.
2. Limitations
   Brittleness and maintenance are significant challenges for lexicon-based systems. The rules are handcrafted and can be brittle, struggling to handle linguistic constructions not explicitly encoded in the system. Furthermore, lexicons and rules require constant manual updates to keep pace with evolving language, such as new slang and new contexts. These systems also have difficulty handling nuance and context. They fundamentally struggle with context-dependent sentiment, like the "unpredictable" example, and implicit sentiment, as they cannot perform commonsense reasoning. Additionally,

they suffer from poor generalization and domain dependency. A rule set and lexicon meticulously crafted for one domain, such as hotel reviews, will likely perform poorly on another, like political analysis, without significant adaptation.

3.3 ML Approaches for Text Sentiment Analysis

Lexical-based methods are limited by their reliance on extensive manual labor for rule and lexicon creation, as well as their difficulty in capturing context-dependent sentiment. To address these challenges, ML methods have shifted from explicitly programming linguistic rules to a data-driven approach. This approach paved the way for a paradigm shift in sentiment analysis. Instead of instructing a system on how to identify sentiment, an ML model learns the complex patterns, nuances, and correlations associated with sentiment directly from a large corpus of labeled examples.

This approach treats sentiment analysis as a classic text classification task. The core principle involves two main stages: first, transforming raw, unstructured text into a structured, numerical format through a process known as feature engineering; and second, training a statistical model on these numerical features to learn a mapping function that can predict the sentiment of new, unseen texts. This section details this pipeline, covering the critical techniques for text representation, the application of ML algorithms, and the practices for model training and evaluation.

3.3.1 Text Preprocessing and Feature Engineering for Text Sentiment

The performance of any traditional ML algorithm is fundamentally dependent on the quality and relevance of the features it is given. Feature engineering is the process of extracting and selecting the most informative features from raw data to create a representation that a model can effectively learn from. For text, this means converting a sequence of words into a fixed-length numerical vector.

Tokenization is the foundational step of breaking down a stream of text into its constituent units or tokens. While splitting by whitespace is a simple start, robust tokenization for sentiment analysis must handle the idiosyncrasies of digital text:

- Contractions: Splitting "don't" into "do" and "n't" or "not" preserves the negation.
- Hyphenation: Words like "state-of-the-art" may need to be treated as a single token to retain their meaning.

- Social Media Constructs: Special tokenizers are often required to correctly handle usernames (@user), hashtags (#sentiment), and URLs, either by isolating them or normalizing them to generic tokens (e.g., <USER>, <HASHTAG>).

To reduce the dimensionality of the feature space and focus on content-bearing words, two normalization techniques are commonly applied:

- Stop Word Removal
  This involves filtering out high-frequency function words that carry little semantic weight with respect to sentiment (e.g., "a," "an," "the," "in," "is"). While generally useful, this step requires caution in sentiment analysis, as some stop words can be part of critical phrases (e.g., the "not" in "not good").
- Stemming and Lemmatization
  Both aim to reduce inflectional forms of a word to a common base form. Stemming uses crude heuristic rules to chop off word endings. It is fast but can be inaccurate. Lemmatization, in contrast, uses vocabulary and morphological analysis to return the dictionary form of a word. Lemmatization is more computationally intensive but more accurate, often preserving semantic integrity better. Examples of stemming and lemmatization are shown in Table 3.1.

  A simple BoW model, where each token is a feature, loses all word order information. *N*-grams are contiguous sequences of n items from a given text, and they serve to capture local context.
- Word *N*-grams
  Unigrams ($n = 1$) are individual words. Bigrams ($n = 2$) and trigrams ($n = 3$) are sequences of two and three words, respectively. Using bigrams like "not good" as a single feature is far more informative for sentiment than having separate features for "not" and "good."

Table 3.1 Comparison of stemming and lemmatization.

Original Word	Stemming	Lemmatization (with POS)
Studies	Studi	Study (as a verb)
Better	Better	Good (as an adjective)
Meeting	Meet	Meeting (as a noun)
Was	Wa	Be (as a verb)

- Character N-grams
  These are sequences of characters. For example, the word "happy" contains the character 3-grams "hap," "app," "ppy." They are robust to misspellings and out-of-vocabulary (OOV) words, making them useful for noisy user-generated content.

Once text is tokenized, the features must be weighted. A simple frequency count is a start, but it overvalues common words. Term frequency-inverse document frequency (TF-IDF) is a superior weighting scheme that evaluates how important a word is to a document in a collection or corpus.

The TF measures how often a term t appears in a document d:

$$\mathrm{TF}(t,d) = \frac{\text{Number of times term } t \text{ appears in document } d}{\text{Total number of terms in document } d} \tag{3.1}$$

The IDF measures how much information the word provides (i.e., whether it is common or rare across all documents). Let D be the total set of documents in the corpus.

$$\mathrm{IDF}(t,D) = \log \frac{|D|}{|\{d \in D : t \in d\}| + 1} \tag{3.2}$$

The "+1" in the denominator is a smoothing term to prevent division by zero for terms not in the corpus.

The TF-IDF score is the product of these two values, rewarding terms that are frequent in a document but rare across the corpus:

$$\text{TF-IDF}(t,d,D) = \mathrm{TF}(t,d) \times \mathrm{IDF}(t,D) \tag{3.3}$$

The final feature vector for a document is composed of the TF-IDF scores for every term in the vocabulary.

Going beyond word presence, syntactic information can provide valuable clues. POS tagging assigns a grammatical category to each word. For sentiment analysis, adjectives (JJ), adverbs (RB), and verbs (VB) are often potent indicators. One can engineer features based on the count or TF-IDF of words belonging to these specific POS categories.

To bridge the gap between lexical and ML methods, lexicon-based scores can be integrated as features in a hybrid model. For a given document, one can compute:

- The total count of positive and negative words based on a lexicon.
- The sum of sentiment scores for all words in the text using a scored lexicon.
- The ratio of positive to negative words.

These engineered features provide the model with explicit sentiment signals, which can complement the patterns learned from n-grams.

The use of n-grams can lead to a feature space with tens or hundreds of thousands of dimensions, most of which are sparse. This "curse of dimensionality" can degrade model performance and increase computational cost. Feature selection aims to select a subset of the most relevant features. Common techniques for text include:

- Chi-squared (χ^2) Test
  Measures the lack of independence between a feature and the sentiment class. Higher scores indicate a stronger association.
- Mutual Information
  Measures how much information the presence/absence of a feature contributes to making the correct sentiment classification decision.

3.3.2 Application of Traditional ML Algorithms to Text Sentiment

With a numerical feature matrix in hand, various supervised learning algorithms can be applied. Each has its own assumptions and strengths.

The Naive Bayes classifier is a probabilistic model based on Bayes' theorem. It is naive because it makes a strong independence assumption: the presence of a particular feature in a class is unrelated to the presence of any other feature. For a document d and a class c, the probability is:

$$P(c|d) \propto P(c) \prod_{i=1}^{n} P(w_i|c) \tag{3.4}$$

where $P(c)$ is the prior probability of the class and $P(w_i|c)$ is the probability of term w_i occurring in a document of class c. Despite its simplistic assumption, Naive Bayes is remarkably effective for text sentiment classification, serving as a strong and fast baseline.

Support vector machines (SVMs) have historically been one of the most powerful and popular algorithms for text classification. The objective of an SVM is to find an optimal hyperplane that separates the data points of different classes in the high-dimensional feature space. The optimal hyperplane is the one that maximizes the margin, which is the distance between the hyperplane and the nearest data points from each class. For nonlinearly separable data, SVMs use the kernel trick to project the data into a higher-dimensional space where a linear separation is possible. The linear kernel is often highly effective for high-dimensional, sparse text data.

Logistic regression is another powerful linear model that is widely used for classification. Despite its name, it is a classification algorithm, not a regression one. It models the probability that a given input point belongs to a particular class. It passes a linear combination of the input features through a sigmoid function, which squashes the output to a value between 0 and 1.

$$\sigma(z) = \frac{1}{1 + e^{-z}} \tag{3.5}$$

$$z = w \cdot x + b \tag{3.6}$$

This output σ can be interpreted as the probability of the positive class. Logistic regression is known for its simplicity, interpretability, and strong performance.

Decision tree learns a hierarchy of if/else rules based on the input features, creating a tree-like structure. They are highly interpretable but prone to overfitting.

Ensemble methods combine the predictions of multiple individual models to produce a more robust and accurate final prediction. A popular ensemble technique is Random Forests, which are an ensemble of many decision trees. It introduces randomness by training each tree on a bootstrapped sample of the data and by considering only a random subset of features at each split. This decorrelates the trees and significantly reduces overfitting. Another powerful ensemble method is gradient boosting machines (GBMs), which build models in a sequential, stagewise fashion. Each new model is trained to correct the errors made by the previous ones. Highly optimized implementations of this idea, such as XGBoost and LightGBM, are often state-of-the-art performers for classification tasks on structured or tabular data.

3.3.3 Model Training, Hyperparameter Tuning, and Evaluation Strategies for Text

The final component of the ML pipeline is the process of training, refining, and fairly evaluating the chosen model.

The labeled dataset must be split into at least two, and ideally three, sets. Training set is used to train the model. Validation set is used to tune the model's hyperparameters and make decisions about the model architecture without peeking at the final test data. Test set is used only once at the very end of the process to provide an unbiased estimate of the model's performance on unseen data. A common split is 70% training, 15% validation, and 15% test.

Hyperparameter tuning involves optimizing the settings of an algorithm that are not learned from the data but are set prior to training. Techniques like grid search and random search are used with the validation set to find the optimal configuration. Grid search exhaustively tries all combinations of a predefined set of hyperparameter values, while random search samples a fixed number of combinations randomly.

Evaluation is a crucial step in assessing model performance. Model performance is typically assessed using standard classification metrics, which are usually derived from a confusion matrix. These metrics provide a comprehensive view of how well the model is performing in terms of accuracy, precision, recall, F1-score, and other relevant measures.

By rigorously following this process of feature engineering, model selection, and evaluation, ML approaches provide a robust and scalable framework for text sentiment analysis, significantly outperforming purely lexical methods in both accuracy and adaptability. They form the bridge to the even more powerful deep learning architectures discussed in the next section.

3.4 Deep Learning Approaches for Text Sentiment Analysis

While traditional ML models brought a data-driven paradigm to sentiment analysis, their performance is fundamentally constrained by the quality of handcrafted features. The process of feature engineering, though powerful, is often laborious and requires significant domain expertise. It implicitly limits the model's learning capacity to the features predefined by the human engineer. Deep learning represents a significant leap forward by automating the feature learning process. These methods, based on multilayered artificial neural networks, can learn hierarchical representations of data directly from the raw text, discovering intricate and abstract patterns that are often missed by manual feature engineering.

The core advantage of deep learning in this context is its ability to learn effective representations of words and their compositions. This section traces the evolution of these powerful techniques, beginning with the foundational concept of word embeddings, moving through the seminal neural architectures like convolutional and recurrent neural networks (RNNs), and culminating in the current state-of-the-art Transformer-based pretrained language models (PLMs) and the emergent paradigm of large language models (LLMs).

3.4.1 Word Embedding as Input Features

Deep learning models cannot process raw text directly. They require numerical input. A simple one-hot encoding is prohibitively high-dimensional, sparse, and fails to capture any semantic relationship between words. Word embedding solves this problem by representing words as dense, low-dimensional, real-valued vectors. These vectors are learned such that words with similar meanings have similar vector representations in the geometric space. This is famously illustrated by the vector arithmetic: vector ('King') – vector ('Man') + vector ('Woman') ≈ vector ('Queen').

Word2Vec [4, 5], developed by Mikolov, is a family of models that learn embeddings from local word context. It features two distinct structures, as illustrated in Figure 3.1.

1. Continuous Bag-of-words (CBOW)
   This model learns to predict a target word from its surrounding context words. For example, given the context {"The," "cat," "on," "the"}, it predicts the target word "sat." The input vectors of the context words are averaged before being used for prediction.
2. Skip-gram
   This model works in the opposite direction. Given a target word (e.g., "sat"), it learns to predict its surrounding context words (e.g., "The," "cat," "on," "the"). Skip-gram is generally slower to train but performs better for infrequent words.

While Word2Vec is based on local context windows, GloVe [6] incorporates global corpus statistics. It is trained on a global word-word co-occurrence matrix, which tabulates how frequently words co-occur in the corpus. The training objective is to learn word vectors such that their dot product equals the logarithm

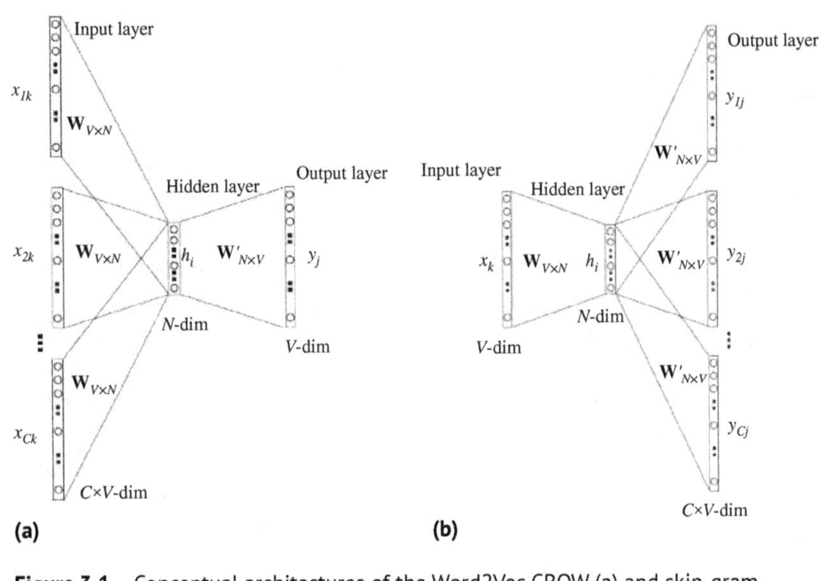

Figure 3.1 Conceptual architectures of the Word2Vec CBOW (a) and skip-gram (b) models.

of their co-occurrence probability. This allows GloVe to capture both local context and global statistical information, often resulting in high-quality embedding.

A limitation of Word2Vec and GloVe is that they treat each word as an atomic unit, making them unable to handle OOV words or understand word morphology. FastText [7] addresses this by representing each word as a bag of character n-grams. For example, the word "apple" with $n = 3$ would be represented by the character n-grams <ap, app, ppl, ple, le>. The final word vector is the sum of its character n-gram vectors. This subword information allows FastText to generate vectors for OOV words and to recognize that words like "love" and "loving" are morphologically related.

The aforementioned methods produce static embedding. The word "bank" has the same vector in "riverbank" and "investment bank." This is a major limitation, as word meaning is highly context-dependent. Contextual embeddings address this by generating a different embedding for a word each time it appears, based on its specific context in a sentence. Early models like ELMo (embeddings from language models) [8] pioneered this approach by using a bidirectional LSTM (BiLSTM). This concept of dynamic, context-aware representations is the cornerstone of the Transformer-based models discussed later, which have largely superseded static embeddings in state-of-the-art NLP.

3.4.2 Neural Network Architectures for Text Sentiment

Once words are converted into embeddings, neural networks can be used to learn how to compose them to classify the sentiment of a sentence or document. Inspired by the success in computer vision, a convolutional neural network (CNN) can be adapted for text classification. A sentence is represented as a matrix where each row is the embedding for a word. 1D convolutions are then applied. A filter of a specific height (e.g., 2, 3, or 4 words) slides over the sentence matrix, acting as a detector for local patterns or n-grams.

The seminal architecture by Kim in 2014 was the first to apply CNN to text classification. The model's structure, as shown in Figure 3.2, uses multiple filters of varying window sizes to capture bi-grams, tri-grams, and 4-grams, simultaneously. After the convolution operation, a max-over-time pooling layer is applied to each filter's output, extracting the single most important feature detected by that filter. These pooled features are then concatenated and fed into a final fully connected softmax layer for classification. Multichannel CNN can further enhance this approach by using different sets of word embedding, such as Word2Vec and GloVe, as separate "channels," analogous to the R, G, and B channels in an image. In applications, CNN is highly effective for sentence-level sentiment analysis, where the presence of key phrases, such as "not very good," serves as a strong signal regardless of their position in the sentence.

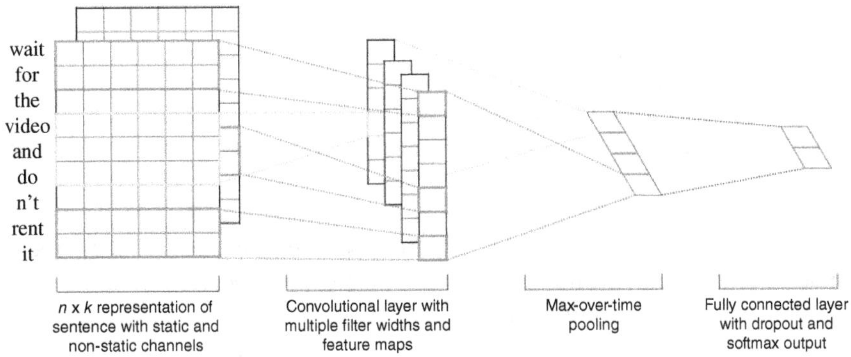

Figure 3.2 Architecture of a CNN for sentence classification.

RNN is designed to process sequential data. A basic RNN processes a sentence word by word, maintaining a hidden state vector h_t that acts as its memory of the sequence seen so far. The hidden state at time step t is a function of the input at that step x_t and the previous hidden state h_{t-1}.

$$h_t = f(Wh_{t-1} + Ux_t + b) \tag{3.7}$$

However, simple RNNs suffer from the vanishing gradient problem, making them unable to capture long-range dependencies. Long short-term memory (LSTM) and gated recurrent unit (GRU) networks were designed to solve this. They introduce gating mechanisms (input, forget, and output gates in LSTMs) that allow the network to selectively remember or forget information over long sequences, making them ideal for modeling language.

Unidirectional and bidirectional architectures differ in how they process text. A standard RNN or LSTM processes text in a unidirectional manner, moving from left to right. However, for sentiment analysis, context from both directions is crucial. To address this, a BiLSTM is used [9], which consists of two LSTMs—one processing the sequence forward and the other processing it backward. At each time step, the hidden states of these two LSTMs are concatenated, providing a representation of the word that is aware of both its past and future context. Furthermore, LSTM is naturally suited for sentiment analysis because it can model the cumulative effect of a sequence. For example, it can learn how a word like "but" can flip the sentiment established earlier in the sentence.

To leverage the best of both worlds, hybrid architectures were developed. A common approach is to use a CNN layer first to extract robust local and n-gram features, and then feed the output of the CNN's pooling layer into an LSTM. This allows the model to first learn key local phrases and then model the sequential dependencies between them.

A key insight is that not all words contribute equally to the sentiment of a sentence. An attention mechanism allows a model to learn to dynamically assign different weights to different parts of the input sequence when making a prediction [10, 11]. For a BiLSTM, instead of just using the final hidden state, an attention layer computes a weighted average of all hidden states, where the weights indicate the importance of each word.

Self-attention, a specific type of attention, allows words within the same sentence to attend to each other, helping the model to resolve co-references and understand complex relationships. This mechanism is the core component of the Transformer architecture. Meanwhile, attention mechanisms enhance both interpretability and performance. They improve model performance by helping it focus on salient features and offer a degree of interpretability. By visualizing the attention weights, one can see which words the model considered most important for its decision. For example, in the sentence "The service was quick, but the food was awful," the attention would be high on "awful."

3.4.3 Transformer-based Models and PLMs

The introduction of the Transformer architecture [12] and the concept of pretraining marked a revolution in NLP. The Transformer dispenses with recurrence entirely and relies solely on a multiheaded self-attention mechanism. This allows it to process all words in a sequence in parallel and to model dependencies between any two words, regardless of their distance. For classification tasks like sentiment analysis, the Transformer encoder stack is typically used [13].

Bidirectional encoder representations from transformers (BERT) [14] is a landmark PLM. The key idea is to pretrain a deep Transformer model on a massive unlabeled text corpus to learn a general-purpose understanding of language. This pretrained model can then be fine-tuned for specific downstream tasks with a much smaller labeled dataset.

1. Pretraining Objectives
   BERT achieves its powerful language representation capabilities through two novel pretraining tasks. First, the masked language model (MLM) randomly masks 15% of the input tokens and requires the model to predict the original masked tokens based on the unmasked context from both the left and right sides. Second, the next sentence prediction (NSP) task provides the model with two sentences, A and B, and asks it to predict whether B is the actual sentence that follows A in the original text.

2. Fine-tuning Strategies for Sentiment Classification
   To fine-tune BERT for sentiment analysis, a single linear classification layer is added on top of the final hidden state of the special [CLS] token. The entire model is then trained end-to-end on the labeled sentiment dataset with a low learning rate. This process adjusts the pretrained weights to specialize them for the sentiment task.
3. Variants
   Numerous variants have improved upon BERT, including RoBERTa [15] for more robust pretraining, ALBERT [16] for parameter reduction to enhance efficiency, and DistilBERT [17] for a smaller, faster, distilled version.

   The generative pretrained Transformer (GPT) series are autoregressive models, meaning they are pretrained to predict the next word in a sequence. While this makes them naturally suited for text generation, they can also be adapted for classification. The modern approach is not to fine-tune the entire model but to use prompt-based learning. For sentiment analysis, one might feed the model a prompt like:

   Review: "This movie was fantastic!"
   Sentiment: Positive
   Review: "I was so disappointed with this product."
   Sentiment:.

The model then generates the most likely completion, which would be Negative. This is known as few-shot learning. If no examples are provided, it is zero-shot learning.

The landscape of PLMs is vast and includes models like XLNet [18], an autoregressive model that learns bidirectional context; T5 [19], which frames all NLP tasks as text-to-text problems; and ELECTRA [20], which uses a more efficient pretraining task. However, PLMs pretrained on general corpora may struggle with specialized domains such as finance or biomedical. To address this, domain adaptation is employed. This process involves further pretraining a general PLM on a corpus from the target domain, such as financial news articles, before fine-tuning it on the specific task. This adaptation adjusts the model's knowledge to the new domain's vocabulary and context, significantly improving performance.

3.4.4 LLMs for Text Sentiment Analysis

LLM is an extension of the PLM paradigm, but at a vastly larger scale, with hundreds of billions of parameters. This scale unlocks emergent abilities, particularly for performing tasks with zero or few examples, fundamentally changing the application workflow.

With LLM, the focus shifts from model training to prompt engineering. The goal is to design a natural language prompt that effectively instructs the model to perform sentiment analysis. A zero-shot prompt might be as simple as:

> Classify the sentiment of the following text as positive, negative, or neutral. Text: "The flight was delayed, but the crew was very helpful." Sentiment:

Few-shot prompting relies on the LLM's in-context learning ability. By providing a few examples of the task within the prompt itself, the model learns the task on-the-fly without any gradient updates or changes to its weights.

A recent advance is instruction fine-tuning [21], where a base LLM is further trained on a massive collection of tasks described via natural language instructions (e.g., "Summarize this document," "Translate this to French," "What is the sentiment of this review?"). This enables models such as Flan-T5 and InstructGPT to excel at understanding and following user instructions for new tasks, resulting in superior zero-shot performance.

LLM offers several advantages, including state-of-the-art performance, often achieving the highest accuracy, especially in zero-shot or few-shot learning scenarios. They also significantly reduce the need for large, task-specific labeled datasets, making them highly efficient. Additionally, LLM is flexible enough to perform complex tasks, such as aspect-based sentiment analysis (ABSA), or provide explanations for their predictions when given the right prompt. However, these models also face several challenges. Training LLM is prohibitively expensive for most organizations, and access is typically limited to paid APIs. This raises issues regarding reproducibility and consistency, as API-based models can be updated by their providers without notice, leading to potential changes in performance. Furthermore, LLMs can inherit and amplify biases from their training data, and they may hallucinate or generate plausible-sounding but incorrect explanations. Finally, sending sensitive data, such as customer feedback, to an external API poses significant data privacy concerns.

3.5 Advanced Topics in Text-based Sentiment Analysis

While the models discussed previously are proficient at document-level classification, they often fall short of the nuanced understanding required for sophisticated real-world applications and fundamental linguistic inquiry. The frontier of sentiment analysis research lies in moving beyond coarse-grained polarity to address more complex, context-dependent, and human-like interpretation tasks. This section explores four such critical research areas that represent profound challenges in the field: understanding sentiment at a fine-grained aspect level, deciphering nonliteral language like sarcasm, bridging linguistic and cultural divides, and making the reasoning of black-box models transparent.

3.5.1 ABSA for Text

Arguably the most significant advanced topic, ABSA [22] shifts the focus from the sentiment of the entire text to the sentiment expressed toward specific aspects or features of an entity. A single product review, for instance, can contain multiple sentiments about different aspects. The sentence, "The phone's camera is brilliant, but the battery life is disappointingly short," expresses a positive sentiment toward the "camera" and a negative sentiment toward the "battery life." ABSA aims to automatically extract these fine-grained opinion units. The task is typically decomposed into several subtasks, which can be solved sequentially or with a single end-to-end model. The description and example of these subtasks are shown in Table 3.2.

Aspect term extraction (ATE) is fundamentally a sequence labeling task [23]. The goal is to label each word in a sentence with a tag indicating whether it is part of an aspect term. The most common tagging scheme is BIO (begin, inside, outside). Traditional approaches relied on conditional random fields (CRFs) with handcrafted features. Modern deep learning methods, particularly BiLSTM-CRF models [24], have become the standard, as they can effectively learn sequence dependencies without manual feature engineering.

Unlike ATE, aspect category detection (ACD) classifies the sentence into one or more predefined aspect categories [25], such as FOOD, SERVICE, and AMBIENCE for restaurant reviews, even if the category is not explicitly mentioned. This can be treated as a multi-label text classification problem, where standard models from Naive Bayes to deep learning architectures can be applied.

Given an aspect term, aspect sentiment classification (ASC) determines its associated sentiment [26]. This is a context-dependent classification task. Early methods would use the words in a window around the aspect term as features.

Table 3.2 Core subtasks of ABSA.

Subtask	**Description**	**Example: "The Service was Slow but the Pizza was Delicious."**
Aspect term extraction	Identify the explicit mentions of aspects in the text	service, pizza
Aspect category detection	Group explicit aspect terms into predefined, broader categories	service: SERVICE, pizza: FOOD
Aspect sentiment classification	Determine the sentiment polarity for each identified aspect	(service, negative), (pizza, positive)

More advanced deep learning models, particularly LSTM with target-dependent attention, have proven highly effective [27]. These models use the aspect term's representation to guide the attention mechanism, forcing the model to focus on the opinion words most relevant to that specific aspect.

Solving ABSA as a pipeline of separate tasks can lead to error propagation. Consequently, significant research has focused on end-to-end models that extract aspect-sentiment pairs in a single pass. Recent Transformer-based models frame this as a generative task. For example, a T5 model can be fine-tuned to take a sentence as input and generate a structured text output like: "[ASPECT] service [SENTIMENT] negative [ASPECT] pizza [SENTIMENT] positive."

3.5.2 Sarcasm, Irony, and Figurative Language Detection

The detection of nonliteral language, particularly sarcasm and irony, remains one of the most difficult open problems in sentiment analysis [28]. Sarcasm is characterized by a fundamental incongruity between the literal meaning of an utterance and its intended meaning. A model that relies on surface-level lexical cues will invariably fail, as in "I love waiting 40 minutes for a coffee. Best service ever."

1. Modeling Incongruity
   Successful sarcasm detection hinges on the ability to model this incongruity. This can manifest in several ways.
   - Sentiment Incongruity:
     A clash between explicitly positive language and a negative situation or context (e.g., positive words in a 1-star review).
   - Contextual Incongruity
     An utterance that is incongruous with the broader discourse context. For social media, this is a powerful signal. A reply like "What a brilliant idea!" to a demonstrably poor suggestion is likely sarcastic. Advanced models incorporate hierarchical attention to model both the response and the original post it replies to.
   - Author-specific Context
     Some models attempt to learn an author's baseline behavior. If a user frequently posts sarcastic comments, a new ambiguous post from them is more likely to be sarcastic. This involves modeling a user's historical data.
2. Methodological Approaches
   The methodological approaches to automatic sarcasm detection have evolved significantly, transitioning from handcrafted heuristics to sophisticated deep contextual modeling. Early systems attempted to capture sarcasm by engineering features based on linguistic and pragmatic theories, such as identifying explicit lexical patterns like interjections and heavy punctuation, quantifying

sentiment incongruity through the co-occurrence of positive and negative words, and leveraging pragmatic cues like hashtags or emoticons. While useful for explicitly marked cases, these methods were often brittle and failed to generalize to more subtle forms of irony. The paradigm shifted with the advent of deep learning, which automates the discovery of these complex cues. Recurrent networks like LSTMs learned to model sequential sentiment shifts, while CNNs excelled at identifying indicative local *n*-gram patterns. The current state-of-the-art is dominated by Transformer-based models such as BERT and RoBERTa. Their self-attention mechanisms are uniquely suited for this task, as they can capture the long-range semantic dissonance between words that constitutes the core of sarcastic incongruity. The research frontier now pushes even further, developing models that explicitly reason about context. For instance, context-aware hierarchical architectures analyze an utterance in relation to its conversational history, while other cutting-edge methods train models to measure the semantic contrast between a sarcastic sentence and a generated literal counterpart, thereby learning to explicitly quantify the ironic gap. These advanced techniques are moving the field toward a more robust, context-dependent understanding of nonliteral language.

3.5.3 Multilingual and Cross-lingual Sentiment Analysis

While sentiment is a universal human experience, its linguistic expression and cultural context vary dramatically across the globe. This presents a significant challenge for sentiment analysis, which has historically been dominated by research and resources in English. This field addresses the critical need to build systems that function effectively across different languages and is typically divided into two related but distinct tasks.

Multilingual sentiment analysis aims to develop a single, unified model capable of processing and classifying text from multiple languages. The goal is a versatile system that can be deployed in a diverse linguistic environment. Cross-lingual sentiment analysis focuses on a transfer learning scenario. The objective is to leverage abundant labeled data from a high-resource language (e.g., English) to build a sentiment analysis model for a low-resource language (e.g., Swahili and Nepali) where such data is scarce or nonexistent.

The dominant paradigm for addressing these challenges, particularly for cross-lingual transfer, leverages multilingual pretrained language model (mPLM) like M-BERT [29] and XLM-R [30]. These models are pretrained on a massive, combined corpus containing text from over 100 languages. The underlying hypothesis is that during this process, they learn a shared, language-agnostic representation space where semantically similar concepts are close to each other, regardless of the source language.

By fine-tuning such a model on English-labeled sentiment data, it learns to map texts to a positive or negative region within this shared semantic space. Due to the language-agnostic nature of this space, the model can then correctly classify a French or Japanese sentence by mapping it to the appropriate region, even without ever having seen a single labeled example in those languages. This powerful capability is known as zero-shot cross-lingual transfer.

Despite their success, mPLMs face key research challenges. The first one is that the fixed capacity of an mPLM must be distributed across many languages. This can lead to the model's performance on any single language being suboptimal compared to a dedicated monolingual model that can devote its entire capacity to the nuances of that one language. The second one is that sentiment cues are not always universal. A word, phrase, or concept considered positive in one culture may be neutral or negative in another. mPLMs primarily learn from statistical co-occurrences and can struggle to capture these deep cultural semantics. For example, expressions of modesty or directness are valued differently across cultures and can be easily misinterpreted by a model trained predominantly on text, leading to culturally biased or inaccurate sentiment classifications.

3.5.4 Explainable AI for Text Sentiment Analysis

As sentiment analysis models, especially deep learning architectures, have become more powerful, they have also become more opaque. The shift toward black-box models creates a critical need for transparency. Explainable AI (XAI) addresses this by seeking to answer the question of why a model made a certain prediction. This is essential for debugging models, building user trust, ensuring fairness, identifying hidden biases, and complying with regulations in high-stakes domains.

Several primary methodologies have been developed to bring explainability to text sentiment analysis.

1. Perturbation-based Methods
   These model-agnostic techniques, such as local interpretable model-agnostic explanations (LIME) [31] and SHapley Additive exPlanations (SHAP) [32], explain a single prediction by creating a local, interpretable approximation of the complex model.

   While LIME is often visualized using image superpixels, in text sentiment analysis, it operates by perturbing the input sentence through word removal. The algorithm generates thousands of variations of the original text and feeds them into the black-box classifier. By observing how the sentiment probability changes when specific words are absent, LIME learns a simple linear model to assign importance weights to each word.

For example, if a model predicts a movie review as "Negative," LIME might reveal that removing the word "boring" causes the negative probability to drop from 90 to 55%, whereas removing "movie" only drops it to 89%. This identifies "boring" as the pivotal feature driving the sentiment classification.

2. Gradient-based Methods
   Specific to neural networks, these methods, including saliency maps and integrated gradients, compute the gradient of the output prediction with respect to the input features (i.e., the word embeddings). The magnitude of the gradient is interpreted as the feature's importance, indicating how much a small change in that feature's value would affect the final decision.
3. Attention-based Explanations
   For Transformer-based models, visualizing the attention weights provides an intuitive way to see which words the model focused on when processing the sequence. However, the faithfulness of this approach has been a subject of significant academic scrutiny.

   A substantial body of research has challenged the reliability of using attention weights as a direct explanation for a model's reasoning. Studies have demonstrated that it is possible to find vastly different attention distributions that still result in the same prediction. In sentiment analysis, a model might place high attention weights on neutral nouns like "movie" or punctuation, rather than on the actual sentiment-bearing adjectives, yet still make the correct classification due to other internal signals. Furthermore, attention weights do not always correlate well with other feature importance metrics like gradients. While attention highlights complex internal model dynamics, it should be interpreted with caution and not be treated as a definitive, faithful explanation of the model's reasoning process.
4. Generative Explanations
   A new frontier in XAI involves using LLMs to generate natural language explanations. Instead of just highlighting salient words, the model is prompted to provide a human-readable justification for its decision. For instance, an explanation might be: "The sentiment was classified as negative because the text contains the phrase 'terribly slow service,' which indicates dissatisfaction with the customer experience." This form of explanation is often more intuitive and directly useful for end-users, representing a promising direction for creating truly transparent AI systems.

3.6 Case Study

This section serves as a practical, in-depth tutorial that applies the theoretical concepts from this chapter to a real-world problem. We tackle one of the most classic benchmarks in sentiment analysis: the IMDB movie review dataset (https://ai.stanford.edu/~amaas/data/sentiment/). By building, training, and evaluating three models of increasing complexity, we will provide a clear, step-by-step guide that is both actionable and illustrative of the field's evolution.

3.6.1 Dataset

The task is a straightforward binary classification problem: given the text of a movie review, classify its sentiment as either positive or negative. The IMDB is the standard dataset for this task. It contains 50,000 polarized movie reviews, carefully split into 25,000 for training and 25,000 for testing. The dataset is balanced between positive and negative classes, making accuracy a reliable evaluation metric. Its clean structure and clear objective make it an ideal environment for comparing different modeling approaches.

3.6.2 Data Preprocessing

Before any model can be trained, the raw text data must be rigorously cleaned and prepared. This crucial step ensures that the models receive meaningful, standardized input, which directly impacts performance. First, a cleaning process is applied to each review, which includes removing HTML tags (e.g., <br />) common in web-scraped data and converting all text to lowercase to ensure uniformity.

Following cleaning, the text is tokenized, or broken into individual words. The subsequent steps diverge depending on the model's requirements. For deep learning models like the LSTM and BERT, these word tokens are converted into numerical integer sequences using a vocabulary mapping. Because neural networks require fixed-size inputs, these sequences are then padded (or truncated) to a uniform length. This ensures that every review, regardless of its original length, is represented by a vector of the same dimension.

3.6.3 Modeling Approaches and Implementation

We implement and compare three distinct models, each representing a key paradigm in text sentiment classification. This progression from a traditional baseline to an advanced BERT will illustrate the evolution of techniques.

1. Logistic Regression
   First, we establish a baseline using a traditional ML approach. This model is highly efficient and interpretable, serving as an essential reference point. It operates on the BoW principle, where the sentiment is inferred from the presence and frequency of words, irrespective of their order.
   The architecture is a two-stage pipeline. The preprocessed text is first converted into a high-dimensional numerical vector using the TF-IDF weighting scheme. TF-IDF evaluates the importance of a word by considering its frequency in a specific document while penalizing words that are common across all documents.
   These TF-IDF vectors are then used as input for a logistic regression classifier. This linear model learns a set of weights for each feature and calculates the probability of a review being positive by passing the weighted sum through a sigmoid function.

$$P(\text{positive}|\text{x}) = \frac{1}{1 + e^{-(\boldsymbol{w} \cdot \boldsymbol{x} + b)}} \tag{3.8}$$

2. BiLSTM
   The second model is a classic deep learning architecture designed to overcome the primary limitation of the baseline. Its inability to understand word order. By processing text as a sequence, this model can capture contextual nuances that depend on syntax and sentence structure.
   We employ a BiLSTM network. At its core, an RNN processes a sequence one element at a time, maintaining a hidden state h_t that serves as a memory of the preceding context.
   LSTM is an advanced type of RNN that uses gating mechanisms to effectively learn long-range dependencies. A bidirectional LSTM enhances this by using two separate LSTMs: one processes the sequence from left-to-right, and the other from right-to-left. The outputs from both are concatenated at each time step, providing a rich representation for each word that is aware of both its past and future context. The final model architecture consists of an embedding layer (to map word indices to dense vectors), the BiLSTM layer, a dropout layer for regularization, and a final dense output layer with a sigmoid activation function.
3. DistilBERT
   The final model represents the modern, state-of-the-art approach to NLP tasks, leveraging transfer learning from a massive, PLM. This method has consistently achieved top-tier results across a wide range of benchmarks.
   We use DistilBERT, a smaller, faster, and more lightweight version of BERT that retains most of its language understanding capabilities. Unlike the other models, we do not train this one from scratch. Instead, we take the pretrained

DistilBERT model and fine-tune it on our IMDB dataset. The architecture's power stems from the Transformer's self-attention mechanism, which allows every word in a sentence to dynamically weigh the importance of all other words, enabling it to model complex, long-range dependencies directly.

The fine-tuning process involves adding a single, new classification layer on top of the pretrained DistilBERT base. The entire network is then trained for a small number of epochs with a very low learning rate, which adapts the model's general linguistic knowledge to the specific task of movie review sentiment classification.

3.6.4 Comparative Results and Analysis

After training all three models on the IMDB training set, we evaluate them on the unseen test set. The results reveal a clear hierarchy of performance and complexity, as shown in Table 3.3.

The results demonstrate a clear progression. The TF-IDF baseline establishes a benchmark, proving that word frequencies alone carry a significant sentiment signal. The BiLSTM provides a significant improvement, which can be attributed directly to its ability to process word order and model sequential context. This allows it to correctly interpret phrases like "not at all good," which might confuse a BoW model.

The fine-tuned DistilBERT model achieves a substantial leap in performance, outperforming the BiLSTM by over 3%. This superior accuracy is a testament to the power of transfer learning. The model does not learn about language from the 25,000 movie reviews alone; it leverages a vast, preexisting knowledge of English grammar, syntax, and semantics learned from billions of words. This allows it to capture subtle contextual nuances, resolve ambiguities, and understand complex sentence structures far more effectively than a model trained from scratch. For instance, in a review like, "The plot was predictable, a flaw that would have sunk a lesser film, but the powerful acting made it a must-see," the Transformer is best equipped to weigh the final clause as the determinant of the overall positive sentiment. This case study confirms that for achieving state-of-the-art results in sentiment analysis, fine-tuning pretrained Transformers is the dominant and most effective strategy.

Table 3.3 Model comparison on IMDB test set.

Model	Accuracy (%)	F1-Score (%)
TF-IDF + Logistic regression	83.90	83.93
Bidirectional LSTM	90.00	90.06
Fine-tuned DistilBERT	93.10	93.08

3.7 Summary and Future Directions in Text-based Sentiment Analysis

This chapter has systematically charted the evolution of text-based sentiment analysis, tracing its progression from interpretable but brittle lexical and rule-based systems to the data-driven power of ML. We have demonstrated how the field transitioned from a reliance on manual feature engineering, exemplified by TF-IDF with linear models, to the automated representation learning of deep learning. The introduction of architectures like LSTMs enabled the modeling of sequential context, while the advent of Transformer-based PLMs such as BERT marked a paradigm shift. By leveraging transfer learning, these models have established a new state-of-the-art, demonstrating a profound ability to understand linguistic nuance, as confirmed in our comparative case study. As computational models have grown in complexity, so too has their capacity to approximate the intricate ways sentiment is expressed in human language.

Looking ahead, the frontier of text-based sentiment analysis is pushing beyond simple polarity classification toward a more holistic understanding of opinion. Future research will increasingly focus on more granular and complex tasks, such as causal sentiment analysis and the integration of argument mining to understand the reasoning structure behind an opinion. Within the dominant LLM paradigm, key challenges remain. The drive for more efficient, controllable, and less biased models is paramount for practical deployment. Furthermore, developing truly faithful XAI techniques for these black-box models is critical for building trust and enabling diagnostics. Ultimately, the goal is to bridge the gap between pattern recognition and genuine comprehension, creating systems that not only classify sentiment but also begin to understand the human experience it represents.

References

1 Wiebe, J., Wilson, T., & Cardie, C. (2005). Annotating expressions of opinions and emotions in language. *Language Resources and Evaluation*, 39, 165–210.
2 Tausczik, Y. R., & Pennebaker, J. W. (2010). The psychological meaning of words: LIWC and computerized text analysis methods. *Journal of Language and Social Psychology*, 29(1), 24–54.
3 Hutto, C., & Gilbert, E. (2014). VADER: A parsimonious rule-based model for sentiment analysis of social media text. *Proceedings of the International AAAI Conference on Web and Social Media*, 8(1), 216–225.

4 Mikolov, T., Chen, K., Corrado, G. S., & Dean, J. (2013). Efficient estimation of word representations in vector space. In International Conference on Learning Representations. https://api.semanticscholar.org/CorpusID:5959482.

5 Mikolov, T., Sutskever, I., Chen, K., Corrado, G., & Dean, J. (2013). Distributed representations of words and phrases and their compositionality. *Advances in Neural Information Processing Systems*, 26, 3111–3119.

6 Pennington, J., Socher, R., & Manning, C. D. (2014). GloVe: Global vectors for word representation. In Proceedings of the 2014 Conference on Empirical Methods in Natural Language Processing (EMNLP), Doha, Qatar, (pp. 1532–1543).

7 Bojanowski, P., Grave, E., Joulin, A., & Mikolov, T. (2017). Enriching word vectors with subword information. *Transactions of the Association for Computational Linguistics*, 5, 135–146.

8 Peters, M. E., Neumann, M., Iyyer, M., Gardner, M., Clark, C., Lee, K., & Zettlemoyer, L. (2018). Deep contextualized word representations. In Proceedings of the 2018 Conference of the North American Chapter of the Association for Computational Linguistics: Human Language Technologies, Volume 1 (Long Papers), New Orleans, USA, (pp. 2227–2237).

9 Xu, G., Meng, Y., Qiu, X., Yu, Z., & Wu, X. (2019). Sentiment analysis of comment texts based on BiLSTM. *IEEE Access*, 7, 51522–51532.

10 Xie, J., Chen, B., Gu, X., Liang, F., & Xu, X. (2019). Self-attention-based BiLSTM model for short text fine-grained sentiment classification. *IEEE Access*, 7, 180558–180570.

11 Ayetiran, E. F. (2022). Attention-based aspect sentiment classification using enhanced learning through CNN-BiLSTM networks. *Knowledge-Based Systems*, 252, 109409.

12 Vaswani, A., Shazeer, N., Parmar, N., Uszoreit, J., Jones, L., Gomez, A. N., Kaiser, Ł., & Polosukhin, I. (2017). Attention is all you need. *Advances in Neural Information Processing Systems*, 30, 5998–6008.

13 Bashiri, H., & Naderi, H. (2024). Comprehensive review and comparative analysis of transformer models in sentiment analysis. *Knowledge and Information Systems*, 66(12), 7305–7361.

14 Devlin, J., Chang, M.-W., Lee, K., & Toutanova, K. (2019). BERT: Pre-training of deep bidirectional transformers for language understanding. In Proceedings of the 2019 Conference of the North American Chapter of the Association for Computational Linguistics: Human Language Technologies, Volume 1, Minneapolis, USA, (pp. 4171–4186).

15 Liu, Y., Ott, M., Goyal, N., Du, J., Joshi, M., Chen, D., Levy, O., Lewis, M., Zettlemoyer, L., & Stoyanov, V. (2019). RoBERTa: A robustly optimized BERT pretraining approach. arXiv preprint arXiv:1907.11692.

16 Lan, Z., Chen, M., Goodman, S., Gimpel, K., Sharma, P., & Soricut, R. (2019). ALBERT: A lite BERT for self-supervised learning of language representations. arXiv preprint arXiv:1909.11942.

17 Sanh, V., Debut, L., Chaumond, J., & Wolf, T. (2019). DistilBERT, a distilled version of BERT: Smaller, faster, cheaper and lighter. arXiv preprint arXiv:1910.01108.

18 Yang, Z., Dai, Z., Yang, Y., Carbonell, J., Salakhutdinov, R., & Le, Q. V. (2019). XLNet: Generalized autoregressive pretraining for language understanding. *Advances in Neural Information Processing Systems*, 32, 5753–5763.

19 Raffel, C., Shazeer, N., Roberts, A., Lee, K., Narang, S., Matena, M., Zhou, Y., Li, W., & Liu, P. J. (2019). Exploring the limits of transfer learning with a unified text-to-text transformer. arXiv preprint arXiv:1910.10683.

20 Clark, K., Luong, M.-T., Le, Q. V., & Manning, C. D. (2020). ELECTRA: Pre-training text encoders as discriminators rather than generators. arXiv preprint arXiv:2003.10555

21 Wei, J., Bosma, M., Zhao, V. Y., Guu, K., Yu, A. W., Lester, B., Du, N., Dai, A. M., & Le, Q. V. (2021). Finetuned language models are zero-shot learners. arXiv preprint arXiv:2109.01652.

22 Zhang, W., Li, X., Deng, Y., Bing, L., & Lam, W. (2022). A survey on aspect-based sentiment analysis: Tasks, methods, and challenges. *IEEE Transactions on Knowledge and Data Engineering*, 35(11), 11019–11038.

23 Augustyniak, Ł., Kajdanowicz, T., & Kazienko, P. (2021). Comprehensive analysis of aspect term extraction methods using various text embeddings. *Computer Speech & Language*, 69, 101217.

24 Kumar, A., Verma, S., & Sharan, A. (2021). ATE-SPD: Simultaneous extraction of aspect-term and aspect sentiment polarity using Bi-LSTM-CRF neural network. *Journal of Experimental & Theoretical Artificial Intelligence*, 33(3), 487–508.

25 Chebolu, S. U. S., Rosso, P., Kar, S., & Solorio, T. (2022). Survey on aspect category detection. *ACM Computing Surveys*, 55(7), 1–37.

26 Brauwers, G., & Frasincar, F. (2022). A survey on aspect-based sentiment classification. *ACM Computing Surveys*, 55(4), 1–37.

27 Ouyang, J., Xuan, C., Wang, B., & Yang, Z. (2024). Aspect-based sentiment classification with aspect-specific hypergraph attention networks. *Expert Systems with Applications*, 248, 123412.

28 Wang, Z., Hu, S. J., & Liu, W. D. (2024). Product feature sentiment analysis based on GRU-CAP considering Chinese sarcasm recognition. *Expert Systems with Applications*, 241, 122512.

29 Pires, T., Schlinger, E., & Garrette, D. (2019). How multilingual is multilingual BERT? In Proceedings of the 57th Annual Meeting of the Association for Computational Linguistics, Florence, Italy, (pp. 4996–5001).

30 Conneau, A., Khandelwal, K., Goyal, N., Chaudhary, V., Wenzek, G., Guzmán, F., Grave, E., Ott, M., Zettlemoyer, L., & Stoyanov, V. (2020). Unsupervised cross-lingual representation learning at scale. In Proceedings of the 58th Annual Meeting of the Association for Computational Linguistics (pp. 8440–8451).
31 Ribeiro, M. T., Singh, S., & Guestrin, C. (2016). "Why should I trust you?": Explaining the predictions of any classifier. In Proceedings of the 22nd ACM SIGKDD International Conference on Knowledge Discovery and Data Mining, San Francisco, USA, (pp. 1135–1144).
32 Lundberg, S. M., & Lee, S.-I. (2017). A unified approach to interpreting model predictions. In I. Guyon, U. Von Luxburg, S. Bengio, H. Wallach, R. Fergus, S. Vishwanathan, & R. Garnett (Eds.), *Advances in neural information processing systems* (pp. 4765–4774). Curran Associates, Inc.

4

Implicit Sentiment Analysis

The preceding chapter detailed the methodologies for analyzing sentiment that is explicitly stated in text, a domain where affective content is largely conveyed through overtly positive or negative lexical choices. While these techniques form the basis of sentiment analysis, they operate on the assumption that opinions are transparently articulated. However, a vast and arguably more interesting landscape of sentiment lies submerged beneath the surface of literal expression. Human communication is rich with nuance, subtlety, and indirection. We often convey our strongest feelings not by what we say but by what we imply. A statement like "The phone's battery lasted just long enough for me to call a tow truck" contains no explicit sentiment words, yet it powerfully communicates a negative experience. Similarly, the sarcastic remark, "What a brilliant idea to schedule a meeting at 7 AM," uses positive language to express profound disapproval.

This is the domain of implicit sentiment analysis, a challenging frontier that pushes beyond mere pattern recognition toward a semblance of genuine linguistic comprehension. To unlock this deeper layer of opinion, a system cannot simply count sentiment words; it must reason. It must leverage commonsense knowledge about the world, understand context in its broadest sense, and detect the subtle incongruities that signal nonliteral intent. The ability to decode implicit sentiment is critical for any application aiming for a truly insightful understanding of human opinion, from discerning true customer satisfaction in seemingly factual feedback to identifying sophisticated forms of online rhetoric.

This chapter ventures into this complex territory. We will begin by dissecting the very nature of implicit sentiment, establishing a clear framework that distinguishes it from its explicit counterpart and delineates its core computational challenges: the commonsense reasoning gap and the semantic incongruity problem. Subsequently, we systematically explore the major methodological paradigms developed to address these challenges, tracing an evolutionary path from early knowledge-driven systems to context-aware deep learning models, and culminating in the emergent reasoning capabilities of large language models (LLMs). Through this exploration, we illuminate the techniques that allow machines to look beyond the words on the page and begin to grasp the sentiment hidden within.

4.1 Defining Implicit Sentiment

Before embarking on an exploration of the methodologies for its analysis, a formal and rigorous definition of implicit sentiment is paramount. It represents a departure from the literal, where affective meaning is not encoded directly in lexical items but is instead woven into the pragmatic and inferential fabric of the discourse. Understanding this phenomenon requires a conceptual framework that can not only distinguish it from its explicit counterpart but also categorize its diverse manifestations and identify the core computational problems it presents.

This section lays that essential groundwork. We begin by establishing a clear dichotomy between explicit and implicit sentiment to delineate our focus. We will then propose a framework centered on the two foundational computational problems that underpin this field, the commonsense reasoning gap and the semantic incongruity problem, and conclude by presenting a taxonomy of common implicit sentiment expressions. This systematic definition will provide the necessary conceptual scaffolding for the technical discussions that follow.

4.1.1 From Explicit to Implicit

To comprehend the challenges inherent in implicit sentiment, one must first draw a firm distinction between it and its explicit counterpart [1], which formed the primary focus of the preceding chapter. This distinction is foundational to the entire field of opinion mining.

Explicit sentiment represents the most direct and transparent form of opinion expression. It is realized on the linguistic surface through the use of words and phrases that carry clear, conventionalized affective valence. These include sentiment-laden adjectives, verbs, nouns, and adverbs. The computational analysis of explicit sentiment, a field pioneered by researchers, is fundamentally a problem of detecting these lexical cues and their syntactic modifiers. While nontrivial, it operates on a relatively straightforward mapping from word to sentiment, assuming that opinions are, for the most part, honestly and directly articulated.

Implicit sentiment, in contrast, operates on a deeper, inferential level. It is the sentiment that is not stated but must be inferred by the reader, or the computational model, through a process of reasoning that goes beyond the literal meaning of the words used [2]. This inference is typically driven by one of two mechanisms: commonsense reasoning or the detection of contextual incongruity. In a statement like, "I had to charge the phone three times during my workday," the sentiment is derived from the commonsense knowledge that frequent charging indicates poor battery life, which is a highly undesirable attribute for a portable device. The sentiment is not in the words themselves but in the implication of the fact they describe. This requires an inferential leap that connects the stated event to a known human value or goal, a process that relies on a vast base of world knowledge often modeled in resources like SenticNet.

This distinction is fundamental to the pursuit of a truly insightful understanding of human opinion. A sentiment analysis system that operates only on the explicit level captures only the most obvious, and often least nuanced, expressions of feeling. The importance of implicit analysis lies in its ability to unlock the vast reservoir of opinions that are otherwise invisible. For a business, this transforms seemingly objective feedback into actionable intelligence; the factual complaint about battery life is a far more useful data point for product improvement than a generic "I don't like it." In the social and political spheres, it allows for the detection of subtle rhetoric, sarcasm, and opinions veiled by politeness or social convention. Ultimately, a model that can interpret implicit sentiment is one that moves from simple sentiment detection to a more sophisticated form of affective comprehension, providing a more accurate, complete, and actionable picture of the user's true state of mind [3].

4.1.2 The Two Foundational Problems

The challenge of understanding implicit sentiment, while multifaceted, can be systematically deconstructed into two core, often intertwined, computational problems. This framework not only helps in categorizing the various phenomena of implicit expression but also provides a clear rationale for the different methodological approaches that will be discussed later in this chapter.

1. The Commonsense Reasoning Gap

   This first and most fundamental problem arises when sentiment is concealed within objective-sounding, factual statements. The text itself lacks any overt affective coloring; its sentiment can only be unlocked by applying external world knowledge or commonsense reasoning to understand the implications of the stated facts. For a computational model, this represents a gap between the text it can process and the vast repository of human knowledge it typically lacks.

   Consider the product review: "The instruction manual for this 'easy-to-assemble' furniture was a hundred pages long." A model operating on lexical cues alone would find no negative words. However, a human reader immediately infers a negative sentiment. This inference follows a logical chain:

- Fact: The manual is 100 pages long.
- Commonsense Knowledge: (a) Products advertised as "easy-to-assemble" should not require extensive instructions. (b) Long, complex manuals are a source of frustration and are indicative of poor design.
- Inference: The product is difficult to assemble and not as advertised.
- Implicit Sentiment: Negative.

To bridge this reasoning gap, a model must somehow access and apply this type of world knowledge, a task that has been a long-standing grand challenge in artificial intelligence.

2. The Semantic Incongruity Problem

This second problem occurs when the surface polarity of the language used is intentionally inconsistent with the intended, underlying sentiment. This is the domain of nonliteral and figurative language, where meaning is generated by a clash or contradiction between different elements of the text or between the text and its context. The canonical example is sarcasm.

In the statement, "I just love how the app crashes every time I open it," the positive sentiment word "love" is semantically incongruous with the negative event it describes. A human reader instantly recognizes this clash as a marker for sarcasm, inverting the polarity of "love" to understand the true negative sentiment. The core task for a model is not to consult an external knowledge base, but rather to detect this internal semantic contradiction within the sentence or its immediate context. Other forms of incongruity include irony and certain metaphors, where the juxtaposition of concepts creates the affective meaning.

These two problems define the landscape of implicit sentiment analysis. While some expressions fall neatly into one category, many sophisticated cases may require both commonsense reasoning and incongruity detection to be fully understood. The following Table 4.1 provides a clear comparative framework to solidify these core concepts before we delve into specific types of implicit expressions.

4.1.3 A Taxonomy of Implicit Sentiment Expressions

The phenomena that fall under the umbrella of implicit sentiment are diverse. To develop effective computational methods, it is crucial to understand the specific characteristics of these different forms of expression. The following taxonomy categorizes the most common types, linking them back to the foundational problems of reasoning and incongruity.

Table 4.1 A comparative framework of explicit and implicit sentiment.

Dimension	Explicit Sentiment	Implicit Sentiment
Linguistic cues	Direct, affective keywords (e.g., "good," "hate," "amazing")	Absence of direct affective words; relies on factual statements or conflicting cues
Inference required	Low. Primarily lexical lookup and syntactic parsing	High. Requires commonsense reasoning, world knowledge, or detection of semantic incongruity
Core challenge	Correctly identifying sentiment words and their scope (negation and intensification)	Bridging the commonsense reasoning gap or resolving semantic incongruity
Example	"The camera quality is excellent"	"The camera ran out of battery after 20 photos"
Primary modeling focus	Accurate feature representation of words and phrases	Modeling external knowledge, deep contextual understanding, or multistep reasoning

1. Sentiment from Factual Consequence
   This is sentiment inferred from the desirable or undesirable consequences of a stated, objective fact. It is a pure manifestation of the commonsense reasoning gap. The text itself is effectively neutral, but its implication is charged with sentiment. For example, in the statement, "This car gets 5 miles to the gallon," the negative sentiment is derived not from the words but from the real-world knowledge that such low fuel efficiency is expensive and environmentally unfriendly. The analytical challenge here is for a model to access and apply this external knowledge to correctly interpret the fact's implication.
2. Sarcasm and Irony
   These are the canonical examples of the semantic incongruity problem. They involve a deliberate inversion of literal meaning to convey the opposite sentiment, often for humorous or critical effect. Sarcasm typically involves a speaker feigning praise to express contempt, as in, "I was absolutely thrilled to spend my Saturday rebooting my computer." Irony is a broader concept where there is a discrepancy between appearance and reality, such as in, "His speech on the importance of clarity was as clear as mud." In both cases, the model's primary task is to detect the internal contradiction between linguistic elements or between the text and its context.
3. Metaphor and Simile
   Sentiment is often conveyed through analogy. A metaphor implicitly transfers properties from one concept (the source) to another (the target), as in,

"This new software is a Swiss Army knife." This conveys positive sentiment by implying the software is versatile and useful, properties associated with a Swiss Army knife. A simile does this explicitly with "like" or "as," such as, "The user interface is like a maze." This implies negative sentiment by associating the UI with confusion and difficulty. Solving this requires a form of analogical reasoning, accessing knowledge about the source domain and applying its attributes to the target domain, thus engaging the commonsense reasoning faculty.

4. Rhetorical Questions
   A rhetorical question does not seek an answer but is posed to assert a strong opinion or create a dramatic effect. The sentiment is embedded in the pragmatic function of the utterance, not its literal form. For instance, the question, "Since when is it acceptable to charge extra for basic features?" is not a genuine inquiry; it is a forceful expression of negative sentiment toward a company's pricing strategy. To analyze this, a model must move beyond semantic interpretation and begin to understand the pragmatic intent behind different forms of speech acts, which again relies on an assumed base of shared social and value-based knowledge.

4.1.4 Chapter Roadmap

Having defined the terrain of implicit sentiment and deconstructed its foundational challenges, the commonsense reasoning gap and the semantic incongruity problem, we are now equipped to explore the computational methodologies designed to navigate this complex landscape. The remainder of this chapter is structured around three distinct, yet progressively sophisticated, methodological paradigms. Each represents a major school of thought in the quest to build models that can interpret sentiment beyond the literal.

The Knowledge-augmented Paradigm: Our first exploration focuses on methods that directly attempt to solve the commonsense reasoning gap. This paradigm operates on the premise that implicit sentiment is a problem of knowledge deficit that can be remedied by explicitly injecting external, human-curated knowledge into models. We examine techniques ranging from feature engineering with lexical-semantic resources to advanced neural architectures that integrate structured knowledge from graphs directly into their learning process.

The Contextual Representation Learning Paradigm: Next, we will examine a paradigm that represents a philosophical shift from external knowledge to internal context. These methods, dominant in the deep learning era, posit that nuanced meaning can be learned from rich contextual data alone. We investigate how recurrent and hierarchical neural networks, enhanced with attention mechanisms, capture the cues that signal nonliteral language. This exploration will culminate in the analysis of large pretrained language models (PLMs) and how the process of fine-tuning enables a deep, implicit understanding of context.

The Prompt-based Reasoning Paradigm: Finally, we address the most recent and transformative approach, driven by the emergent capabilities of LLMs. This paradigm shifts the focus from training specialized models to guiding general-purpose reasoning engines. We delve into how carefully crafted prompts and advanced techniques like chain-of-thought (CoT) can instruct these models to perform complex, multistep reasoning, tackling both the commonsense gap and semantic incongruity in a flexible, zero-shot manner. This represents a move from implicit pattern recognition to explicit, interpretable reasoning.

By systematically examining these three paradigms, this chapter will trace the evolution of thought in implicit sentiment analysis, highlighting the theoretical underpinnings, technical implementations, and inherent trade-offs of each major approach.

4.2 The Knowledge-augmented Paradigm: Injecting Commonsense for Implicit Sentiment Reasoning

The most straightforward and intuitive reaction to the commonsense reasoning gap is to regard it as an issue of insufficient information. For instance, if a model cannot grasp that "the phone's battery died in 3 hours" is a negative statement due to the lack of real-world knowledge that poor battery life is unfavorable, then the rational solution is to supply it with such knowledge. This fundamental concept has given rise to the knowledge-augmented paradigm, which is the first major school of thought in addressing implicit sentiment. This approach is based on the assumption that the key to achieving deeper understanding is to explicitly incorporate structured human knowledge into computational models, thus equipping them with the context necessary to make accurate inferences.

This section systematically investigates the evolution of this paradigm, from early efforts that depended on handcrafted features to advanced neural architectures that can dynamically reason over knowledge graphs. We start by looking into the theoretical challenge of aligning discrete, symbolic knowledge with the continuous vector spaces of neural networks. Then, we follow the progression of techniques, beginning with feature engineering from lexical resources, moving on to the integration of knowledge graph embeddings (KGEs), and finally arriving at the use of graph neural networks (GNNs) to model the multistep reasoning process needed for complex implicit sentiment analysis. Throughout this exploration, the central theme remains the explicit endeavor to bridge the commonsense gap by making machines more knowledgeable.

4.2.1 Aligning Symbolic Knowledge with Vector Spaces

At the heart of the knowledge-augmented paradigm lies a fundamental challenge that has defined a significant portion of modern AI research: the alignment of two disparate representations of information. On one side, we have symbolic knowledge, the structured, human-readable format of classical AI and logic. This knowledge is typically represented in discrete structures like ontologies or knowledge graphs, composed of entities and the explicit, logical relationships that connect them. A knowledge triple such as (battery, hasProperty, and lifespan) is precise, interpretable, and amenable to formal reasoning. However, this symbolic world is inherently rigid, often incomplete, and struggles to capture the continuous, graded nature of real-world semantics.

On the other side lies the distributed representation in a vectorial space, the native domain of neural networks. Here, meaning is not discrete but is instead represented as dense, low-dimensional vectors. Semantic relationships are not defined by explicit links but are encoded by proximity and direction in a high-dimensional geometric space. This representation is powerful for learning complex patterns from unstructured data and for handling ambiguity and nuance. Yet, it is a black box, lacking the explicit structure and verifiable reasoning paths of its symbolic counterpart. It excels at learning correlation from data, but not necessarily causation or factual relations.

The central theoretical challenge, therefore, is to bridge this inherent schism. Aligning symbolic knowledge with vector spaces is the task of creating a principled mapping between these two worlds, enabling them to inform and enrich one another. As illustrated in Figure 4.1, this alignment must create a shared space where both text and knowledge can coexist and interact.

This alignment process must address several key questions before it can be applied to implicit sentiment analysis:

1. Entity Representation
   How can a discrete entity from a knowledge graph be given a meaningful representation within a continuous vector space? The symbolic node battery lifespan needs to be transformed into a vector that captures its semantic essence and its relationship to other concepts. This process is known as KGE.
2. Relational Modeling
   How can a logical relationship, such as isA or causes, be modeled as a mathematical operation between vectors? The goal is to make the vector space itself reflect the structure of the knowledge graph. For example, a successful alignment would ensure that the vector operation $v_{\text{cat}} - v_{\text{animal}}$ is geometrically similar to $v_{\text{dog}} - v_{\text{animal}}$, thereby capturing the isA relationship.

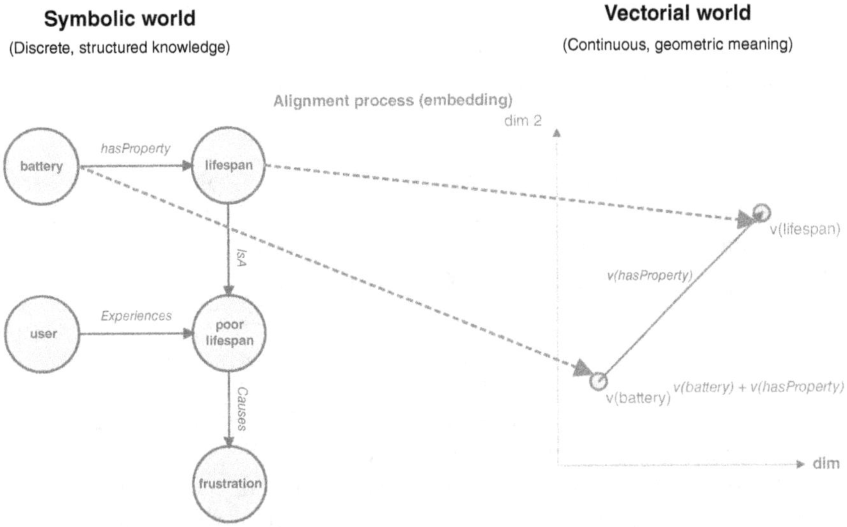

Figure 4.1 Conceptual illustration of the alignment challenge between the discrete, structured symbolic world of knowledge graphs and the continuous, geometric vectorial world of neural embeddings.

3. Knowledge Fusion and Integration
   How can this external, structured knowledge effectively guide or constrain the learning process of a neural network without overwhelming the nuanced patterns learned from the text itself? The fusion must be synergistic, not merely additive. The model needs to learn when to rely on factual knowledge and when to trust the textual context.

   Answering these questions is the prerequisite for any successful knowledge-augmented system. The techniques detailed in the following sections, from simple feature engineering to sophisticated GNNs, can all be seen as different practical attempts to solve this core alignment problem.

4.2.2 Feature Engineering with Lexicons and Knowledge Graphs for Implicit Cues

The primary objective of the alignment process is to manually extract meaningful signals from structured knowledge sources and engineer them into numerical features. This approach treats the knowledge base as a rich repository from which to explicitly craft features that can then be fed into a traditional supervised machine learning classifier, such as an SVM or logistic regression model. This pipeline, while laborious, makes the model's reliance on external knowledge entirely transparent.

Standard sentiment lexicons, which map individual words like "good" or "bad" to polarity scores, are often insufficient for implicit sentiment, as the text frequently lacks such explicit affective words. The solution lies in using more advanced, concept-level lexicons that associate multi-word concepts with affective information.

A canonical example is SenticNet [4, 5], a resource that links commonsense concepts to a vector of emotional and polarity values. The feature engineering process using such a resource typically involves the steps outlined in Table 4.2.

The final feature vector, let's call it X_{lex}, can be formally represented as:

$$\boldsymbol{x}_{\text{lex}} = \left[c_{\text{pos}}, c_{\text{neg}}, s_{\text{avg}}, e_{\text{joy}}, e_{\text{frustration}}, \ldots\right] \tag{4.1}$$

where c_{pos} and c_{neg} are counts of positive/negative concepts, s_{avg} is the average polarity, and e_i are binary flags for specific emotions. This vector provides strong, explicit signals of implicit sentiment to the classifier.

While concept lexicons provide valuable information, they often miss the nuanced relationships between concepts. Knowledge graphs like ConceptNet [6] are particularly adept at capturing this relational knowledge. Feature engineering from a graph is more complex and focuses on the paths and connections between concepts mentioned in the text.

Consider the implicit sentiment in "My new phone gets hot enough to fry an egg." A lexicon might not contain "fry an egg" as a negative concept. A knowledge graph, however, allows for multi-hop reasoning. The reasoning process for this example is illustrated in Figure 4.2, which ultimately allows for the inference of a negative sentiment polarity.

Table 4.2 Feature engineering workflow with a concept-level lexicon.

Step	**Description**	**Example: "I was on Hold for an Hour to Resolve a Simple Billing Issue."**
Concept extraction	Parse the input text to identify phrases that match concepts in the lexicon	Extracted concepts: on_hold, billing_issue
Affective lookup	For each concept, retrieve its associated polarity and emotional scores from the lexicon	on_hold -> Polarity: −0.8, Emotion: frustration. billing_issue -> Polarity: −0.6, Emotion: annoyance
Feature creation	Aggregate the retrieved scores into a numerical feature vector for the entire document	Features could include: neg_concept_count: 2; avg_polarity: −0.7; has_frustration: 1

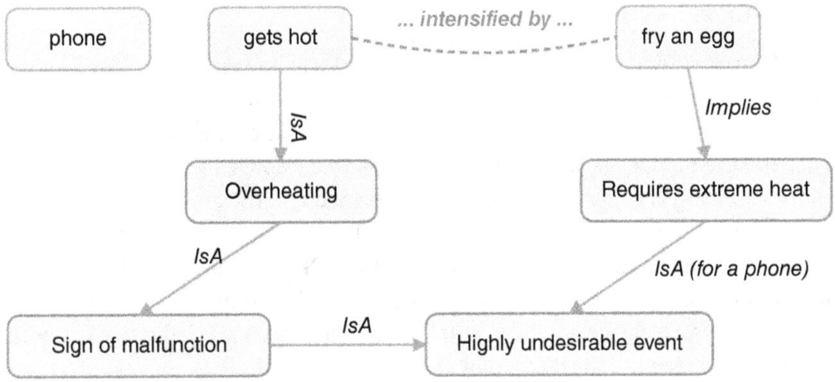

Figure 4.2 A simplified reasoning path in a knowledge graph for the sentence "My new phone gets hot enough to fry an egg." The model can traverse this path to infer negative sentiment.

The feature engineering workflow for graphs involves the following steps.

1. Entity Linking
   Identify key concepts in the text and link them to nodes in the knowledge graph.
2. Path Finding
   Search the graph for semantic paths connecting the identified entities to known affective concepts.
3. Path-based Feature Creation
   To convert the discovered relational information into numerical features, several key steps are taken. First, a binary feature known as path existence is created to indicate whether a semantic path of a certain type, such as CausesPain or HasProperty, exists between concepts. Second, path length is measured as the shortest path distance between two key concepts, with the understanding that a shorter path may imply a more direct and stronger sentiment-bearing relationship. Finally, relationship type counts are calculated as a vector that tallies the occurrences of different relationship types, such as the number of cause relationships, along the paths.

   In essence, these feature engineering techniques act as a manual bridge between the symbolic and vectorial worlds. They distill complex relational knowledge into a set of numerical clues that a machine learning model can easily digest. However, this process is highly dependent on the quality and coverage of the knowledge source, requires significant feature engineering effort, and can be brittle. This inherent limitation motivated the shift toward more integrated neural architectures that can learn to utilize this knowledge automatically.

4.2.3 KGE-enhanced Neural Networks

While feature engineering provides a transparent way to incorporate knowledge, it is labor-intensive, and its effectiveness is ultimately capped by the ingenuity of the handcrafted features. This approach creates a pipeline where errors can propagate, and the model cannot learn to reinterpret the knowledge-based features in light of a new textual context. A more sophisticated and integrated approach is to directly enhance neural networks with KGEs. This method automates the fusion process, allowing the model to learn how to best utilize external knowledge in the context of the specific task. This is achieved by first learning a vector representation for the knowledge graph itself, and then fusing these knowledge vectors with the textual representations learned by the neural network.

Before knowledge can be fused into a neural network, the discrete, symbolic graph must be converted into the continuous vector space that neural networks operate on. Knowledge representation learning (KRL), also known as KGE, is a family of techniques designed for this exact purpose. KRL models learn low-dimensional vector representations for the entities and relations in a knowledge graph, with the goal of preserving the graph's original structure through geometric relationships in the new vector space.

A seminal and highly intuitive KRL model is TransE [7]. TransE models relationships as simple translations in the embedding space. For a given knowledge triple (head, relation, tail), denoted as (h, r, t), the model learns vector embeddings for each component, such that the embedding of the head entity plus the embedding of the relation is geometrically close to the embedding of the tail entity. This structural relationship is captured by the following objective:

$$h + r \approx t \tag{4.2}$$

The model is trained by minimizing a margin-based ranking loss function, which encourages the score of a valid triple (a "positive sample") to be higher than the score of a corrupted, invalid triple (a "negative sample," e.g., replacing h or t with a random entity). For instance, the model learns vectors such that vector('battery') + vector('hasProperty') is close to vector('lifespan'). This simple yet powerful principle allows the rich semantics of the knowledge graph to be captured in a format that neural networks can readily process. While more advanced models like TransH [8], RotatE [9], and ComplEx [10] have been developed to handle more complex relation patterns, TransE provides the foundational principle for this line of research.

Once pretrained embeddings for a knowledge graph are available, the next challenge is to fuse this knowledge with the representations learned from text. This fusion should be synergistic, allowing the model to dynamically decide when and how much to rely on the external knowledge. Several techniques have been proposed to achieve this.

1. Concatenation or Initialization
   The simplest method. For a word in the text that corresponds to an entity in the knowledge graph, its pretrained KGE is concatenated with its standard word embedding. This combined vector, which now contains both textual-contextual and world-knowledge information, is then fed into a neural network like a BiLSTM.
2. Gated Fusion
   A more dynamic approach involves using a gating mechanism, inspired by the architecture of long short-term memory (LSTMs). A gate, which is essentially a small neural network layer with a sigmoid activation, learns a weight vector g between 0 and 1. This gate controls the flow of information from the knowledge embedding (e_k) into the final representation. The updated representation e_{fused} could be calculated as:

$$e_{\text{fused}} = g \odot e_k + (1 - g) \odot e_t \tag{4.3}$$

   where e_t is the text-based embedding and $\odot$ is element-wise multiplication. This allows the model to learn to pay more attention to knowledge when it is relevant to the context.
3. Attention-based Fusion
   The most flexible method uses an attention mechanism. The text representation is used as a "query" to "attend" to a set of relevant KGEs. The model learns to dynamically assign higher weights to the knowledge concepts that are most pertinent for understanding the sentiment of the current word or phrase, effectively selecting the most useful pieces of knowledge on the fly.

4.2.4 Implicit Sentiment Reasoning with GNN

While the fusion techniques discussed previously successfully integrate knowledge at the entity level, they do not explicitly model the multi-hop reasoning process that humans often use to decipher complex implicit sentiment. Consider the statement, "The new OS update made my trusty old photo editor obsolete." A human understands this is negative by following a chain of reasoning: (OS update, causes, software obsolete) → (software obsolete, isA, negative event) → (negative event, evokes, frustration). The sentiment is not tied to a single concept but emerges from the relationships between concepts. To computationally model this kind of chained inference, a more powerful tool is needed: GNN.

GNN is a class of neural networks designed to operate directly on graph-structured data. They provide a principled way to learn representations of nodes by aggregating information from their neighbors. This iterative aggregation process naturally mimics multi-hop reasoning, as information from distant nodes propagates across the graph over several layers of the network.

The GNN-based workflow for implicit sentiment analysis, as illustrated in Figure 4.3, is more sophisticated than simple embedding fusion.

1. Subgraph Construction
   For a given input sentence, a relevant, localized reasoning subgraph is extracted from a large, global knowledge graph. This subgraph is typically seeded with entities identified in the text and expanded to include their N-hop neighbors. This step focuses the reasoning process on the most relevant part of the knowledge base.
2. Graph Propagation with a GNN
   A GNN is applied to this subgraph. The initial representation of each node in the subgraph is its pretrained knowledge embedding. The GNN then updates these representations iteratively. In each layer, the representation of a node is updated by aggregating the vector representations of its neighboring nodes.

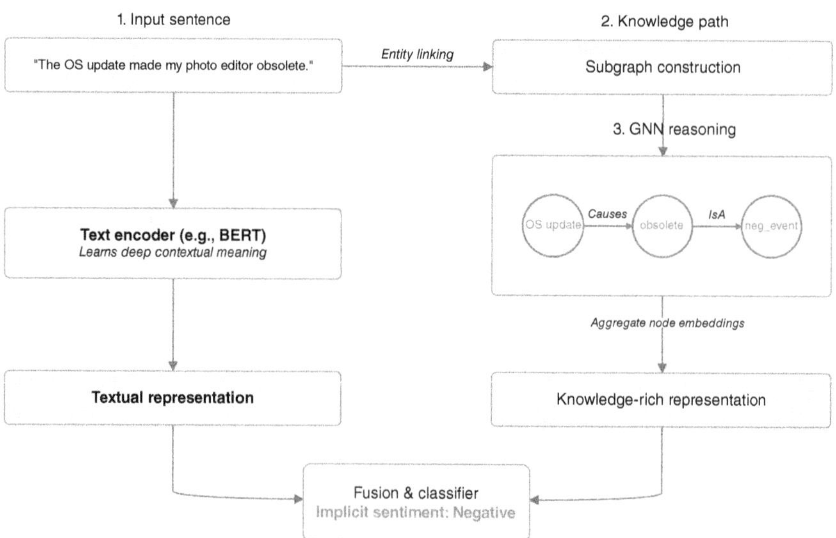

Figure 4.3 The workflow for implicit sentiment analysis using a GNN. A sentence-specific subgraph is constructed, reasoned over by the GNN, and the resulting knowledge-rich representation is fused with a textual representation for final classification.

3. Information Fusion and Classification
   After several layers of propagation, the final node representations from the GNN are contextualized by the reasoning process over the graph structure. The representations of the initial seed entities are then selected from the GNN's output. These knowledge-rich, reasoned representations are fused with the textual representations learned from a parallel text encoder. This final, combined vector, containing both deep textual context and structured reasoning, is fed into a classifier to predict the sentiment.

   By operating directly on the graph structure, GNN provides a more powerful and dynamic way to model the explicit reasoning paths needed to bridge the commonsense gap. They move beyond simply knowing that a concept is negative to modeling how a series of interconnected concepts leads to a negative conclusion, representing a significant step toward more human-like reasoning in sentiment analysis.

4.3 The Contextual Representation Learning Paradigm: Learning Implicit Sentiment Understanding from Context

The knowledge-augmented paradigm provides a powerful and interpretable framework for tackling implicit sentiment, particularly the commonsense reasoning gap. It operates by treating intelligence as something that can be explicitly structured and injected. However, this approach is fundamentally constrained by the coverage and static nature of existing knowledge bases. The contextual representation learning paradigm is rooted in the distributional hypothesis of linguistics, the idea that a word's meaning is defined by the company it keeps. Proponents argue that the subtle cues required to decipher implicit sentiment, especially those related to semantic incongruity like sarcasm, are already encoded within the rich, complex patterns of linguistic context. The challenge, therefore, is to build models with sufficient capacity to learn deep, dynamic, and context-aware representations that can automatically capture these nuanced signals. It posits that by observing a word in a vast and diverse range of contexts, a model can implicitly learn the commonsense associations that a knowledge graph seeks to make explicit.

This section explores this context-centric paradigm as a complementary approach to knowledge augmentation. We begin with its theoretical underpinnings and trace its evolution from recurrent neural networks (RNNs) that model sequential context to the deep contextual understanding enabled by PLMs like BERT (bidirectional encoder representations from transformers). We also examine advanced techniques like contrastive learning designed to sharpen a model's ability to differentiate subtle sentiments based purely on context.

4.3.1 The Distributional Hypothesis and the Primacy of Context in Implicit Analysis

The conceptual bedrock of the contextual representation learning paradigm is the distributional hypothesis, a principle with deep roots in linguistics. This hypothesis posits that words that occur in similar contexts tend to have similar meanings. For decades, this idea has been the driving force behind statistical semantics and is the direct theoretical ancestor of modern word embeddings like Word2Vec and GloVe, which operationalize this principle by learning vector representations where contextual similarity translates to geometric proximity.

While this principle is foundational for all modern NLP, it takes on a special significance in the field of implicit sentiment analysis. The contextual paradigm extends the distributional hypothesis with a crucial corollary: if a word appears in a context that is anomalous or incongruous with its typical usage, its meaning is likely being modulated or inverted. This is the core principle for tackling the semantic incongruity problem. For example, the word "love" typically co-occurs with positive concepts ("love my family," "love this song"). When a model observes it in a highly atypical context, such as "love waiting in line for 3 hours," the distributional anomaly itself becomes a powerful signal for nonliteral meaning (i.e., sarcasm).

Furthermore, this paradigm posits that by observing language at a massive scale, a model can also begin to address the commonsense reasoning gap, though implicitly. While a knowledge graph explicitly states (battery_dies_quickly, IsA, negative_event), a language model trained on billions of sentences will have observed the phrase "battery dies quickly" countless times, predominantly in contexts associated with complaints, problems, and negative reviews. Through sheer statistical association, the model learns an implicit link between the factual event and the negative sentiment, effectively learning a form of distributional common sense without ever consulting a structured knowledge base.

Therefore, in this paradigm, context is given primacy. The central assumption is that the signals needed to decipher implicit sentiment are not necessarily missing and in need of external injection but are already present, encoded within the intricate, high-dimensional patterns of language use. The challenge shifts from knowledge engineering to building models with sufficient capacity and the right architectural biases to automatically discover and leverage these deep contextual signals. RNNs, with their ability to process sequences, represented the first major step in this direction.

4.3.2 Sequential Pattern Detection with RNNs

The first deep learning architecture to fully operationalize the principle of context-driven analysis is RNN. Unlike feed-forward networks, which process inputs independently, RNNs are specifically designed to handle sequential data like text. RNN processes a sentence word-by-word, maintaining a hidden state vector that serves as a dynamic memory of the sequence seen thus far. This inherent ability to model sequential dependencies made RNNs, particularly their more advanced variants like LSTMs and gated recurrent units (GRUs), the natural choice for learning from linguistic context.

For implicit sentiment analysis, the key was to leverage these architectures not just for general classification but to specifically detect the subtle patterns of semantic incongruity and long-range dependencies that signal nonliteral meaning.

One of the most significant breakthroughs in applying RNN to nuanced NLP tasks was the integration of the attention mechanism. A standard BiLSTM produces a rich, context-aware representation for each word, but for classification, it often just uses the final hidden state, which can be a bottleneck. The attention mechanism overcomes this by allowing the model to look back over the entire sequence and dynamically decide which words are most important for the final decision.

This is particularly powerful for detecting semantic incongruity, the hallmark of sarcasm. Consider the sentence: "I just love how this new update drains my battery." A standard model might be confused by the conflict between "love" and "drains." An attention-based BiLSTM can learn to identify this conflict. When making its final prediction, it can assign high attention weights to both "love" and "drains," recognizing that the interaction between these two distant, sentiment-conflicting words is the most critical piece of evidence.

The process, which is formalized below, is conceptually visualized in Figure 4.4, showing how attention highlights the key conflicting words in a sarcastic sentence.

1. A BiLSTM processes the input sentence to produce a sequence of hidden states $H = [h_1, h_2, \ldots, h_n]$, where each h_i is the concatenated forward and backward state for the i-th word.
2. An attention mechanism computes an attention score for each hidden state, indicating its importance. This is often done by comparing each h_i to a learnable context vector u_w.

$$e_i = \boldsymbol{u}_w^T \tanh\left(\boldsymbol{W}_w \boldsymbol{h}_i + \boldsymbol{b}_w\right) \tag{4.4}$$

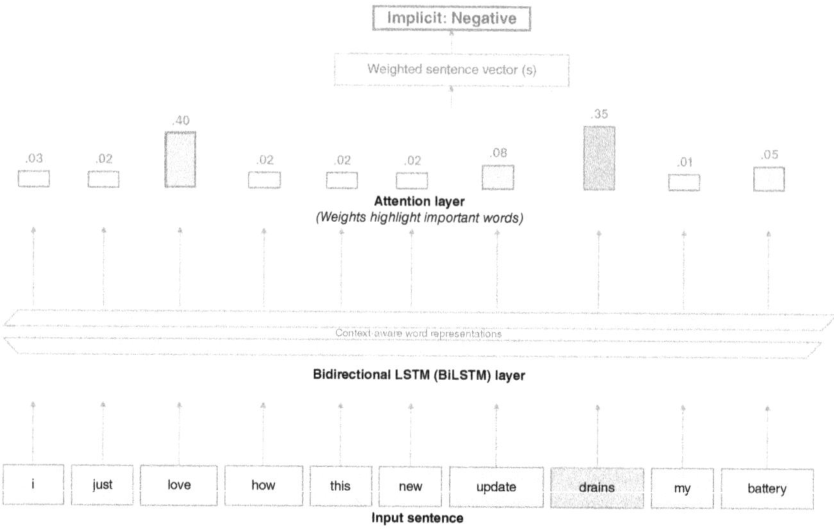

Figure 4.4 An attention-based BiLSTM for sarcasm detection. The attention mechanism learns to assign higher weights to the semantically incongruous words ("love" and "drains"), enabling the model to correctly identify the implicit negative sentiment.

3. These scores are normalized into a probability distribution (the attention weights) using a softmax function.

$$\alpha_i = \frac{\exp(e_i)}{\sum_j \exp(e_j)} \tag{4.5}$$

4. A single, fixed-length sentence vector s is computed as the weighted sum of the hidden states.

$$s = \sum_i \alpha_i \boldsymbol{h}_i \tag{4.6}$$

5. This vector s, which now selectively focuses on the most salient words, is fed into a final softmax layer for classification.

The attention mechanism can be extended to model structure at a higher level, which is crucial for implicit sentiment that unfolds across multiple sentences. A single sarcastic sentence might be easy to spot, but sometimes the sentiment is only apparent when considering the entire document's context.

The hierarchical attention network (HAN) [11] was designed for this purpose. It mirrors the natural structure of a document by employing a two-level attention mechanism.

- Word-level Attention: A first BiLSTM-with-attention is used to process each sentence individually, creating a vector representation for each sentence that focuses on its most important words.
- Sentence-level Attention: A second, higher-level BiLSTM-with-attention then takes this sequence of sentence vectors as its input. It learns to assign attention weights to each sentence, identifying which sentences are most critical for determining the overall sentiment of the document.

This hierarchical structure allows the model to capture document-level phenomena. For instance, a review might start with several factual, neutral-sounding sentences describing a product's features, but a single, concluding sentence might subtly frame that information in a negative light. The HAN can learn to place a high attention weight on that crucial final sentence to make the correct implicit sentiment classification for the entire document. This ability to weigh information at both the word and sentence level represented a significant step toward deep contextual understanding.

4.3.3 Deep Contextual Understanding with PLM

While RNN-based architectures represented a significant step forward, their ability to understand context is ultimately limited. They learn from scratch on a specific, often small, task-specific dataset. This means they lack a broader, more general understanding of language and the world. The advent of PLM, particularly the Transformer-based architecture of models like BERT [12], marked a paradigm shift in NLP and, by extension, in implicit sentiment analysis.

The core innovation of PLM is the pretraining and fine-tuning workflow. A massive model is first pretrained on an enormous, unlabeled text corpus. During this phase, the model is forced to learn the fundamental statistical patterns, syntactic structures, and semantic relationships of language to solve self-supervised tasks like predicting masked words. The result is not just a model but a rich, prepackaged foundation of linguistic knowledge that can then be rapidly adapted, or fine-tuned, for a wide range of specific downstream tasks, including implicit sentiment analysis.

PLMs like BERT address the challenges of implicit sentiment in a fundamentally different way than the paradigms discussed so far. Unlike knowledge-augmented models that are explicitly given structured facts, BERT learns a form of implicit knowledge through its massive-scale pretraining. Consider our recurring example: "The phone's battery died in 3 hours." BERT does not know that poor battery life is bad in a symbolic sense. Instead, it has learned a deep, distributional representation where the vector for our example sentence is located in a region of the embedding space that is extremely close to the region of explicitly negative sentences. It has, in effect, learned the distributional common sense that was previously elusive. This allows PLMs to often handle cases of implicit sentiment from factual consequences without any external knowledge injection, blurring the lines between the knowledge-driven and context-driven paradigms.

PLMs truly excel at tackling the semantic incongruity problem due to the core component of their architecture: the self-attention mechanism. Unlike an RNN's sequential memory, self-attention allows every word in a sentence to directly interact with every other word. This makes it exceptionally good at detecting the long-range dependencies and contradictions that characterize implicit sentiment.

When fine-tuning a PLM for implicit sentiment detection, the process is straightforward yet powerful:

1. A pretrained BERT model is taken.
2. A simple classification layer is added on top of the final representation of the special [CLS] token, which is designed to aggregate sentence-level information.
3. The entire model is then trained end-to-end on a labeled implicit sentiment dataset.

During fine-tuning, the self-attention mechanism, already pretrained to understand complex linguistic relationships, learns to specialize in spotting incongruity. For the sentence "I just love how this new update drains my battery," the self-attention heads can learn to create a strong connection between "love" and "drains." The model learns that when these two concepts, which are semantically distant and conflicting in its pretrained worldview, are brought together in this syntactic construction, it is a powerful indicator of implicit sentiment. Figure 4.5 illustrates

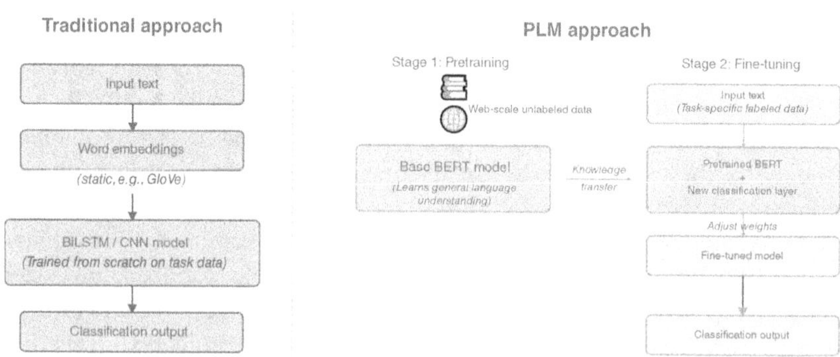

Figure 4.5 A comparison between the traditional approach (left), where a model is trained from scratch on task data, and the PLM fine-tuning approach (right), which leverages a massive pretrained model and adapts it. The PLM approach effectively transfers a vast amount of general linguistic knowledge to the specific task of implicit sentiment detection.

the conceptual difference between the traditional deep learning approach and the PLM-based fine-tuning approach for this task.

By leveraging the deep contextual understanding baked into their pretrained weights, PLMs have consistently set new state-of-the-art performance benchmarks on the implicit sentiment detection tasks, often outperforming more complex, specialized architectures with far less task-specific training data.

4.3.4 Contrastive Learning for Implicit Sentiment Differentiation

While fine-tuning PLMs on standard classification objectives is highly effective, it may not be optimal for tasks requiring the differentiation of very subtle semantic nuances, a common feature of implicit sentiment. For instance, the factual statement "The phone's screen is 6.9 inches" might be implicitly positive for a user who values large screens but negative for one who prefers compact devices. A standard classifier might struggle to distinguish these without strong contextual cues.

Contrastive learning [13] offers a more powerful training objective for such scenarios. Instead of learning to predict a specific class label for a single input, contrastive learning trains a model to pull semantically similar examples closer together in the embedding space while pushing dissimilar examples further apart. This forces the model to learn a more structured and discriminative representation space, focusing on the subtle features that truly differentiate meanings.

The application of contrastive learning to implicit sentiment typically follows this structure.

1. **Constructing Pairs**
   For each input sentence (the "anchor," x_i), we need to construct positive and negative pairs.

   A positive pair $\left(x_i, x_i^+\right)$ consists of the anchor and another sentence that shares the same implicit sentiment, even if the surface words are different. This can be created through data augmentation techniques like back-translation or by using sentences from the same class in a batch.

   A negative pair $\left(x_i, x_j^-\right)$ consists of the anchor and a sentence with a different implicit sentiment. These are typically other samples from the training batch that belong to a different class.
2. **The Training Objective**
   The model, usually a Transformer-based encoder, maps each sentence into an embedding vector. The training objective is to minimize a contrastive loss function, such as the InfoNCE loss [14]. The core idea of this loss is to make the embedding of the anchor (v_i) more similar to the embedding of its positive pair $\left(v_i^+\right)$ than to the embeddings of all its negative pairs $\left(v_i^-\right)$.

The simplified form of the InfoNCE loss for a single positive pair and N negative pairs can be expressed as:

$$L_i = -\log \frac{\exp\left(\mathrm{sim}(v_i, v_i^{+})/\tau\right)}{\exp\left(\mathrm{sim}(v_i, v_i^{+})/\tau\right) + \sum_{j=1}^{N} \exp\left(\mathrm{sim}(v_i, v_j^{-})/\tau\right)} \tag{4.7}$$

where v_i, v_i^{+}, and v_j^{-} are the sentence embeddings produced by the model. $\mathrm{sim}(a, b)$ is a similarity function, typically the cosine similarity between two vectors. τ is a temperature hyperparameter that controls the sharpness of the distribution, essentially scaling how much the model should focus on hard-to-distinguish negative examples.

By minimizing this loss over the entire dataset, the model is learning a simple decision boundary. It is forced to learn what makes "The battery lasted all day" (positive) fundamentally similar to "I never have to worry about charging" (positive), while simultaneously pushing both far away from "The battery died in 3 hours" (negative). This results in a more robust and semantically organized embedding space, which has been shown to significantly improve performance on challenging implicit sentiment classification tasks, especially in low-data regimes. This technique essentially sharpens the model's ability to perceive subtle differences based purely on context.

4.4 The Prompt-based Reasoning Paradigm: Guiding Large Models for Implicit Sentiment Interpretation

The paradigms discussed thus far, whether augmenting models with explicit knowledge or training them to learn from deep context, share a common workflow: they aim to create a specialized model, fine-tuned or explicitly designed for the singular purpose of sentiment analysis. The final and most recent paradigm represents a radical departure from this philosophy. Driven by the vast scale of LLMs, this new approach does not seek to build a specialized tool but rather to effectively communicate a task to a general-purpose reasoning engine. The focus shifts from model training to model instruction.

This prompt-based reasoning paradigm operates on the principle that models with sufficient scale exhibit emergent abilities, such as multistep reasoning, that are not present in smaller models and were not explicitly programmed. By interacting with these models through carefully crafted natural language prompts, we can guide them to perform complex implicit sentiment analysis on the fly, often without any task-specific training data. This section explores this transformative approach. We first examine the theoretical underpinnings of emergent abilities and in-context learning (ICL), then delve into the practical experience of prompt engineering for this task, and finally analyze advanced techniques like CoT that make the model's implicit reasoning process explicit and verifiable.

4.4.1 Emergent Abilities and ICL in LLM

The prompt-based paradigm is not merely an incremental improvement. It is enabled by fundamentally new phenomena observed in language models of immense scale [15]. Understanding this paradigm requires grasping two core concepts that differentiate LLMs from their smaller, pretrained predecessors: emergent abilities and ICL.

Emergent abilities refer to capabilities that are not present in smaller-scale models but appear, often sharply and unpredictably, once a model's size, training data, and compute cross certain thresholds [16]. While a smaller model like BERT can be fine-tuned to classify sentiment, it cannot, for instance, explain why a sentence is sarcastic in a zero-shot setting. A sufficiently large LLM can exhibit emergent abilities such as performing multistep reasoning, following complex instructions, and decomposing problems into intermediate steps. For implicit sentiment analysis, the most relevant emergent ability is a form of robust, flexible commonsense reasoning. These models appear to have internalized such a vast and nuanced representation of the world from their training data that they can perform the inferential leaps necessary to bridge the commonsense gap without being explicitly programmed or fine-tuned to do so. This emergent reasoning power is the raw material that the prompt-based paradigm seeks to harness.

ICL is the remarkable mechanism through which these emergent abilities are activated and steered. ICL describes a model's capacity to learn a new task at inference time, simply by being shown a few examples within the context of the prompt itself, without any updates to its underlying weights or parameters. This is a form of rapid, temporary learning that is distinct from the slow, permanent learning of fine-tuning.

4.4.2 Zero-shot and Few-shot Implicit Sentiment Analysis via Prompt Engineering

The primary interface for interacting with an LLM is no longer code or complex configurations, but natural language itself. The practice of designing effective natural language instructions to guide an LLM is known as prompt engineering. For implicit sentiment analysis, this means crafting prompts that can steer the model's emergent reasoning abilities toward the correct interpretation without any task-specific training. This is accomplished through two main strategies: zero-shot and few-shot prompting.

In a zero-shot setting, the model is given a task description and an input to be analyzed, but it is provided with zero prior examples of the task. The model must rely entirely on its pretrained knowledge and its ability to understand the instruction. This is the most challenging yet most flexible way to use an LLM.

A simple zero-shot prompt for implicit sentiment analysis might look like this:

Instruction: Analyze the implicit sentiment of the following product review. The sentiment can be "Positive," "Negative," or "Neutral." Explain your reasoning.
Review: "This laptop gets hot enough to be uncomfortable on my lap after about 20 minutes."
Sentiment:

For a sufficiently capable LLM, this prompt is often enough to elicit a correct response (e.g., Negative) along with a reasonable explanation (e.g., "The laptop overheating causes physical discomfort, which is a significant flaw and indicates a negative user experience."). The success of zero-shot prompting is a direct testament to the model's emergent ability to generalize from its pretraining to a completely new task formulation.

While powerful, zero-shot performance can be brittle. The model might misinterpret the desired output format or struggle with particularly ambiguous cases. Few-shot prompting significantly improves reliability by leveraging the model's ICL capability. In this approach, the prompt includes a small number of complete examples that demonstrate the task.

These examples serve several critical functions:

- Task Specification
  They clarify the exact nature of the task in a way that is often more precise than a natural language instruction alone.
- Format Specification
  They show the model the desired output format such as the exact labels to use and whether an explanation is needed.
- Reasoning Pattern Demonstration
  For complex tasks, they can implicitly demonstrate a desired reasoning pattern.

A simple few-shot prompt for implicit sentiment analysis might look like this:

Analyze the implicit sentiment (Positive/Negative) of the review.

Review: "The package arrived a week late."
Sentiment: Negative
Review: "The user manual was only two pages long."
Sentiment: Positive

Review: "This laptop gets hot enough to be uncomfortable on my lap after about 20 minutes."
Sentiment:

By conditioning its prediction on the two provided examples, the LLM is better able to understand the task and produce the correct Negative output. The selection of these few-shot examples is a critical part of prompt engineering; well-chosen, diverse examples can dramatically improve performance.

The performance of prompt engineering for implicit sentiment thus involves carefully crafting the task instruction, selecting high-quality and representative examples, and structuring the prompt in a clear, unambiguous way. These techniques allow us to effectively tap into the vast, latent capabilities of LLM, turning them into powerful zero-shot or few-shot implicit sentiment analyzers without the need for costly data collection and model training cycles.

4.4.3 CoT: Making the Reasoning Process for Implicit Sentiment Explicit

While few-shot prompting can effectively guide an LLM to produce the correct final answer, it still largely treats the model as a black box. We see the input and the final output, but the intermediate reasoning steps the model might have taken to arrive at its conclusion remain hidden within its vast network of parameters. This lack of transparency is a significant drawback for high-stakes applications and for understanding and debugging model failures.

CoT [17] prompting was a landmark discovery that directly addresses this issue by making the model's reasoning process explicit. The key insight is remarkably simple yet profound by modifying the few-shot exemplars in the prompt to include the intermediate reasoning steps used to get from the problem to the answer, the LLM can be coaxed into generating its own explicit, step-by-step reasoning chain before providing its final conclusion.

A standard few-shot prompt simply maps an input to an output. A CoT prompt, in contrast, demonstrates the entire reasoning process.

Analyze the implicit sentiment of the review and provide your reasoning.

Review: "The user manual was only two pages long."
Reasoning: A very short manual implies the product is simple and easy to set up. Simplicity and ease of use are desirable qualities in a product. Therefore, the sentiment is positive.
Sentiment: Positive
Review: "I had to charge the phone three times today."

Reasoning:
Sentiment:

When presented with this prompt, the LLM learns the desired format for its response. It understands that it must first generate a "Reasoning": section before the final "Sentiment": label. For the final example, it would then produce a full response, such as:

Reasoning: Charging a phone multiple times in a single day indicates that the battery life is very poor. Poor battery life is a major flaw in a mobile device and a significant source of user frustration. Therefore, the sentiment is negative.
Sentiment: Negative

The impact of CoT on complex reasoning tasks like implicit sentiment analysis is transformative.

- Improved Accuracy
  For problems that cannot be solved impulsively and require multiple steps of inference, forcing the model to generate a reasoning chain significantly improves its final accuracy. This process seems to allow the model to decompose the problem, focus on intermediate steps, and allocate more computational resources to the task, reducing the likelihood of intuitive but incorrect answers. It's the difference between a quick guess and a considered judgment.
- Enhanced Interpretability
  This is the most significant benefit for implicit sentiment analysis. CoT provides a transparent window into the model's thought process. It moves the reasoning from an opaque, internal state to an explicit, human-readable text. This allows us to verify the reasoning by checking if the model's logic is sound and debug errors by pinpointing where exactly its reasoning went wrong. A correct answer accompanied by sound reasoning is far more trustworthy than a correct answer from a black box.

  For implicit sentiment, the generated reasoning chain is often more valuable than the final polarity label itself. It provides the reason behind the sentiment, which is the core goal of deep user understanding. CoT transforms the LLM from a simple classifier into an explainable reasoning engine.

4.4.4 Advanced Prompting Strategies for Robust Reasoning

While CoT prompting significantly improves the reasoning capabilities of LLM, the single reasoning path it generates can sometimes be flawed or land on an incorrect conclusion due to the probabilistic nature of the model. To address this and enhance the robustness of the reasoning process, several advanced prompting strategies have been developed. These techniques aim to move from a single, potentially fragile line of reasoning to a more resilient, aggregated result.

Self-consistency [18] addresses the fragility of a single reasoning chain by leveraging a core statistical principle: a consensus drawn from a diverse sample is more reliable than a single data point. Instead of generating one best reasoning path, this technique employs a stochastic decoding strategy to produce multiple, varied reasoning chains from the same initial prompt.

The underlying mechanism consists of two stages. First, a diverse set of candidate reasoning paths is generated by the language model. Each path represents a potentially different way of thinking through the problem. Second, the final answers derived from each of these paths are aggregated, and the most frequent answer is selected through a majority vote. This process effectively marginalizes outlier or flawed reasoning paths that may occur due to the probabilistic nature of the model. By relying on the collective agreement of multiple reasoning processes, self-consistency significantly increases the robustness and accuracy of the final outcome.

The linear, step-by-step nature of CoT, even when diversified by self-consistency, is not always optimal for problems that require exploration, evaluation, and backtracking. The tree-of-thoughts (ToT) [19] framework generalizes the linear chain into a more flexible tree structure, allowing for a more deliberate and strategic exploration of the problem space.

The ToT paradigm operates by decomposing the reasoning process into a series of thoughts, where each thought is a coherent unit of text that contributes to solving the problem. At each step, instead of generating just one subsequent thought, the model is prompted to propose multiple potential next thoughts, thereby creating branches in a reasoning tree. Crucially, the ToT framework equips the language model with the ability to act as an evaluator. It can assess the value or promise of different branches based on heuristics or self-reflection. This evaluation allows a search algorithm to systematically navigate the tree, expanding promising nodes while pruning or backtracking from those deemed unviable. This structured exploration enables the model to look ahead, compare different reasoning directions, and make more globally optimal decisions, which is essential for tasks characterized by high ambiguity or a complex solution space.

4.5 Research Frontiers and Open Challenges in Implicit Sentiment Analysis

As the methodologies for implicit sentiment analysis evolve from knowledge-driven systems to powerful reasoning engines, the frontier of research is pushed further, revealing new layers of complexity and ambition. The goal is no longer simply to classify a text's hidden polarity but to achieve a far more granular, causal, and holistic understanding of human opinion. This section explores three key research frontiers that are shaping the future of the field: the pursuit of implicit aspect-based sentiment, the shift toward causal inference in opinion analysis, and the expansion into multimodal contexts. These areas represent the next grand challenges, promising to unlock an even deeper level of affective comprehension.

4.5.1 Implicit Aspect-based Sentiment Analysis

Aspect-based sentiment analysis (ABSA) has traditionally focused on opinions where both the aspect and its associated sentiment are explicitly mentioned (e.g., "The camera is amazing"). However, a significant portion of opinions about specific features is conveyed implicitly. Implicit aspect-based sentiment analysis (implicit ABSA) is the challenging task of identifying sentiment toward aspects that are not directly stated in the text. This frontier combines the core difficulties of ABSA with the inferential hurdles of implicit analysis.

There are two primary challenges within implicit ABSA:

Implicit Aspect Extraction: This involves identifying that an opinion is being expressed about an aspect category even when no specific term for that aspect is present. For instance, the review "The phone barely fits in my pocket" expresses a negative sentiment. The explicit term is "phone," but the implicit aspect being critiqued is the size or portability of the device. Solving this requires a model to map factual descriptions to a predefined ontology of aspect categories, a task that heavily relies on commonsense reasoning. A model must understand that pocket-fit relates directly to the physical dimensions of an object.

Implicit Sentiment Toward an Explicit Aspect: This occurs when an aspect is mentioned, but the sentiment toward it is conveyed through a factual statement. In the sentence, "The laptop's fan sounds like a jet engine during video calls," the aspect fan is explicit. The sentiment, however, is implicit. It requires the commonsense knowledge that a "jet engine" is extremely loud, and loud fan noise is a highly undesirable characteristic for a laptop. This task demands the same reasoning capabilities discussed throughout this chapter but applied at a much more granular, aspect-specific level.

Current research in implicit ABSA is increasingly leveraging LLMs. By providing LLMs with a clear definition of aspect categories and using CoT prompting, researchers are guiding these models to first identify the relevant implicit aspect and then reason about the sentiment toward it. The ultimate goal is to build systems that can produce a complete, structured summary of opinions, capturing not just "the camera is good" but also that "it feels like a brick in the hand" implies negative sentiment toward weight and ergonomics.

4.5.2 Toward Causal Inference in Opinion Analysis

Traditional sentiment analysis, both explicit and implicit, is fundamentally a correlational task. It identifies what sentiment is present but rarely addresses why it is being expressed in a particular way. The frontier of causal inference in opinion analysis seeks to move beyond correlation to understand the underlying causal factors that shape an opinion and its expression. This involves answering questions like: "What event caused this user to become sarcastic?" or "Is the user's negative sentiment a result of a product failure or a misunderstanding of its features?"

This pursuit introduces several new research dimensions:

- Causal Event and Reason Extraction
  The goal is to identify the specific events or reasons that led to the expressed sentiment. For example, in "After the latest update, the app started crashing," the causal task is to extract latest update as the cause for the negative sentiment associated with crashing.
- Counterfactual Reasoning
  This involves asking "what if" questions to understand the sensitivity of an opinion. For instance, "Would the user's sentiment have been positive if the battery had lasted all day?" Answering such questions requires models that can not only understand the stated world but also reason about hypothetical, alternative worlds.
- Distinguishing Cause from Justification
  Users often provide justifications that are not the true underlying cause of their sentiment. A user might complain about a minor UI issue, but the root cause of their frustration could be a major data-loss bug they experienced earlier. Causal models must learn to disentangle these complex human behaviors.

This research direction has profound implications. For a business, understanding the root cause of customer dissatisfaction is far more valuable than simply knowing that the customer is unhappy. For social science, it enables a deeper analysis of how events shape public discourse. While still in its nascent stages, this shift from "what" to "why" represents a move toward a more explanatory and actionable form of artificial intelligence, leveraging techniques from causal machine learning and integrating them with the reasoning capabilities of LLMs.

4.5.3 Multimodal Sarcasm Detection

The final frontier discussed here involves breaking free from the confines of text-only analysis. Sentiment, especially complex forms like sarcasm, is an inherently multimodal phenomenon. The same sentence, "That's just great," can be genuinely positive, brutally sarcastic, or dryly ironic, and the disambiguating signal often lies outside the words themselves. Multimodal sarcasm detection aims to build models that can jointly interpret cues from different data streams—typically text, acoustics (speech), and vision—to achieve a more accurate and robust understanding.

- Acoustic Cues
  The tone of voice is a powerful indicator. Sarcasm is often characterized by a slower speech rate, a flattened pitch contour, and nasalization. A model could learn that a positive sentence delivered with a deadpan, monotonic tone is likely sarcastic.
- Visual Cues
  Facial expressions and gestures are equally important. A smile delivered with a rolling of the eyes, a smirk, or a mismatch between the expression in the eyes and the mouth are classic visual markers of nonliteral intent.

The primary challenge in this area is multimodal fusion: how to effectively combine information from these disparate and often asynchronous modalities. As will be detailed in the next chapter, this involves learning joint representations that can capture the complex interplay between words, tone, and facial expressions. For instance, a model must learn to detect the incongruity not just between words in a sentence, but between the positive polarity of the words and the negative valence of the facial expression accompanying them. The development of large-scale, multimodal datasets and sophisticated fusion architectures (often involving multiheaded attention across modalities) is driving progress in this area, providing a natural bridge from our discussion of implicit sentiment in text to the broader world of multimodal analysis.

4.6 Case Study: A Deep Dive into Reasoning-based Implicit Sentiment Interpretation with LLMs

To ground the theoretical discussions of the preceding sections in a practical application, this case study provides a deep dive into using a modern LLM to solve the core challenge of implicit sentiment analysis. We will demonstrate how the prompt-based reasoning paradigm, specifically using CoT prompting, can be applied to not only classify but also explain implicit sentiment in real-world product reviews. This case study will showcase the methodology, analyze its outputs, and critically evaluate its strengths and inherent limitations, thereby providing a comprehensive understanding of the state-of-the-art in practice.

4.6.1 Task Definition and Data Source

1. Task Definition
   The task is defined as follows: given a product review that does not contain explicit, high-polarity sentiment words (e.g., "good," "bad," "love," "hate"), the system must perform two actions:
   - Classify the implicit sentiment of the review as "Positive," "Negative," or "Neutral."
   - Generate a step-by-step natural language explanation (a reasoning chain) that justifies the classification based on commonsense or contextual inference.

   The emphasis is on the generated explanation, as this provides the interpretable insight that makes the analysis valuable.
2. Data Source
   For this case study, we will use illustrative examples drawn from the Amazon Customer Reviews Dataset. This large-scale dataset contains millions of product reviews across various categories. We specifically select reviews that are rated with a low star rating (1 or 2 stars) or a high star rating (4 or 5 stars) but whose text is predominantly factual or nonliteral. These reviews serve as excellent examples of naturally occurring implicit sentiment. For instance, a 1-star review stating, "The box arrived empty," is a perfect example of implicit negative sentiment requiring commonsense inference.

4.6.2 CoT Prompting

As established in Section 4.4, CoT prompting is the ideal technique for this task because it explicitly instructs the model to generate the required reasoning chain. We will use a few-shot CoT prompt to guide an LLM (e.g., a model from the GPT or Claude series).

A successful prompt is carefully engineered to provide clear instructions, high-quality examples, and a well-defined output structure. Our prompt architecture consists of three key components:

Role-playing Instruction: The prompt begins by assigning a persona to the LLM to prime it for the desired analytical mindset.

Few-shot Demonstrations (Exemplars): We provide two diverse examples that demonstrate the complete, desired reasoning process—one positive and one negative. These examples teach the model the expected format and the style of reasoning.

The Query: The final part of the prompt is the new, unseen review that the model must analyze.

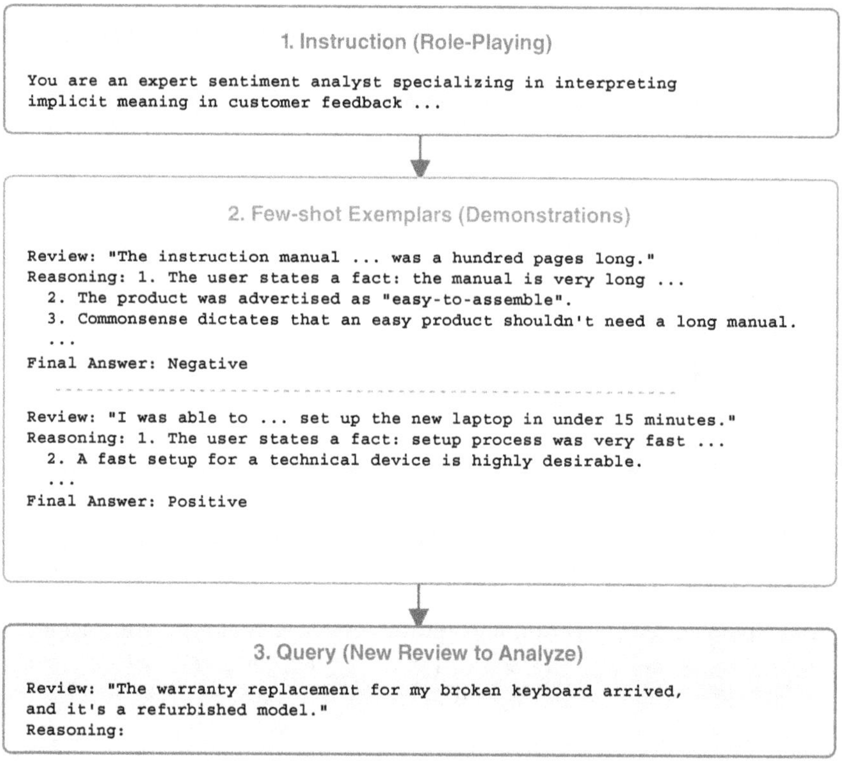

Figure 4.6 The architecture of the few-shot CoT prompt, comprising an initial instruction, detailed examples demonstrating the reasoning process, and the final query.

Figure 4.6 illustrates the complete architecture of the prompt used in this case study.

You are an expert sentiment analyst specializing in interpreting implicit meaning in customer feedback. Your task is to analyze the following product reviews, provide a step-by-step reasoning chain, and then conclude with a final sentiment label.

Example:

Review: "The instruction manual for the 'easy-to-assemble' bookshelf was a hundred pages long."

Reasoning:

1. *The user states a fact: the manual is very long (100 pages).*
2. *The product was advertised as "easy-to-assemble."*

3. *Commonsense knowledge dictates that an easy-to-assemble product should not require a long, complex manual.*
4. *This implies the product is actually difficult to assemble and does not meet the user's expectations.*
5. *Difficulty and unmet expectations are sources of user frustration.*

Therefore, the implicit sentiment is negative.

Final Answer: Negative

Review: "The warranty replacement for my broken keyboard arrived, and it's a refurbished model."

Reasoning:

1. *The user's original product (a keyboard) was broken, which is already a negative starting point.*
2. *They received a warranty replacement, which is the expected procedure.*
3. *The key piece of information is that the replacement is a "refurbished model," not a new one.*
4. *Commonsense knowledge suggests that customers generally expect a new, unused item as a replacement for a faulty product they purchased new, especially under warranty.*
5. *Receiving a refurbished (i.e., used and repaired) item can feel like a downgrade and implies the company is cutting costs at the customer's expense.*
6. *This feeling of being undervalued and receiving a lesser-quality item leads to disappointment.*

Therefore, the implicit sentiment is negative.

Final Answer: Negative

This generated output perfectly demonstrates the power of CoT. The model successfully deconstructs the problem: it identifies the key factual statements (Step 1–3), invokes the relevant social and consumer expectations (Step 4–5), connects those expectations to an emotional outcome (Step 6), and arrives at a logical conclusion. The explanation is clear, interpretable, and provides deep insight into the source of the negative sentiment.

4.6.3 Critical Evaluation and Analysis

While the CoT approach is powerful, a critical academic evaluation requires an analysis of its performance across different scenarios, including its failure modes.

A qualitative review of the model's outputs on a variety of reviews from the dataset reveals several strengths:

- Handling Sarcasm
  For a review like, "I love how this 'premium' travel mug leaks coffee all over my shirt," the model correctly identifies the semantic incongruity between "love" and "leaks," and between "premium" and a product failure.
- Multi-hop Reasoning
  For reviews like, "The printer ink cartridge ran out after printing only 20 pages," the model can produce a chain like: (20 pages is a very low yield) -> (low yield means high cost-per-page) -> (high cost is a negative attribute) -> Negative.
- Nuance Recognition
  The model can distinguish between "The phone is heavy" (potentially neutral or negative) and "The phone feels substantial and solid in the hand" (positive), demonstrating its sensitivity to phrasing.

The primary failure mode of this approach is when the LLM's "commonsense" knowledge is flawed, incomplete, or misaligned with a specific context. We can categorize these errors:

- Lack of Niche Knowledge
  For a highly specialized product (e.g., scientific equipment), the model might lack the domain-specific knowledge to interpret a factual statement correctly. A review stating "The oscilloscope showed a 3% signal jitter" might be interpreted as neutral, whereas an expert would know this is unacceptably high and thus negative.
- Cultural Misinterpretation
  Common sense can be culturally specific. A comment about a product being "very loud" could be positive in a context where loudness equates to power (e.g., a rock concert speaker) but negative in most others. The model may default to the most common interpretation and miss the cultural nuance.
- Over-reasoning or Hallucination
  Sometimes the model can "overthink" a simple problem, inventing complex, unfounded reasons for a sentiment. For a neutral statement like "The charging cable is black," the model might hallucinate a reasoning chain about how black cables are harder to find in the dark, leading to an incorrect negative classification. This highlights that the reasoning is plausible, but not necessarily grounded in the user's actual experience.

To appreciate the leap forward that LLM-based reasoning represents, it is useful to compare its performance to the context-driven models discussed in Section 4.3 (e.g., a fine-tuned BERT or BiLSTM).

Let's take the refurbished keyboard example. A BERT model fine-tuned for sentiment classification would likely struggle with this sentence and might classify it as "Neutral." The reason is that the sentence contains no strong negative polarity words. The model would learn vector representations for "warranty," "replacement," and "refurbished," but it has no inherent, structured knowledge about the complex consumer expectations governing warranty claims. It might learn that "broken" is negative, but it has no robust way to connect the concept of "refurbished" to the context of a "warranty replacement" to infer the user's disappointment. It can learn correlations from its fine-tuning data, but it cannot perform the multi-step, knowledge-driven inference that the CoT-prompted LLM executes explicitly. This case study thus clearly illustrates that for complex implicit sentiment that hinges on world knowledge and reasoning, the prompt-based paradigm offers a fundamentally more powerful and interpretable solution.

4.7 Conclusion

This chapter has journeyed into the complex and nuanced world of implicit sentiment, moving beyond the analysis of explicitly stated opinions to explore the vast landscape of inferred and unstated feelings. We have established that the core of this challenge lies in surmounting two fundamental obstacles: the commonsense reasoning gap, which requires world knowledge to interpret factual statements, and the semantic incongruity problem, which demands sensitivity to nonliteral language like sarcasm and irony. Our exploration of the methodologies designed to tackle these problems has revealed a clear and fascinating evolutionary trajectory in the field of artificial intelligence itself.

4.7.1 Recapitulation of Challenges and Methodological Paradigms

We traced the development of three distinct paradigms. The first, the knowledge-augmented paradigm, represented a direct attempt to solve the reasoning gap by explicitly injecting structured, symbolic knowledge into models, first through feature engineering and later through more sophisticated fusion with KGEs and GNNs. The second, the contextual representation learning paradigm, shifted the focus inward, operating on the premise that sufficient linguistic knowledge could be learned implicitly from the deep, distributional patterns within massive text corpora. This approach, culminating in PLMs like BERT, proved exceptionally powerful for detecting semantic incongruity.

Finally, we arrived at the current state-of-the-art: the prompt-based reasoning paradigm. Powered by the emergent abilities of LLMs, this approach reframes the task entirely. Through techniques like CoT prompting, it transforms the analysis from a classification problem into an explicit, interpretable reasoning process, capable of addressing both commonsense gaps and semantic incongruity in a flexible, zero-shot manner.

4.7.2 From Sentiment Classification to Computational Empathy

Looking forward, the ultimate goal of this research frontier extends beyond mere classification. The ability to understand implicit sentiment is a critical stepping stone toward a much grander ambition: achieving genuine affective comprehension. The path forward involves tackling even deeper challenges, such as discerning the causal roots of an opinion and interpreting sentiment in rich, multimodal contexts.

The true north for this field is the development of systems that possess a form of computational empathy—the ability not just to identify an emotion, but to understand its context, its cause, and its implications from a human-centric perspective. As models continue to evolve, the distinction between analyzing text and understanding the person behind the text will become increasingly blurred. The journey through implicit sentiment is, therefore, not just a technical challenge; it is an integral part of the larger quest to create more insightful, responsive, and ultimately, more understanding artificial intelligence.

References

1 Mao, Y., Liu, Q., & Zhang, Y. (2024). Sentiment analysis methods, applications, and challenges: A systematic literature review. *Journal of King Saud University: Computer and Information Sciences*, 36(4), 102048.

2 Zhao, Y., Mamat, M., Aysa, A., & Ubul, K. (2024). A dynamic graph structural framework for implicit sentiment identification based on complementary semantic and structural information. *Scientific Reports*, 14(1), 16563.

3 Li, Z., Zou, Y., Zhang, C., Zhang, Q., & Wei, Z. (2021). Learning implicit sentiment in aspect-based sentiment analysis with supervised contrastive pre-training. In Proceedings of the 2021 Conference on Empirical Methods in Natural Language Processing, Punta Cana, Dominican Republic, (pp. 246–256).

4 Cambria, E., Speer, R., Havasi, C., & Hussain, A. (2010). SenticNet: A publicly available semantic resource for opinion mining. In AAAI Fall Symposium: Commonsense Knowledge, Volume 10, Arlington, USA.

5 Cambria, E., Zhang, X., Mao, R., Chen, M., & Kwok, K. (2024). SenticNet 8: Fusing emotion AI and commonsense AI for interpretable, trustworthy, and explainable affective computing. In 26th International Conference on Human-Computer Interaction (HCII 2024), Washington, DC, USA, (pp. 197–216). Cham: Springer.

6 Speer, R., & Havasi, C. (2013). ConceptNet 5: A large semantic network for relational knowledge. In The People's Web Meets NLP: Collaboratively Constructed Language Resources (pp. 161–176). Berlin, Heidelberg: Springer.

7 Bordes, A., Usunier, N., Garcia-Duran, A., Weston, J., & Yakhnenko, O. (2013). Translating embeddings for modeling multi-relational data. *Advances in Neural Information Processing Systems*, 26, 2787–2795.

8 Wang, Z., Zhang, J., Feng, J., & Chen, Z. (2014). Knowledge graph embedding by translating on hyperplanes. *Proceedings of the AAAI Conference on Artificial Intelligence*, 28(1), 1112–1119.

9 Sun, Z., Deng, Z. H., Nie, J. Y., & Tang, J. (2019). Rotate: Knowledge graph embedding by relational rotation in complex space. arXiv preprint arXiv:1902.10197.

10 Trouillon, T., Welbl, J., Riedel, S., Gaussier, É., & Bouchard, G. (2016). Complex embeddings for simple link prediction. *Proceedings of the 33rd International Conference on Machine Learning (ICML)*, 48, 2071–2080.

11 Yang, Z., Yang, D., Dyer, C., He, X., Smola, A., & Hovy, E. (2016). Hierarchical attention networks for document classification. In Proceedings of the 2016 Conference of the North American Chapter of the Association for Computational Linguistics: Human Language Technologies, San Diego, USA, (pp. 1480–1489).

12 Devlin, J., Chang, M.-W., Lee, K., & Toutanova, K. (2019). BERT: Pre-training of deep bidirectional transformers for language understanding. In Proceedings of the 2019 Conference of the North American Chapter of the Association for Computational Linguistics: Human Language Technologies, Volume 1, Minneapolis, USA, (pp. 4171–4186).

13 Khosla, P., Teterwak, P., Wang, C., Sarna, A., Tian, Y., Isola, P., Maschinot, A., Liu, C., & Krishnan, D. (2020). Supervised contrastive learning. *Advances in Neural Information Processing Systems*, 33, 18661–18673.

14 Oord, A. V. D., Li, Y., & Vinyals, O. (2018). Representation learning with contrastive predictive coding. arXiv preprint arXiv:1807.03748.

15 Brown, T., Mann, B., Ryder, N., Subbiah, M., Kaplan, J. D., Dhariwal, P., Neelakantan, A., Shyam, P., Sastry, G., Askell, A., & Amodei, D. (2020). Language models are few-shot learners. *Advances in Neural Information Processing Systems*, 33, 1877–1901.

16 Wei, J., Tay, Y., Bommasani, R., Raffel, C., Zoph, B., Borgeaud, S., Yogatama, D., Bosma, M., Zhou, D., Metzler, D., & Fedus, W. (2022). Emergent abilities of large language models. arXiv preprint arXiv:2206.07682.

17 Wei, J., Wang, X., Schuurmans, D., Bosma, M., Xia, F., Chi, E., Le, Q. V., & Zhou, D. (2022). Chain-of-thought prompting elicits reasoning in large language models. *Advances in Neural Information Processing Systems*, 35, 24824–24837.

18 Wang, X., Wei, J., Schuurmans, D., Le, Q., Chi, E., Narang, S., Chowdhery, A., & Zhou, D. (2022). Self-consistency improves chain of thought reasoning in language models. arXiv preprint arXiv:2203.11171.

19 Yao, S., Yu, D., Zhao, J., Shafran, I., Griffiths, T., Cao, Y., & Narasimhan, K. (2023). Tree of thoughts: Deliberate problem solving with large language models. *Advances in Neural Information Processing Systems*, 36, 11809–11822.

5

Multimodal Sentiment Analysis

The preceding chapters have established the foundational principles of sentiment analysis, primarily within the textual domain. However, a reliance on linguistic information alone constitutes a significant abstraction from the inherently multimodal nature of human communication. The semantic content of an utterance is frequently modulated, reinforced, or even contradicted by concurrent signals from other modalities. Paralinguistic cues embedded in speech, such as prosody and vocal intensity, and nonverbal signals conveyed through facial expressions and body gestures, provide a rich layer of information that is inaccessible through text-only analysis. Consequently, phenomena such as sarcasm, irony, and sincerity are often disambiguated not by lexical choice, but by this crucial, co-occurring nonverbal context.

To transcend the limitations of unimodal analysis, this chapter introduces the paradigm of multimodal sentiment analysis (MSA). The central objective of MSA is to develop computational models capable of synergistically integrating information from disparate data channels—typically text, audio, and video—to achieve a more accurate and robust appraisal of human sentiment. The discussion will proceed systematically. First, we will address the fundamental challenges of unimodal feature representation for visual and acoustic data, alongside the critical task of intermodal alignment. Subsequently, we will provide a comprehensive survey of modality fusion strategies, tracing their evolution from early, feature-level concatenation to sophisticated, attention-based deep learning architectures. Finally, these theoretical concepts will be contextualized through a practical case study, demonstrating the application of these techniques and elucidating the performance gains attainable through a multimodal approach. Ultimately, this chapter provides the theoretical framework and practical methodologies necessary for constructing analytical systems that more closely approximate the holistic and nuanced perceptual capabilities of human beings.

5.1 Introduction to MSA

While language provides the explicit scaffolding for communication, a substantial portion of affective information is conveyed through parallel nonverbal channels. The prosody of a voice, the fleeting expression on a face, or a simple hand gesture can fundamentally alter, reinforce, or even entirely contradict the literal meaning of words. To ignore these signals is to risk a superficial or incorrect interpretation of sentiment. This chapter, therefore, transitions our focus from a unimodal to a multimodal paradigm, exploring how computational systems can achieve a more robust and human-like understanding of emotion by integrating and analyzing data from linguistic, acoustic, and visual streams. We begin by establishing the cognitive rationale for this approach, connecting it to the challenge of implicit sentiment, and defining the core concepts that will guide our technical exploration of multimodal representation, fusion, and modeling.

5.1.1 The Cognitive Basis of Multimodal Communication

Human communication is an intrinsically multimodal phenomenon, a coordinated process in which information is simultaneously encoded and transmitted across multiple channels. From a cognitive science perspective, language did not evolve in isolation but as part of an integrated system that includes gesture, facial expression, and vocal intonation. These channels are not merely redundant carriers of the same information; rather, they function in a complex, synergistic relationship, each contributing unique, complementary, and sometimes conflicting information to the overall message. The cognitive processing of a communicative act, therefore, involves the implicit and often subconscious integration of these parallel streams of data to form a coherent interpretation.

The limitations of a purely linguistic approach become starkly evident when considering the functional roles of nonverbal channels in sentiment expression. The acoustic modality, encompassing paralinguistic cues such as pitch, loudness, tempo, and voice quality, serves as a primary vehicle for conveying emotional arousal and valence. For instance, a high-pitched, rapid speech pattern is almost universally associated with states of high arousal like excitement or fear, whereas a low-pitched, slow pattern often signals low arousal, such as sadness or contemplation. These vocal cues provide a continuous, analog layer of emotional coloring that contextualizes the discrete, symbolic information carried by words.

Similarly, the visual modality, particularly through facial expressions, offers a direct window into affective states. The work of Ekman and Friesen [1] on the Facial Action Coding System (FACS) systematically demonstrated how combinations of minute muscle movements in the face correspond to a set of basic, cross-culturally recognized emotions (e.g., happiness, sadness, anger, fear, surprise, and disgust). A smile accompanying the utterance "I am fine" reinforces the positive sentiment. Conversely, the same utterance delivered with a furrowed brow and tightened lips signals distress, fundamentally altering the perceived meaning.

Perhaps the most compelling argument for multimodal analysis stems from the phenomenon of intermodal incongruity, where signals from different channels present conflicting information. This incongruity is not a processing error but a sophisticated communicative strategy often employed to convey complex social and emotional states like sarcasm, irony, or politeness. A classic example is the sarcastic utterance, "That's just great," where the positive lexical content is deliberately contradicted by a flat, monotonic vocal contour and a dismissive facial expression. A unimodal, text-based system would invariably misinterpret this as positive sentiment, failing to capture the speaker's true, negative evaluation. The detection of such sentiment relies entirely on the ability to identify and resolve the conflict between the linguistic and nonlinguistic channels.

In summary, the very fabric of human communication is woven from multiple threads. Language provides the core semantic content, but the acoustic and visual modalities supply the essential affective texture, context, and nuance. To disregard these nonverbal channels is to analyze an impoverished and potentially misleading representation of the original communicative act. Therefore, the pursuit of a computational system capable of robustly and accurately understanding human sentiment necessitates a multimodal approach, one that mirrors the integrative perceptual processes inherent to human cognition.

5.1.2 Bridging Implicit and Explicit Sentiment

The challenge of implicit sentiment analysis, as delineated in the preceding chapter, presents a formidable obstacle for unimodal systems. Such systems struggle because the sentiment is not encoded in the explicit lexical content but is instead embedded within the broader context. Often, this context is not textual but sensory. MSA offers a natural and powerful solution to this problem by reintroducing the very channels of information that are absent in pure text.

Consider the archetypal case of sarcasm. The statement, "This is a fantastic idea," when viewed as a text string, carries unambiguously positive sentiment. A text-based model would almost certainly classify it as such. However, if this statement is delivered with a flat, monotonic tone and accompanied by a subtle eye-roll, the human observer instantly decodes the true, negative sentiment. In this scenario, the sentiment is only implicit from the perspective of the linguistic modality. From a multimodal perspective, the negative sentiment is made explicit by the incongruous signals from the acoustic and visual channels. These nonverbal cues serve a meta-communicative function: they provide instructions on how to interpret the literal words.

Therefore, many of the most difficult problems in implicit sentiment analysis are artifacts of a self-imposed, single-modality limitation. Multimodality provides the necessary affective grounding for language. It anchors ambiguous or polysemous linguistic expressions to a tangible emotional reality expressed through voice and vision. By equipping our models with the ability to perceive these cross-modal relationships, particularly the crucial signals of congruence and incongruity, we transform the problem of implicit sentiment detection from a task of inferring missing information to one of integrating available, explicit information from multiple sources. In this light, MSA is not merely an alternative approach; it is arguably the most direct and conceptually sound methodology for resolving the ambiguities that plague text-only systems.

5.1.3 Core Concepts: Modality, Fusion, and Task Definition

To establish a rigorous foundation for the technical discussions that follow, it is essential to define the core terminology and formal notation used in MSA.

A modality refers to a channel or type of information through which sentiment is expressed and perceived. In MSA, we are primarily concerned with the three dominant modalities in human communication:

- Linguistic Modality (M_L): This encompasses the semantic content of an utterance, represented as a sequence of words or tokens.
- Acoustic Modality (M_A): This includes the paralinguistic properties of speech, such as prosody (pitch and energy), vocal intonation, and rate of speech.
- Visual Modality (M_V): This comprises nonverbal cues captured visually, most notably facial expressions, head movements, and body gestures.

A single multimodal data instance or utterance, is thus a composite of information from these streams. For computational modeling, raw data from each modality is transformed into a numerical feature representation. We denote these unimodal feature vectors as $x_L \in R^{d_L}$, $x_A \in R^{d_A}$, and $x_V \in R^{d_V}$, where d_L, d_V, and d_V represent the dimensionality of the feature space for each modality, respectively.

Fusion is the central mechanism in MSA, referring to the process of integrating information from multiple modalities to generate a unified representation for a final prediction. Conceptually, fusion can be represented as a function $\mathcal{F}$ that operates on the unimodal feature vectors:

$$z = \mathcal{F}(x_L, x_A, x_V)$$

Here, Z is the resulting joint representation that ideally captures the complex intermodal dynamics. The design of this fusion function $\mathcal{F}$ is a principal challenge in MSA, with strategies ranging from simple concatenation to sophisticated, attention-based neural architectures.

The ultimate objective of an MSA system is to learn a mapping from a multimodal input instance U to a sentiment label y. The nature of y defines the specific task:

1. Sentiment Classification
   A discrete prediction task where y belongs to a predefined set of categories. Common variants include:
   Polarity Classification: $y \in \{\text{positive, neutral, negative}\}$
   Emotion Recognition: $y \in \{\text{angry, happy, sad, surprised, ...}\}$
2. Sentiment Regression
   A continuous prediction task, typically used to measure sentiment intensity. In this case, y is a real-valued scalar within a specific range (e.g., $y \in [-1, +1]$), where -1 denotes maximum negative intensity and $+1$ denotes maximum positive intensity.

   The learning process involves training a model M to minimize a loss function $\mathcal{L}(y, \hat{y})$, where $\hat{y} = M(U)$ is the model's prediction. The choice of $\mathcal{L}$ depends on the task, with cross-entropy loss being standard for classification and mean squared error (MSE) for regression.

5.2 Representation and Alignment of Multimodal Data

With the conceptual framework of MSA established, we now turn to the foundational practical challenge: transforming raw, heterogeneous data from linguistic, acoustic, and visual streams into a structured, machine-readable format. Before any fusion can occur, each modality must be independently processed to extract salient, sentiment-relevant features. This process, known as representation, converts unstructured data like text strings, audio waveforms, and video pixels into meaningful numerical vectors. However, extracting features is only half the battle. These modalities unfold over time at different granularities, creating a temporal desynchronization. Therefore, a second critical step, alignment, is required to establish a meaningful correspondence between events across the different data streams. This section addresses these two prerequisite steps in sequence, first delving into the techniques for unimodal feature extraction and subsequently examining the methods and challenges of data alignment, thereby laying the essential groundwork for the fusion strategies discussed later.

5.2.1 Unimodal Feature Engineering

The initial and most fundamental step in any multimodal pipeline is the transformation of raw, heterogeneous data from each modality into structured, numerical representations. This process, known as feature engineering or representation learning, is paramount, as the quality and expressiveness of the resulting features directly constrain the performance of any subsequent fusion model. The techniques employed are highly modality-specific, tailored to extract the most salient affective information from the unique characteristics of text, audio, and visual data streams.

1. Visual Modality Features
   The visual channel, dominated by the human face, provides a rich, high-bandwidth signal for emotional expression. The primary goal of visual feature extraction is to quantify facial muscle movements, head orientation, and eye gaze, all of which are strongly correlated with underlying affective states. While traditional methods relied on handcrafted geometric features, modern approaches almost exclusively employ deep learning, particularly a convolutional neural networks (CNNs), to learn powerful representations directly from pixel data. A standard pipeline for this process is depicted in Figure 5.1. The processing steps are described as follows.
   1. Input Video Frame: A single frame containing a subject's face is selected from the video.
   2. Face Detection: An algorithm (e.g., MTCNN) identifies and crops the face region.
   3. Facial Landmark Localization: A model detects a set of key points on the eyebrows, eyes, nose, and mouth.
   4. Feature Extraction
      Geometric Features: The coordinates and relative distances of landmarks are used to compute geometric descriptors, most notably facial action units (AUs).
      Appearance Features: The aligned and normalized face patch is fed directly into a deep CNN (e.g., a pretrained VGG-Face or ResNet model).
   5. Output Visual Vector (x_V): The process yields a numerical vector x_V representing the facial expression in the frame.

   From this pipeline, two principal categories of features are derived: facial AUs and deep features. The FACS, developed by Ekman and Friesen, provides a systematic taxonomy of all visually discernible facial muscle movements, termed AUs [1]. For instance, AU12 (lip corner puller) is the primary component of a smile, whereas AU4 (brow lowerer) is characteristic of anger or confusion. Automated tools can estimate the

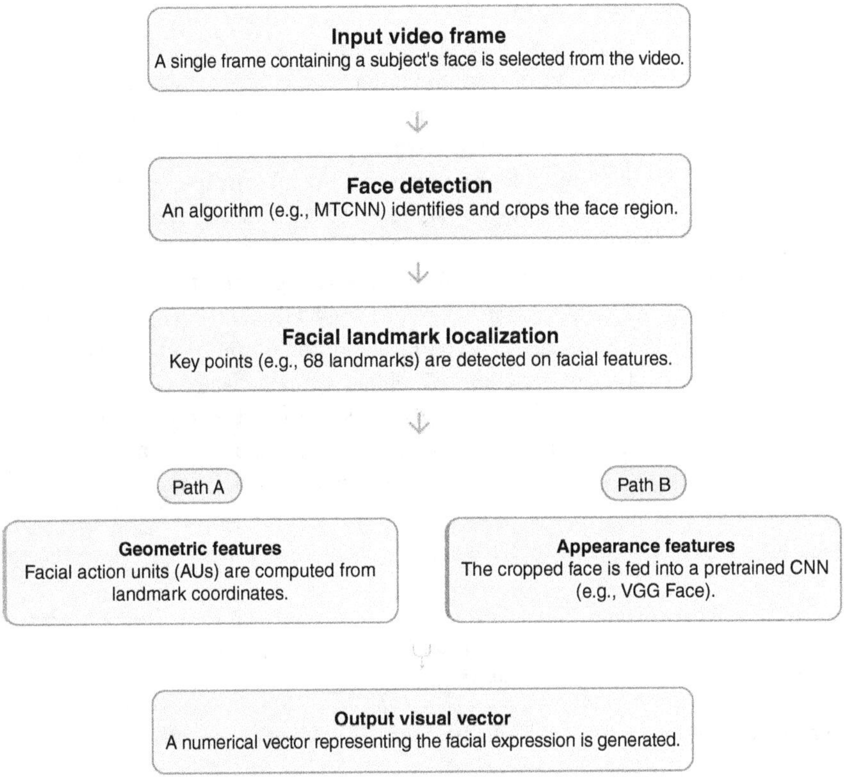

Figure 5.1 A flowchart illustrating the key stages of visual feature extraction.

presence and intensity of these AUs from facial landmarks, producing a low-dimensional and interpretable feature vector. The interpretability of AUs makes them valuable for fine-grained emotional analysis.

In deep learning approach, the raw pixel data from the cropped face region is used directly. The image is passed through a deep CNN, often one that has been pretrained on a massive face recognition or expression recognition dataset (e.g., VGG-Face and FaceNet). The activations from one of the network's penultimate layers are then extracted to serve as the feature vector, x_V. These high-dimensional vectors are less interpretable than AUs but have been shown to capture more subtle and robust textural and shape information, often leading to superior performance in downstream tasks.

2. Acoustic Modality Features
The acoustic modality reveals how something is said, providing critical prosodic and paralinguistic information that colors the semantic content of speech. Feature extraction aims to quantify these vocal characteristics using specialized audio processing toolkits such as openSMILE [2], Praat [3], or Librosa [4]. Table 5.1 provides a summary of the most influential acoustic feature sets in sentiment analysis. A standard practice is to distinguish between two levels of features:

- Low-level Descriptors (LLDs): These are fine-grained features computed over short, overlapping time windows (typically 20–40 ms). They form a time series that captures the dynamic evolution of the speech signal.
- High-level Statistical Functions: To obtain a single, fixed-size feature vector for an entire utterance or segment, statistical functions (e.g., mean, standard deviation, percentiles, and regression coefficients) are applied to the time series. The result is a high-level summary vector, x_A.

Table 5.1 Provides a summary of the most influential acoustic feature sets in sentiment analysis.

Feature Set	Description	Representative Features	Emotional Relevance & Interpretation
Prosodic	Captures the suprasegmental aspects of speech, including rhythm, stress, and intonation contour	Pitch (fundamental frequency, F_0), energy (intensity/loudness), and voicing probability	Directly correlates with emotional arousal. High-arousal states like joy or anger are typically marked by higher pitch, greater energy, and faster speech rate. Low arousal (e.g., sadness) exhibits the opposite pattern
Spectral	Describes the frequency distribution and resonant properties of the vocal tract	MFCCs, formants, and spectral centroid	Correlates with emotion valence and category. The spectral shape of a voice can help differentiate emotions (e.g., anger often has more energy in higher frequency bands compared to sadness.)
Voice quality	Characterizes the periodicity and "purity" of vocal fold vibrations	Jitter (frequency perturbation), shimmer (amplitude perturbation), and harmonics-to-noise ratio (HNR)	Reflects laryngeal tension and vocal stability. Increased jitter and shimmer (more irregular vibrations) are often associated with negative-arousal states like fear, anxiety, or sadness

3. Linguistic Modality Features
The linguistic modality provides the explicit semantic content of the message. As established in Chapter 3, the state-of-the-art in natural language representation has decisively shifted from sparse, count-based methods (e.g., TF-IDF) to dense, contextual embeddings learned by deep neural networks.

Current best practices center on the use of pretrained language models (PLMs), with BERT (bidirectional encoder representations from transformers) [5] and its variants being the most prominent examples. These models are pretrained on vast unlabeled text corpora, enabling them to learn nuanced, context-sensitive representations of language. Unlike static word embeddings, the representation of a word in BERT is a function of its entire surrounding context.

For sentence- or utterance-level sentiment analysis, a common and effective strategy is to input the entire text sequence into the model and extract a single, fixed-size vector that summarizes its meaning. This is typically achieved by using the final hidden state corresponding to a special classification token ([CLS]) that is prepended to the input sequence. This process is formalized as:

$$x_L = \mathrm{BERT}\big(\,[\mathrm{CLS}], w_1, w_2, \ldots, w_n\big)_{[\mathrm{CLS}]} \tag{5.1}$$

where $w_1, \ldots, w_n$ are the tokens of the utterance. The resulting vector, x_L, is not merely an aggregation of word meanings but a rich, context-aware semantic embedding of the entire utterance, primed for integration with features from other modalities in the fusion stage.

5.2.2 Data Alignment and Synchronization

Following the extraction of unimodal features, a critical and nontrivial challenge emerges: temporal alignment. The linguistic, acoustic, and visual data streams are inherently asynchronous, captured at different sampling rates and representing information at different levels of granularity. A video may be recorded at 30 frames per second (FPS), its corresponding audio at 16,000 samples per second (16 kHz), while the transcribed text unfolds at an irregular pace of only a few words per second. Simply concatenating these feature streams would be meaningless without first establishing a coherent temporal correspondence between them.

The core of the problem lies in mapping a single semantic unit, such as a word, to its corresponding acoustic and visual manifestations. The word "excellent," for example, is a discrete textual unit, but its utterance spans a continuous duration in the audio signal and corresponds to a sequence of multiple video frames capturing the dynamic movement of the speaker's face. The goal of alignment is to resolve this asynchrony, ensuring that the features being fused at any given moment are genuinely related to the same underlying event. Figure 5.2 provides a conceptual illustration of this challenge and the principle of segmentation-based alignment.

Several strategies are employed to address this challenge: utterance-level segmentation and forced alignment.

Utterance-level Segmentation: This is the most common and pragmatic approach. The multimodal stream is first segmented into meaningful units, typically corresponding to sentences or utterances defined by pauses in speech. For each segment, a single, fixed-size feature vector is computed for each modality. For text (x_L), this is the sentence embedding. For audio and video $(x_A,\ x_V)$, this is achieved by applying high-level statistical functions to the frame-level features across the entire segment. While this method sacrifices fine-grained temporal dynamics, its simplicity and effectiveness make it a strong baseline.

Forced Alignment: For tasks requiring more granular analysis, forced alignment is used. This technique leverages an automatic speech recognition (ASR) model to determine the precise start and end timestamps for every word in the audio signal. This creates a direct, word-level alignment between the linguistic and acoustic modalities. Visual features can then be synchronized to these word boundaries. While more powerful, this method's accuracy is contingent on the performance of the ASR system and may not perfectly capture nonverbal cues that precede or outlast the spoken word.

Ultimately, whether achieved through explicit preprocessing steps like segmentation or learned implicitly by advanced neural architectures, proper data alignment is an indispensable prerequisite for any meaningful multimodal fusion. It ensures that the model is learning from temporally coherent signals, which is fundamental to discovering the complex interplay between what is said, how it is said, and what is seen.

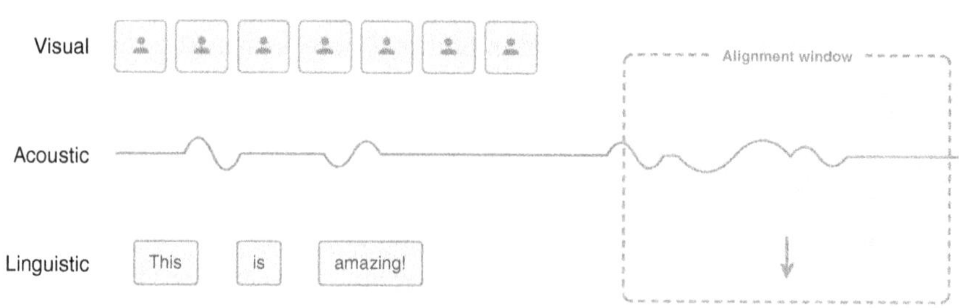

Figure 5.2 Multimodal data alignment schematic.

5.3 Multimodal Fusion Strategies: From Simple Concatenation to Intelligent Interaction

Having successfully transformed raw, asynchronous multimodal data into aligned, unimodal feature vectors (x_L, x_A, x_V), we arrive at the heart of MSA: fusion. This is the critical stage where information from disparate sources is integrated to form a single, cohesive representation from which a final sentiment prediction can be made. The primary objective of this section is to systematically investigate and evaluate the strategies available for combining these feature vectors.

The answer is far from trivial. A naive approach might simply concatenate the vectors, but this often fails to capture the complex, nonlinear relationships that exist between modalities. Human communication is not a simple summation of its parts, as modalities interact in intricate ways. Sometimes, they serve to reinforce the primary message. In other cases, they complement it by adding essential context. Most critically, however, they can even contradict one another, creating complex meanings such as sarcasm or irony. An effective fusion mechanism must therefore be capable of modeling these nuanced dynamics.

This section provides a systematic exploration of multimodal fusion strategies, tracing their conceptual evolution. We begin by examining the classic paradigms of early fusion (feature-level) and late fusion (decision-level), outlining their respective strengths and inherent limitations. We then progress to more sophisticated hybrid and model-level fusion techniques, which represent the state-of-the-art in deep learning. These methods, including tensor-based fusion, gated mechanisms, and attention-based approaches, move beyond simple combination to enable true intermodal interaction, laying the groundwork for the advanced architectures discussed later in this chapter.

5.3.1 Early Fusion and Late Fusion

Before the widespread adoption of end-to-end deep learning architectures, multimodal fusion was predominantly categorized into two distinct paradigms: early fusion and late fusion. These strategies represent foundational concepts that differ fundamentally in when and how they combine information from different modalities. Understanding them is essential for appreciating the evolution and motivation behind more modern, complex fusion techniques.

1. Early Fusion: Feature-level Integration
   Early fusion, also known as feature-level fusion, is the most intuitive approach. It operates on the principle of combining multimodal information at the earliest possible stage, directly after feature extraction. The process involves concatenating the unimodal feature vectors (x_L, x_A, x_V) into a single, high-dimensional vector, Z_{early}. This joint representation is then fed into a single predictive model (e.g., a support vector machine, a decision tree, or a neural network) to make the final sentiment prediction.
   Formally, the fusion process is a simple vector concatenation:

$$Z_{\text{early}} = [x_L; x_A; x_V] \tag{5.2}$$

   where [;] denotes vector concatenation. The resulting vector's dimensionality is the sum of its constituent parts. This architecture, conceptually depicted in Figure 5.3, allows the classifier to discover correlations between the low-level features of different modalities from the outset.
   - Primary Advantage
     Capturing low-level correlations. The signal strength of early fusion lies in its ability to model the raw, fine-grained interdependencies between modalities. The classifier has access to the complete multimodal context simultaneously, enabling it to learn, for example, how a subtle change in vocal pitch (an acoustic feature) co-occurs with a specific facial micro-expression (a visual feature) when a particular word (a linguistic feature) is spoken.
   - Key Disadvantages
     Brittleness in synchronization. This approach is critically contingent upon precise temporal alignment. If the feature streams are even slightly out of sync, the model will learn spurious correlations from concatenated features

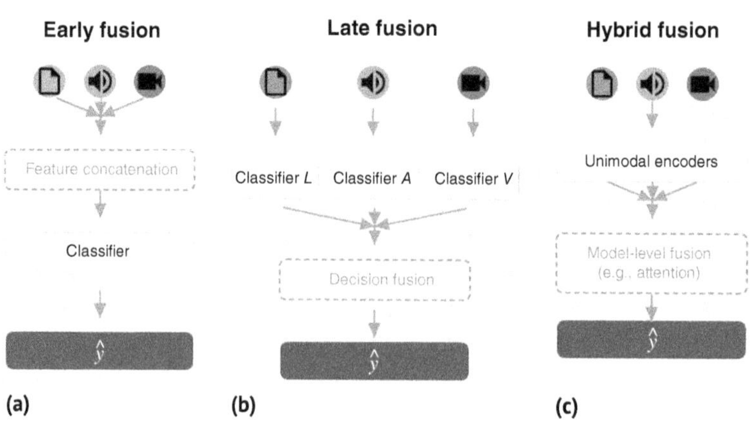

Figure 5.3 A comparison of early, late, and hybrid fusion architectures.

that do not correspond to the same event, introducing significant noise and degrading performance.

The curse of dimensionality. The concatenated feature vector can become exceptionally high-dimensional, which often requires a larger amount of training data to avoid overfitting and can significantly increase computational complexity.

Lack of robustness. The rigid structure of early fusion makes it highly intolerant to missing modalities. If data from one channel is unavailable for a given sample, the entire input vector is compromised, often rendering the sample unusable without complex imputation strategies.

2. Late Fusion: A Committee of Experts

In stark contrast, late fusion, or decision-level fusion, postpones integration to the final possible moment. It can be analogized to a committee of experts, where each expert is a unimodal classifier trained exclusively on a single modality. Each model independently processes its input and formulates a preliminary decision, typically a probability distribution over the sentiment classes or a regression score. These individual decisions are then aggregated to produce a final, collective judgment.

The fusion is performed on the outputs of these unimodal models. Common aggregation methods include majority voting for classification, or a weighted average of the prediction scores:

$$\hat{y} = \sum_{m \in \{L,A,V\}} w_m \hat{y}_m, \text{ where } \sum w_m = 1 \tag{5.3}$$

The weights (w_m) can be uniform or tuned to reflect the empirically determined importance of each modality for the specific task. This approach is illustrated in Figure 5.3.

- Primary Advantage

  Robustness and modularity. The modular design of late fusion is its greatest asset. The system can gracefully handle missing modalities by simply excluding the corresponding expert's vote from the final aggregation. Furthermore, it allows for the use of highly specialized, state-of-the-art architectures for each modality without constraint, and individual models can be trained or updated independently.
- Key Disadvantages

  Neglect of intermodal dynamics. The critical flaw of late fusion is that it prevents any interaction between modalities at the feature level. The experts never communicate during their analysis; they only present their final conclusions. This means that crucial cross-modal information, such as the sarcastic intent revealed by a mismatch between positive words and a negative tone of voice, is completely lost. The system cannot learn the synergistic or contradictory relationships that are fundamental to human communication.

This fundamental trade-off, early fusion's ability to model deep interactions versus late fusion's robustness, defined the landscape of multimodal research for years. The former is powerful but fragile; the latter is resilient but shallow. This dichotomy created a clear need for intermediate strategies that could capture the best of both worlds, motivating the development of the hybrid and model-level fusion techniques we explore next.

5.3.2 Model-level and Hybrid Fusion

The inherent limitations of early and late fusion, the former's rigidity and the latter's representational shallowness, catalyzed the development of more sophisticated strategies that seek to combine their respective strengths. With the advent of deep learning, the focus shifted from a fixed, pre-model fusion point to integrating modalities within the model's architecture itself. This paradigm, broadly termed model-level fusion or hybrid fusion, allows for rich, hierarchical, and dynamically learned interactions between modalities. Instead of simply combining raw features or final decisions, these methods create intermediate representations that are progressively refined through cross-modal influence.

This section explores three prominent families of model-level fusion techniques that have become central to modern MSA: tensor-based fusion, gated mechanisms, and the increasingly dominant cross-modal attention.

1. Tensor-based Fusion: Modeling High-order Interactions
   Simple feature concatenation, as used in early fusion, only captures linear, additive relationships between modalities. However, the interplay between modalities is often multiplicative and far more complex. For instance, the sentiment expressed by a smile (visual) might not just add to but fundamentally amplify or dampen the meaning of a spoken word (linguistic). To model such high-order, multiplicative interactions, tensor-based fusion was proposed.

   A tensor is a multidimensional array that generalizes vectors (1st-order tensors) and matrices (2nd-order tensors). In this context, the unimodal feature vectors (x_L, x_A, x_V) are combined using an outer product rather than concatenation. The outer product of two vectors, say $x_L \in R^{d_L}$ and $x_A \in R^{d_A}$, results in a matrix (a 2nd-order tensor) of size $d_L \times d_A$. Extending this to three modalities, the outer product $x_L \otimes x_A \otimes x_V$ creates a 3rd-order tensor of size $d_L \times d_A \times d_V$. Each element in this tensor represents a specific three-way interaction between individual features from each modality.

   A notable example is the tensor fusion network (TFN) by Zadeh et al. [6]. In TFN, a threefold Cartesian product is computed to create this interaction tensor, which is then passed through a linear layer to project it back to a lower-dimensional space for the final prediction.

- Strength
  It provides a mathematically principled way to explicitly model all possible multilinear interactions between unimodal features, offering a much richer representational capacity than simple concatenation.
- Weakness
  The primary drawback is its computational complexity and high parameter count. The size of the interaction tensor grows exponentially with the dimensionality of the input features, making it susceptible to overfitting and difficult to scale to very high-dimensional feature spaces.

2. Gated Mechanisms: Dynamic Control of Information Flow
   Not all modalities contribute equally to the sentiment of every utterance. In a sarcastic statement, the acoustic and visual channels might carry more weight than the literal text. Conversely, in a complex, nuanced film review, the linguistic content is paramount. Gated mechanisms provide a solution by allowing the model to dynamically control the flow of information from each modality, learning to assign importance on a sample-by-sample basis.

   Inspired by the gating units in long short-term memory (LSTM) and gated recurrent unit (GRU), these mechanisms introduce gate, small neural network, typically with a sigmoid activation, that output a value between 0 and 1. This value acts as a soft switch, determining how much of a feature vector is allowed to pass through.

   For instance, a simple gating mechanism for a feature vector x_m (where $m \in \{L, A, V\}$) can be formulated as:

   $$g_m = \sigma\left(W_m[x_L; x_A; x_V] + b_m\right) \tag{5.4}$$

   $$x'_m = g_m \odot x_m \tag{5.5}$$

   Here, g_m is the gate value for modality m, computed based on the concatenated features of all modalities. The element-wise product ($\odot$) then modulates the original feature vector x_m to produce a refined representation x'_m. Models like the gated multimodal unit (GMU) [7] leverage this principle to learn how to adaptively fuse information based on the input context.

   - Strength
     They introduce a high degree of flexibility and context-awareness. The model can learn to up-weight or down-weight the influence of certain modalities depending on the specific input, making it more robust and interpretable.
   - Weakness
     While powerful, simple gating may not fully capture the fine-grained, element-to-element interactions between modalities in the way that attention mechanisms can.

3. Cross-modal Attention: Focusing on Relevant Intermodal Cues
Perhaps the most impactful innovation in multimodal fusion is the application of attention mechanisms, specifically cross-modal attention. This technique allows the model to dynamically focus on the most relevant parts of one modality while processing another. Instead of simply modulating the importance of an entire modality (as in gating), attention can pinpoint specific features or time-steps that are most influential.

The core principle of attention, which will be explored in depth in Chapter 6, involves computing alignment scores between a "query" vector and a set of "key" vectors. In a cross-modal context, features from one modality act as queries to "attend to" features from another modality, which serve as keys and values.

For example, to understand how acoustic features should influence the representation of linguistic features, we can use the acoustic representation (x_A) to query the linguistic representation (x_L). The model learns to identify which words in the text are most affected by the tone of voice. A simplified formulation is:

$$\text{Attention}(Q, K, V) = \text{softmax}\left(\frac{QK^T}{\sqrt{d_k}}\right)V \tag{5.6}$$

In a cross-modal setting, we might have $Q = x_L$, $K = x_A$, $V = x_A$. This would produce a context vector representing the most relevant acoustic information with respect to the text. This context vector is then integrated with the original linguistic representation.

Models like the multimodal Transformer (MulT) by Tsai et al. [8] extend this concept by using a stack of cross-modal attention layers, allowing for iterative, bidirectional refinement of representations between all pairs of modalities.

- Strength
  It offers the most fine-grained and powerful mechanism for modeling intermodal dynamics. It can capture both global (which modality is more important) and local (which specific features/words/frames are important) dependencies, leading to state-of-the-art performance on many MSA benchmarks. Its ability to handle sequences of varying lengths makes it particularly well-suited for multimodal data.
- Weakness
  The computational cost can be high, particularly the quadratic complexity with respect to sequence length, although various efficient Transformer variants are being developed to mitigate this.

In conclusion, the evolution from simple concatenation to these sophisticated model-level fusion strategies reflects a deeper understanding of the multimodal fusion problem. By enabling direct, learned, and dynamic interactions within the model's hidden layers, these techniques provide the necessary architectural tools to begin unraveling the complex, synergistic tapestry of human communication.

5.3.3 A Core Challenge: Modeling Modality Incongruity

The fusion strategies discussed thus far implicitly assume that modalities work in concert to express a unified emotional state. However, one of the most complex and revealing aspects of human communication is modality incongruity, which refers to instances where the information conveyed by different channels is inconsistent or even contradictory. This phenomenon is not merely noise; it is often a deliberate communicative act used to convey nuanced social and emotional meanings, most notably sarcasm, irony, and deception. A truly robust fusion model must therefore move beyond simply integrating congruent signals and learn to effectively identify, interpret, and resolve these informative conflicts.

Modality incongruity presents a profound challenge to fusion models. Consider the utterance, "I love this," spoken with a flat tone of voice and accompanied by an eye-roll. The linguistic modality carries a strongly positive signal. The acoustic modality provides a neutral or slightly negative signal (lack of enthusiasm). The visual modality delivers a clearly negative signal (disdain). An early fusion model based on simple concatenation would be presented with a confusing, contradictory feature vector, making it difficult for a simple classifier to disentangle the true sentiment. A late fusion model would fare little better; it might receive a positive vote from its linguistic expert and negative votes from its acoustic and visual experts, but it would lack the context to understand why this conflict exists and how to resolve it. It might resort to a simple majority rule, but it would fail to grasp the sarcastic intent, which is an emergent property of the conflict itself.

The ability to handle incongruity is thus a key differentiator for advanced fusion mechanisms. This is where techniques like gated mechanisms and, especially, cross-modal attention demonstrate their superiority. Gated mechanisms can learn to dynamically down-weight a modality that appears to be misleading. In the sarcasm example, the model might learn that when certain acoustic and visual cues are present, the gate for the linguistic channel should be partially closed, reducing its influence on the final prediction. Cross-modal attention offers an even more sophisticated solution. An attention mechanism can learn that the pattern of a positive word co-occurring with a negative tone is, in itself, a powerful feature. The model can learn to use the representation of the eye roll as a query to specifically attend to and reinterpret the representation of the word love. This allows the model to not just resolve the conflict but to understand the conflict as the primary signal.

Therefore, modeling modality incongruity is not just about choosing which modality to trust. It is about learning the rules of conflict, the complex, context-dependent ways in which humans use intermodal discrepancies to craft meaning. The capacity of a fusion model to explicitly represent and reason about these incongruities is a direct measure of its sophistication and its potential to achieve a truly human-like understanding of sentiment.

5.4 Deep Learning Architectures for MSA

The fusion strategies discussed in the previous section provide the conceptual building blocks for integrating multimodal data. However, their practical realization and ultimate performance are contingent upon the underlying model architecture that implements them. The advent of deep learning has revolutionized this landscape, offering powerful, end-to-end frameworks capable of learning both unimodal representations and complex cross-modal fusion dynamics simultaneously. These architectures move beyond the static, predefined fusion points of classic paradigms and embed fusion as an intrinsic, learnable component of the network.

This section delves into the specific deep learning architectures that have defined the state-of-the-art in MSA. We will begin by examining the classic architectures built upon CNN and recurrent neural network (RNN), which laid the groundwork for handling visual and sequential data. We will then transition to the current frontier: attention-driven models, particularly those based on the Transformer architecture, which have demonstrated unparalleled capabilities in modeling long-range dependencies and intricate intermodal relationships. To ground these architectural discussions in a practical context, we will conclude with an overview of the benchmark datasets and evaluation metrics that are commonly used to validate and compare these models.

5.4.1 Classic Architectures with CNNs and RNNs

The initial application of deep learning to MSA was characterized by the synergistic use of two foundational architectures: CNNs, for their unparalleled ability in spatial feature extraction, and RNNs, for their inherent capacity to model sequential data. These pioneering models established a powerful and logical template for end-to-end multimodal learning, typically comprising two distinct stages: a parallel set of unimodal encoders followed by a fusion and prediction stage. This modular, hierarchical approach allows each network to specialize in processing its corresponding data type before their learned representations are integrated.

A representative architecture from this era, as conceptually detailed in Figure 5.4, operationalizes this two-stage process. The first and most crucial stage is dedicated to transforming the raw, high-dimensional, and often sequential input of each modality into a compact, fixed-size, and semantically rich feature vector. This is accomplished through three independent processing streams:

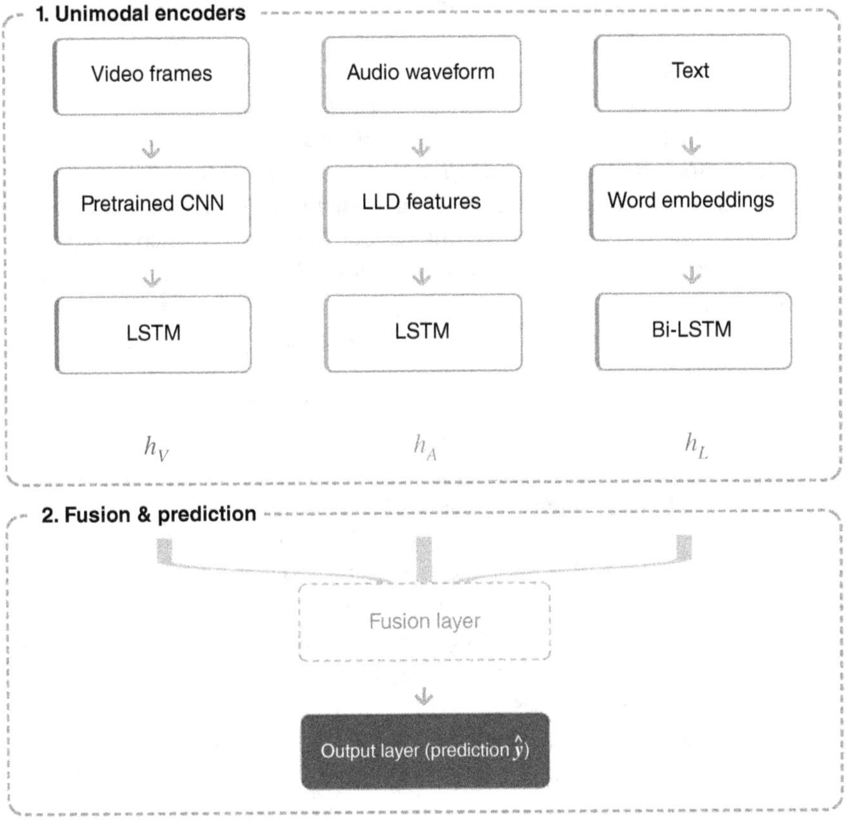

Figure 5.4 A prototypical end-to-end architecture for MSA using parallel CNN and RNN-based encoders. The model is structured in two stages: (1) unimodal encoders, where each modality is independently processed to generate a fixed-size vector representation, and (2) fusion & prediction, where these representations are combined to produce the final sentiment output.

- Visual Encoder
  The input to this stream is a sequence of video frames corresponding to an utterance. First, a pretrained CNN (e.g., ResNet and VGG-Face) is applied to each frame individually. This network, having been trained on massive image datasets, acts as a powerful feature extractor, converting each raw pixel frame into a high-level feature vector that represents facial appearance and expression. The resulting sequence of frame-level vectors is then fed into an RNN, typically LSTM or GRU. The RNN processes this sequence chronologically, capturing the temporal dynamics of the facial expression as it evolves over time. The final hidden state of the LSTM, denoted as h_V, serves as the comprehensive visual representation for the entire utterance.
- Acoustic Encoder
  The process for the audio stream mirrors the visual one. The raw audio waveform is first preprocessed into a sequence of LLDs, such as Mel-frequency cepstral coefficients (MFCCs), pitch, and energy, using a toolkit like openSMILE. This converts the continuous audio signal into a discrete sequence of feature vectors. This sequence is then modeled by a dedicated LSTM, which learns the temporal patterns in prosody, intonation, and voice quality. The final hidden state of this RNN, h_A, encapsulates the salient acoustic information of the speech segment.
- Linguistic Encoder
  For the textual modality, the input is a sequence of words from the transcription. These words are first converted into dense vector representations using pretrained word embeddings like GloVe or Word2Vec. This sequence of vectors is then passed to a bidirectional LSTM (Bi-LSTM). The bidirectional nature of this network allows it to process the sequence in both forward and backward directions, thereby capturing the full context of each word based on both preceding and succeeding words. The final linguistic representation, h_L, is typically formed by concatenating the final hidden states of the forward and backward LSTM passes.

  Once the unimodal encoders have produced their respective summary vectors (h_V, h_A, h_L), the second stage begins.
- Fusion Layer
  The three vectors are brought together in a fusion layer. In many foundational models, this was implemented as a simple concatenation, creating a single, larger vector that combines all the learned unimodal information. This joint vector is then passed through one or more fully connected (dense) layers, which are tasked with learning the cross-modal relationships from this combined representation.

- Output Layer
  Finally, the output from the fusion layer is fed into an output layer to produce the final sentiment prediction, $\hat{y}$. For a classification task (e.g., predicting positive, neutral, or negative), this layer would typically use a softmax activation function to output a probability distribution over the classes. For a regression task (e.g., predicting sentiment intensity on a scale of −1 to 1), a linear activation function might be used.

  This classic architectural blueprint, while since surpassed by more advanced models, was instrumental in demonstrating the viability of end-to-end deep learning for MSA. It established the core principles of specialized unimodal encoding followed by a dedicated fusion mechanism, a paradigm that continues to influence the design of more complex, state-of-the-art systems.

5.4.2 Attention-driven Fusion: The Rise of the Transformer Architecture

While CNN/RNN-based models established a powerful baseline, their architectural properties revealed inherent limitations when faced with the full complexity of multimodal data. RNNs, by their sequential nature, process information chronologically, creating a potential bottleneck where long-range dependencies within a sequence can be lost due to the vanishing gradient problem. Furthermore, their typical fusion mechanisms, often occurring at a single point after unimodal encoding, struggled to capture the deeply interwoven and iterative nature of cross-modal interactions. This created a clear need for an architecture capable of modeling global dependencies and enabling more profound, fine-grained fusion.

The solution emerged with the Transformer architecture [9], a paradigm-shifting model that has since redefined the state-of-the-art across numerous domains, including multimodal learning. The Transformer dispenses with recurrence entirely, relying instead on its core innovation: the self-attention mechanism. This mechanism, and its powerful extension to cross-modal attention, directly addresses the primary challenges of MSA.

1. The Power of Self-attention for Unimodal Context
   Before delving into multimodal fusion, it is crucial to understand the Transformer's foundational mechanism: self-attention. For a single sequence of features (e.g., the word embeddings of a sentence), self-attention allows the model to compute a new representation for each element by attending to all other elements in the same sequence. In essence, it asks for each word: "Which other words in this sentence are most important for understanding my meaning?"

This is achieved by projecting each input element into three distinct vectors: a Query (Q), a Key (K), and a Value (V). The Query represents the current element's request for information. The Keys of all other elements act as labels or indices for the information they hold. The compatibility between a Query and a Key is computed, generating an attention score. These scores are scaled and passed through a softmax function to create a probability distribution, the attention weights. Finally, a weighted sum of all value vectors is computed, producing the output for the current element. This process allows information to flow directly between any two points in the sequence, making it exceptionally effective at capturing long-range dependencies.

2. Cross-modal Attention: Enabling Deep Intermodal Dialogue
The true power of the Transformer for MSA is realized when this attention principle is extended to operate between different modalities. This technique, cross-modal attention, allows one modality to directly query another, learning to focus on the most relevant parts of the source modality to enrich its own representation. This transforms fusion from a single event into a dynamic, iterative dialogue between modalities, occurring at every layer of the network.

A seminal model that operationalizes this concept is the MulT by Tsai et al. [8]. Let the input sequences for the linguistic, acoustic, and visual modalities. The core of MulT is a stack of cross-modal Transformer layers. Within each layer, a modality's representation is iteratively refined by attending to the others.

Consider the crucial task of refining the linguistic representation x_L using the acoustic representation x_A. This is achieved via a cross-modal attention block where the linguistic sequence generates the Queries, while the acoustic sequence provides the Keys and Values.

$$Q_L = X_L W_{Q_L} \tag{5.7}$$

$$K_A = X_A W_{K_A},\ V_A = X_A W_{V_A} \tag{5.8}$$

The resulting context vector, $C_{A \to L}$, represents the acoustic information that is most relevant to each word in the text:

$$C_{A \to L} = \text{Attention}\left(Q_L, K_A, V_A\right) = \text{softmax}\left(\frac{Q_L K_A^T}{\sqrt{d_k}}\right) V_A \tag{5.9}$$

For a sarcastic utterance like "That's great," the query from the word "great" can attend to the entire acoustic sequence and discover that the low-pitch, flat intonation (represented in the acoustic Keys and Values) is highly relevant, thus infusing the representation of "great" with this contradictory acoustic context.

3. Multi-head Attention: Capturing Diverse Relationships
A single attention mechanism might learn to focus on one type of relationship. To capture diverse and complex intermodal relationships simultaneously, the Transformer employs multi-head attention. This mechanism runs the attention process multiple times in parallel with different, learned linear projections for Q, K, and V. Each head can thus specialize in a different aspect of the cross-modal interaction.

$$\text{head}_i = \text{Attention}\left(X_L W_{Q_i}, X_A W_{K_i}, X_A W_{V_i}\right) \tag{5.10}$$

The outputs of all heads are then concatenated and linearly projected back to the original dimension:

$$\text{MultiHead}\left(X_L, X_A\right) = \text{Concat}\left(\text{head}_1, \ldots, \text{head}_h\right) W_O \tag{5.11}$$

In our sarcasm example, one head might learn to associate positive words with flat intonation, while another might focus on aligning spoken words with corresponding lip movements. This allows for a much richer and more multifaceted fusion.

4. The MulT Architecture in Detail
The MulT architecture systematizes this process. In each of its stacked layers, a modality is sequentially passed through a series of cross-modal attention blocks. First, it attends to the acoustic modality to produce an intermediate representation. Then, this intermediate representation attends to the visual modality. This entire update process, a cascade of cross-modal attentions followed by a feed-forward network and residual connections, is performed for all three modalities. This allows for a deeply bidirectional and iterative refinement of representations. With each subsequent layer, the unimodal features become progressively more aware of the context provided by their counterparts.

After passing through the stack of cross-modal Transformer layers, the model produces three highly fused output sequences, x'_L, x'_A, x'_V. These are typically concatenated, pooled, and finally passed to a simple linear classifier for sentiment prediction.

The Transformer's architectural superiority for MSA can be summarized as follows:

- Handling of Unaligned Sequences
  Attention operates on sets of vectors, making it naturally robust to the unaligned, variable-length sequences typical of multimodal data.
- Global Context Modeling
  It effectively captures long-range dependencies both within and between modalities.

- Deep and Iterative Fusion
  It enables a fine-grained, layer-by-layer fusion process, resulting in deeply contextualized representations that far surpass the capabilities of classic single-point fusion methods.

  These properties have firmly established the Transformer as the dominant architectural paradigm in modern MSA, consistently achieving state-of-the-art performance on a wide array of benchmark tasks.

5.4.3 Benchmarks and Tools: Common Datasets and Evaluation Metrics

The rapid progress in developing sophisticated multimodal architectures has been driven and rigorously measured by a set of publicly available, standardized benchmark datasets. These datasets provide the essential raw material for training and evaluating models, and they serve as a common ground for comparing the performance of different fusion strategies and architectures. This section provides an overview of the most influential datasets in the field, along with the standard metrics used for evaluation.

1. Key Public Datasets
   While numerous multimodal datasets exist, a few have emerged as the de facto standards for sentiment analysis research due to their size, quality of annotation, and the challenging nature of their content. Table 5.2 summarizes the key characteristics of these canonical datasets.

   CMU-MOSI (Multimodal Opinion Sentiment and Intensity) [10]: As one of the earliest and most widely used benchmarks, MOSI consists of short monologue video clips where single speakers review products. Its primary annotation is a 7-point sentiment intensity score (from −3 for highly negative

Table 5.2 Overview of mainstream MSA datasets.

Dataset	Domain	Samples	Annotation Type	Key Challenges
CMU-MOSI [10]	YouTube monologues (opinion videos)	2,199	Sentiment intensity (regression): [−3, 3]	Short, opinion-dense utterances; focus on speaker-centric sentiment
CMU-MOSEI [11]	YouTube monologues (diverse topics)	23,453	Sentiment intensity (regression): [−3, 3] & emotion (classification): 6 classes	Larger scale and greater topical diversity; more complex and varied language

Dataset	Domain	Samples	Annotation Type	Key Challenges
IEMOCAP [12]	Dyadic conversations (actor dialogues)	10,000	Emotion (classification): 4–10 classes (e.g., happy, sad, angry, and neutral)	Conversational context (turn-taking); spontaneous, emotionally charged interactions
MELD [13]	Multiparty conversations (Friends TV show)	13,000	Emotion (classification): 7 classes & sentiment (classification): 3 classes	Multiparty conversational dynamics; context from previous utterances is crucial

to +3 for highly positive), making it ideal for regression tasks. The data is pre-segmented into opinionated utterances, and features are often provided, allowing researchers to focus purely on the fusion task.

CMU-MOSEI (Multimodal Opinion Sentiment and Emotion Intensity) [11]: MOSEI is a significant extension of MOSI, featuring a much larger number of samples and covering a far broader range of topics beyond product reviews. This diversity introduces greater linguistic and emotional complexity. In addition to sentiment intensity, MOSEI also includes annotations for six basic emotions (happiness, sadness, anger, fear, disgust, and surprise), enabling multitask learning. Its scale has made it the primary benchmark for developing large, data-hungry models like Transformers.

IEMOCAP (Interactive Emotional Dyadic Motion Capture) [12]: Unlike the monologue-based MOSI and MOSEI, IEMOCAP features dyadic (two-person) conversations between actors performing scripted and improvised scenes. The focus is on categorical emotion recognition (e.g., happy, sad, angry, and neutral). IEMOCAP is crucial for studying sentiment in an interactive, conversational context, where emotions can be influenced by the conversational partner.

MELD (Multimodal EmotionLines Dataset) [13]: MELD takes conversational complexity a step further by sourcing its data from the multiparty dialogues of the TV show Friends. This dataset requires models to understand emotion and sentiment within a rich conversational history, as a character's emotional state often depends on the preceding turns in the conversation. It is a key benchmark for context-aware conversational sentiment analysis.

2. Evaluation Metrics

   The choice of evaluation metric is determined by the specific task defined by the dataset's annotations, classification, or regression.

For classification tasks (e.g., IEMOCAP and MELD):

- Accuracy
  The percentage of correctly classified samples. It is a straightforward metric but can be misleading on datasets with imbalanced class distributions.
- F1-Score
  The harmonic mean of precision and recall. The weighted F1-score, which accounts for class imbalance by weighting the F1-score of each class by its proportion in the dataset, is the most commonly reported metric for emotion recognition.

For regression tasks (e.g., MOSI and MOSEI):

- Mean Absolute Error (MAE)
  The average absolute difference between the predicted scores and the ground-truth scores. It is easily interpretable as the average prediction error.
- Pearson Correlation Coefficient (Corr)
  Measures the linear correlation between the predictions and the ground truth. It indicates how well the model's predictions trend with the true scores, regardless of scale.

In addition to these primary metrics, researchers often report binary accuracy (Accuracy-2, by collapsing scores into positive/negative classes) and other correlation measures to provide a comprehensive performance profile of their models. The use of these standardized datasets and metrics is vital for ensuring that progress in the field is reproducible, quantifiable, and meaningful.

5.5 Case Study: Analyzing Sentiment in YouTube Opinion Videos

The theoretical discussions of fusion strategies and the architectural deep dives into advanced models provide a strong foundation for understanding MSA. However, to truly appreciate the practical application and power of these techniques, it is instructive to walk through an end-to-end implementation. This case study will bridge the gap between theory and practice by demonstrating how to build and analyze a multimodal system for a common and high-impact domain: YouTube opinion videos.

To ensure the scientific rigor and reproducibility of this study, we will base our analysis on a curated selection of video segments from the widely recognized benchmark dataset, CMU-MOSI. This dataset, composed of opinionated monologues from YouTube product reviews, is ideal for our purpose. It not only aligns perfectly with our chosen domain but also provides preexisting, high-quality data including video clips, time-aligned transcriptions, and fine-grained sentiment intensity annotations. By leveraging this established resource, we can focus squarely on the core tasks of feature extraction, model implementation, and nuanced result interpretation.

The objective is to develop a model that can predict the sentiment of these review segments, moving beyond the literal meaning of words to incorporate the crucial emotional cues present in the speaker's tone of voice and facial expressions. The CMU-MOSI dataset contains numerous examples of sarcasm, feigned enthusiasm, and subtle disappointment, making it an ideal testbed for the advanced fusion techniques we have discussed.

We will follow a structured, project-based approach:

- Problem Definition and Data Selection
  We define our precise goal and detail the process of selecting representative samples from the CMU-MOSI dataset for our analysis.
- Feature Extraction and Alignment
  We apply the feature engineering techniques to the selected data to extract linguistic, acoustic, and visual features.
- Model Implementation
  We detail the implementation of a simplified, yet powerful, fusion model inspired by the Transformer architecture.
- Result Analysis and Qualitative Insights
  Finally, we evaluate the model's performance and conduct a qualitative analysis of specific, challenging examples from the dataset to demonstrate the value of the multimodal approach.

  Through this hands-on example, we will solidify the concepts presented in this chapter and provide a practical blueprint for applying MSA to real-world challenges.

5.5.1 Problem Definition and Data Selection

1. Problem Definition
   The primary objective of this case study is to build and evaluate an MSA model capable of predicting the sentiment intensity of a given opinion video segment. Our goal is to demonstrate empirically that by fusing linguistic, acoustic, and visual information, we can achieve a more accurate and robust prediction than a model that relies on text alone, especially in cases of modality incongruity.

   The task is framed as a regression problem. Given a video segment, the model must predict a sentiment score on a continuous scale from -3 (highly negative) to $+3$ (highly positive). This fine-grained intensity score provides a more nuanced evaluation than a simple positive/negative classification.

Our key hypothesis is that the multimodal model's predictions will align more closely with human-annotated ground-truth scores, particularly on challenging samples where the sentiment is expressed implicitly.

2. Data Source

   To ensure scientific validity and reproducibility, our analysis is grounded in the CMU-MOSI dataset. As a canonical benchmark in the field, CMU-MOSI offers several advantages for this case study.

   - Domain Relevance

     It comprises 2,199 opinionated segments, which are extracted from 93 YouTube videos and all focus on reviews of movies, books, and products.

   - High-quality Annotations

     Each segment is meticulously annotated by multiple human annotators for sentiment intensity on a [−3, 3] scale. The dataset provides the average of these scores as the ground-truth label.

   - Preprocessed Data

     The dataset provides pre-segmented video clips, time-aligned transcriptions, and word-level alignments, which significantly streamlines the experimental setup.

     We use the official training, validation, and test splits provided with the dataset to train our model and evaluate its performance fairly.

3. Selection of Illustrative Samples for Qualitative Analysis

   Beyond quantitative evaluation on the test set, a core part of this case study is the qualitative analysis of specific, illustrative examples. To this end, we will preselect a small, curated subset of samples from the validation set that exemplify key multimodal phenomena. These samples will be used in Section 5.5.4 to visually and intuitively demonstrate our model's capabilities. The selection criteria for these samples are as follows:

   Congruent Positive Sentiment: A sample where the text is positive ("this is amazing"), the tone is enthusiastic (high pitch and varied intonation), and the facial expression is joyful (smiling and raised eyebrows). This will serve as a baseline to ensure the model correctly interprets straightforward cases.

   Congruent Negative Sentiment: A sample where the text is negative ("it's terrible"), the tone is disappointed (low energy and slow pace), and the facial expression is negative (frowning and scowling).

   Sarcasm (Incongruity): The most critical category. A sample where the text is explicitly positive (e.g., "Just what I always wanted"), but the acoustic and/or visual cues are clearly negative (e.g., flat, monotonic tone; eye-rolling; a smirk). This type of sample is designed to make a text-only model fail.

Subtle Negative Sentiment: A sample where the text is neutral or mildly positive (e.g., "It works as advertised"), but the sentiment is "leaked" through nonverbal channels, such as a sigh, a hesitant tone, or a lack of facial expression, indicating underlying disappointment.

By defining a clear problem, leveraging a standardized dataset, and preselecting a set of challenging examples for in-depth analysis, we establish a solid and transparent foundation for the remainder of this case study.

5.5.2 Feature Extraction and Alignment

With the problem defined and the data selected, the next step is to process the raw multimodal segments from the CMU-MOSI dataset into aligned, numerical feature vectors. This stage is a direct application of the unimodal feature engineering techniques detailed in Section 5.2.1. For this case study, we will utilize widely available, pretrained models and standard toolkits to ensure the process is both state-of-the-art and reproducible.

The CMU-MOSI dataset conveniently provides data segmented at the utterance level, meaning each data point (a video clip with its transcription) represents a single, coherent opinion. This pre-segmentation greatly simplifies the alignment process, allowing us to adopt an utterance-level alignment strategy. For each utterance, we extract a single, fixed-size feature vector for each of the three modalities.

1. Linguistic Feature Extraction
   For the linguistic modality, our goal is to capture the rich, contextual semantics of the transcribed text. We use a pretrained BERT model, specifically the bert-base-uncased variant, a powerful and widely used baseline.

   The process for each transcribed utterance is as follows:
   - Tokenization
     The input text is tokenized using the standard BERT WordPiece tokenizer. Special tokens, [CLS] at the beginning and [SEP] at the end, are added to the token sequence.
   - Model Inference
     The tokenized sequence is fed into the pre-trained BERT model.
   - Feature Extraction
     We extract the final hidden state corresponding to the [CLS] token. This 768-dimensional vector serves as a comprehensive semantic summary of the entire utterance. We denote this vector as $x_L \in \mathbb{R}^{768}$. This entire process can be efficiently implemented using the popular Hugging Face Transformers library in Python.

2. Visual Feature Extraction

To represent the visual information, we need to capture the dynamic facial expressions of the speaker throughout the utterance. We use a toolkit that automates the pipeline of face detection, landmark localization, and feature extraction. A robust choice for this is OpenFace 2.0.

For each video segment corresponding to an utterance, the process is:

- Frame-level Processing
  OpenFace processes the video frame by frame. In each frame, it detects the speaker's face, localizes 68 facial landmarks, and extracts a rich set of features.
- Feature Selection
  We utilize a subset of the features provided by OpenFace, specifically the facial AUs' intensities and head pose information. This results in a sequence of low-dimensional feature vectors, one for each frame.
- Utterance-level Aggregation
  To create a single feature vector for the entire utterance, we apply high-level statistical functions (functionals) to the frame-level sequence. We compute the mean and standard deviation for each feature across all frames in the segment. This captures both the average expression and the degree of expressiveness. The resulting concatenated vector is our final visual representation, x_V.

3. Acoustic Feature Extraction

For the acoustic modality, we aim to capture the prosodic and spectral characteristics of the speaker's voice. A powerful and standard toolkit for this task is openSMILE (open-source Speech and Music Interpretation by Large-space Extraction).

The process for each audio segment is:

- Configuration
  We use one of openSMILE's standard, large-scale feature set configurations, such as the ComParE 2016 feature set. This set is specifically designed for paralinguistic analysis and includes a comprehensive range of LLDs and functionals.
- Feature Extraction
  The audio file for the utterance is processed by the openSMILE toolkit using the chosen configuration.
- Utterance-level Features
  The toolkit directly outputs a single, high-dimensional feature vector for the entire audio input. This vector contains functionals (e.g., mean, max, and percentiles) of various LLDs like MFCCs, pitch (F_0), and energy. This vector serves as our final acoustic representation, x_A.

At the conclusion of this stage, each of the 2,199 utterances in the CMU-MOSI dataset is represented by a triplet of aligned, fixed-size feature vectors: x_L, x_V, x_A. This structured data is now ready to be fed into our multimodal fusion model for training and evaluation.

5.5.3 Model Implementation

With our aligned feature vectors prepared, we now proceed to the core of the case study: implementing the multimodal fusion model. While state-of-the-art models like MulT involve complex, multilayered architectures, for the purpose of this illustrative study, we construct a simplified yet powerful model. Our architecture is inspired by the Transformer and places a strong emphasis on a clear, interpretable cross-modal attention mechanism to demonstrate the superiority of learned, dynamic fusion over simple concatenation.

Our model is composed of three main components: unimodal encoders, a cross-modal fusion block, and a prediction head.

1. Unimodal Encoders
   Although we have already extracted feature vectors (x_L, x_V, x_A), these features exist in disparate spaces with different dimensionalities. The first step within the model is to project these heterogeneous features into a common, lower-dimensional embedding space where they can be meaningfully compared and fused. This is achieved using three independent linear layers (fully connected layers) with a nonlinear activation function (e.g., ReLU).
   Linguistic encoder:
   $$h_L = \mathrm{ReLU}(x_L W_L + b_L) \tag{5.12}$$
   Visual encoder:
   $$h_V = \mathrm{ReLU}(x_V W_V + b_V) \tag{5.13}$$
   Acoustic encoder:
   $$h_A = \mathrm{ReLU}(x_A W_A + b_A) \tag{5.14}$$
   Here, W_L, W_V, W_A are trainable weight matrices and b_L, b_V, b_A are bias vectors. The outputs, h_L, h_V, h_A are now unimodal embeddings of a uniform dimension, specifically $d_{\text{model}} = 128$.
2. Cross-modal Fusion Block
   This block is the heart of our model. Its purpose is to refine the representation of a primary modality (in our case, the linguistic modality, which carries the core semantic content) by incorporating relevant information from the other contextual modalities (acoustic and visual). We achieve this using two parallel cross-modal attention mechanisms.
   - Acoustic-to-linguistic Attention
     This mechanism allows the linguistic embedding h_L to query the acoustic embedding h_V to find the most relevant acoustic context. Following the standard attention formulation, we define:

Query (Q): Derived from the linguistic embedding $Q_L = h_L W Q_L$
Key (K): Derived from the acoustic embedding $K_A = h_A W_{K_A}$
Value (V): Also derived from the acoustic embedding $V_A = h_A W_{V_A}$
The acoustic context vector is then computed as:

$$C_{A \to L} = \text{Attention}(Q_L, K_A, V_A) \tag{5.15}$$

Since we are dealing with single vectors per utterance rather than sequences, the attention mechanism simplifies. The softmax over a single key is trivial, so the formula effectively learns a gated projection of the acoustic value vector, modulated by the linguistic query. This context vector represents the portion of acoustic information deemed most relevant to the text.

- Visual-to-linguistic Attention
  An identical process is performed in parallel to compute the visual context vector, $C_V \to L$, where the linguistic embedding h_L queries the visual embedding h_V.
- Integration
  The original linguistic embedding h_L is then fused with the context vectors derived from the other two modalities. We use a simple concatenation followed by a linear layer to create the final, fused representation:

$$Z_{\text{fused}} = [h_L; C_{A \to L}; C_{V \to L}] \tag{5.16}$$

This vector Z_{fused} is a powerful representation because it contains not only the original semantic information from the text but also contextually relevant, dynamically weighted information from the speaker's voice and facial expressions.

3. Prediction Head
   The final component is a simple regression head that maps the fused representation to the sentiment intensity score. It consists of one or more fully connected layers.

$$\hat{y} = \text{Linear}(Z_{\text{fused}}) \tag{5.17}$$

The output, $\hat{y}$, is a single scalar value representing the predicted sentiment score on the [−3, 3] scale.

4. Training and Baselines
   The entire model is trained end-to-end using the MSE loss function, which is standard for regression tasks.

$$\text{Loss} = \frac{1}{N} \sum_{i=1}^{N} (y_i - \hat{y}_i)^2 \tag{5.18}$$

We use the Adam optimizer to minimize this loss on the CMU-MOSI training set, using the validation set for hyperparameter tuning.

To demonstrate the value of multimodality, we compare our fusion model against a strong text-only baseline. This baseline will use the exact same architecture for the linguistic encoder and prediction head but will completely omit the acoustic and visual modalities and the fusion block. By comparing the performance of the two models on the test set, we can directly quantify the performance gain attributable to the inclusion of multimodal information and the cross-modal attention mechanism.

5.5.4 Result Analysis and Qualitative Insights

After training both our cross-modal fusion model and the text-only baseline on the CMU-MOSI dataset, we evaluate their performance on the held-out test set. The analysis is twofold: first, we examine the quantitative metrics to establish the overall performance improvement; second, and more importantly, we conduct a qualitative deep dive into the preselected illustrative samples to understand how and why the multimodal model succeeds where the text-only model fails.

1. Quantitative Performance
   The performance of the two models is compared using the standard regression metrics for the MOSI dataset: MAE and the Pearson correlation coefficient (Corr). Additionally, we report the binary classification accuracy (Accuracy-2) by thresholding the predictions at zero (positive vs. negative). The results are summarized in Table 5.3.

   The quantitative results provide clear evidence for the efficacy of the multimodal approach. Our cross-modal fusion model significantly outperforms the text-only baseline across all metrics. It achieves a lower MAE, indicating that its predictions are, on average, closer to the ground-truth scores. The higher correlation coefficient demonstrates that its predictions align more reliably with the trends in human sentiment ratings. The notable 3.7% increase in binary accuracy further confirms that the inclusion of acoustic and visual cues leads to more correct sentiment classifications.

Table 5.3 Performance comparison on the CMU-MOSI test set.

Model	MAE (↓)	Corr (↑)	Accuracy-2 (↑) (%)
Text-only baseline	0.952	0.651	76.50
Cross-modal fusion model (ours)	**0.864**	**0.723**	**80.20**
Performance gain	0.088	0.072	3.70

While these numbers confirm that our model is better, they do not explain why. The true value of multimodality is revealed through a qualitative analysis of specific, challenging cases.

2. Qualitative Insights

We analyze the model's predictions on the illustrative samples we selected in Section 5.5.1. The analysis is presented in Figure 5.5, which visualizes the inputs and compares the predictions of both models against the ground truth.

Case 1: Congruent Positive Sentiment

Utterance: "YEAH IT REALLY IS GOOD I MEAN"

Ground Truth Score: +2.20

Plausible Context: The speaker delivers this line with a genuine smile and a nod, and their voice is enthusiastic with a rising, varied intonation. All modalities are aligned in their positive sentiment.

Analysis: As shown in Figure 5.5, both models correctly identify the positive polarity. The text-only baseline, reading the explicit positive words, predicts a

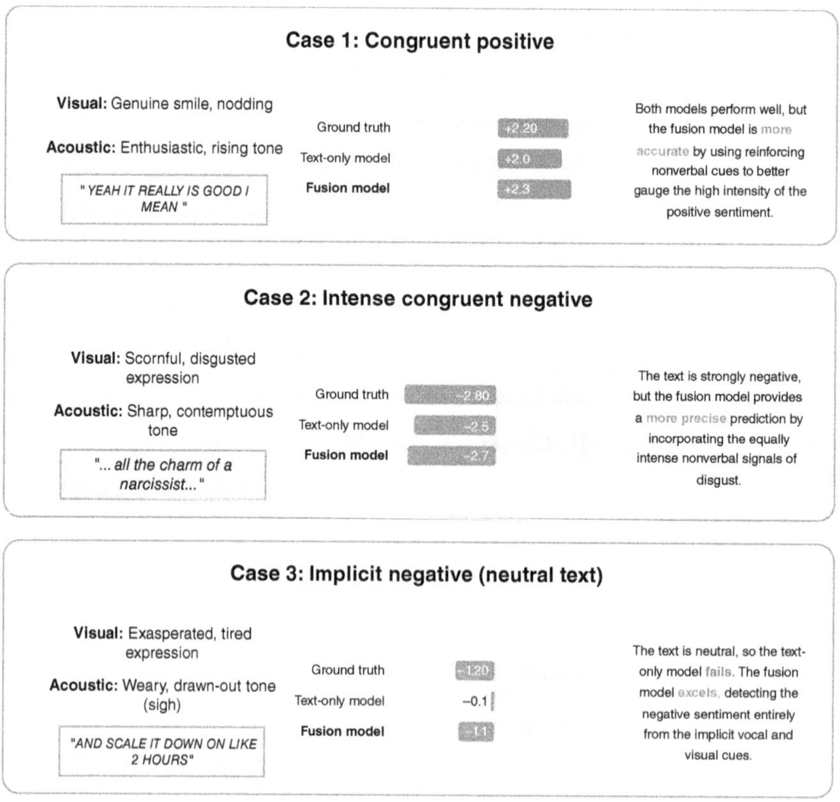

Figure 5.5 Qualitative analysis of model predictions on illustrative samples.

strong score of +2.0. It performs well but slightly underestimates the speaker's high level of enthusiasm. The fusion model, however, predicts +2.3. By integrating the reinforcing positive cues from the visual (smile, nod) and acoustic (enthusiastic tone) channels, it more accurately captures the intensity of the speaker's sentiment, resulting in a prediction much closer to the ground truth.

Case 2: Intense Congruent Negative Sentiment

Utterance: "HE UM HAD ALL THE CHARM OF A NARCISSIST XXX BOY THE WHOLE FILM"

Ground Truth Score: −2.80

Plausible Context: The text itself is sarcastic and deeply negative. The speaker reinforces this with a scornful tone, a disgusted facial expression (e.g., a sneer), and a dismissive hand gesture.

Analysis: This example showcases the models' handling of intense, explicitly negative language. The text-only baseline correctly identifies the strong negativity from phrases like "charm of a narcissist" and predicts a score of −2.5. This is a strong performance, but it doesn't quite reach the extreme level of disdain expressed. The fusion model's prediction of −2.7 is more precise. It confirms the intense negativity of the text with the equally intense negative signals from the speaker's voice and expression, allowing it to more accurately model sentiment at the extreme end of the scale.

Case 3: Implicit Negative Sentiment

Utterance: "AND SCALE IT DOWN ON LIKE 2 HOURS"

Ground Truth Score: −1.20

Plausible Context: The text itself is a neutral, factual statement about duration. However, the speaker conveys their negative feeling (likely frustration or exhaustion) entirely through nonverbal cues: a heavy sigh, a tired or exasperated expression, and a weary, drawn-out tone.

Analysis: This case perfectly demonstrates the fundamental limitation of unimodal analysis. The text-only baseline is completely blind to the sentiment. Seeing no emotional words, it predicts a score of −0.1, effectively identifying the utterance as neutral and failing the task. In stark contrast, the fusion model predicts −1.1. It successfully bypasses the neutral text and extracts the rich sentimental information from the acoustic (weary tone) and visual (exasperated expression) channels. This demonstrates the model's core strength: its ability to find and interpret sentiment even when it is entirely absent from the language itself.

This qualitative analysis provides compelling evidence that the performance gain of our multimodal model is not arbitrary. It stems directly from its ability to model the complex interplay between language, voice, and expression. By learning to interpret not just the content of each modality but the patterns of their interaction, especially patterns of incongruity, the model achieves a deeper, more human-like understanding of sentiment.

5.6 Chapter Summary and Outlook

This chapter has navigated the transition from a unimodal, text-centric view of sentiment to a more holistic and human-like multimodal perspective. We established that to accurately decode the full spectrum of human expression, it is not sufficient to analyze words in isolation. The acoustic and visual channels are not merely supplementary; they are integral components of communication that carry essential information about emotional valence, arousal, and intent. By treating sentiment analysis as a multimodal problem, we gain the ability to resolve ambiguities like sarcasm and to capture the subtle nuances that are lost in pure text.

Our exploration began with the foundational steps of unimodal feature representation, detailing the techniques for converting raw video, audio, and text into structured, numerical feature vectors using tools like pretrained CNNs, acoustic feature extractors, and large language models. We addressed the critical challenge of data alignment, establishing the importance of synchronizing these disparate data streams to enable meaningful fusion.

The core of the chapter focused on multimodal fusion strategies. We traced the evolution of these techniques from the classic paradigms of early (feature-level) and late (decision-level) fusion to the more sophisticated, model-level fusion methods that define the modern deep learning era. We delved into the mechanisms of tensor-based fusion for modeling high-order interactions, gated mechanisms for dynamic information filtering, and, most importantly, the transformative power of cross-modal attention for enabling fine-grained, context-aware intermodal dialogue.

We then examined the concrete deep learning architectures that implement these strategies. We reviewed the foundational CNN/RNN-based models that set the stage for end-to-end learning and culminated in an in-depth analysis of the Transformer architecture. The Transformer, with its inherent ability to model long-range dependencies and its natural extension to cross-modal attention, has emerged as the dominant framework for achieving state-of-the-art performance. Finally, a comprehensive case study grounded these concepts in a practical application, demonstrating empirically how a multimodal model built with these principles can successfully interpret complex, real-world sentiment expressions where a text-only model would fail.

A recurring theme throughout our discussion of advanced fusion and modern architectures has been the pivotal role of the attention mechanism. We have seen it as the key enabling technology that allows models to move beyond static fusion and learn dynamic, context-dependent relationships between modalities. It is the mechanism that empowers a model to ask: "Given these words, which part of the speaker's tone is most important? Given this facial expression, how should I reinterpret the meaning of this phrase?"

While we have introduced its application in a multimodal context, we have only scratched the surface of its full potential and versatility. To truly master modern sentiment analysis, whether it be unimodal or multimodal, one must possess a deep understanding of attention itself. It is the engine that drives not only multimodal fusion but also the very large language models that are redefining the field. Therefore, our journey logically continues in the next chapter, where we will place the attention mechanism under the microscope, dissecting its internal workings, exploring its powerful variants, and demonstrating its broader impact across the entire landscape of sentiment analysis.

References

1. Ekman, P., & Friesen, W. V. (1978). *Facial action coding system: A technique for the measurement of facial movement*. Consulting Psychologists Press.
2. Eyben, F., Wöllmer, M., & Schuller, B. (2010). Opensmile: The Munich versatile and fast open-source audio feature extractor. In Proceedings of the 18th ACM International Conference on Multimedia, Firenze, Italy, (pp. 1459–1462).
3. Boersma, P. (2001). Praat, a system for doing phonetics by computer. *Glot International*, 5(9), 341–345.
4. McFee, B., Raffel, C., Liang, D., Ellis, D. P., McVicar, M., Battenberg, E., & Nieto, O. (2015). Librosa: Audio and music signal analysis in Python. In Proceedings of the 14th Python in Science Conference (SciPy 2015), Austin, USA, (pp. 18–24).
5. Devlin, J., Chang, M. W., Lee, K., & Toutanova, K. (2019). Bert: Pre-training of deep bidirectional transformers for language understanding. In Proceedings of the 2019 Conference of the North American Chapter of the Association for Computational Linguistics: Human Language Technologies, Volume 1, Minneapolis, USA, (pp. 4171–4186).
6. Zadeh, A., Chen, M., Poria, S., Cambria, E., & Morency, L. P. (2017). Tensor fusion network for multimodal sentiment analysis. arXiv preprint arXiv:1707.07250.
7. Arevalo, J., Solorio, T., Montes-y-Gomez, M., & González, F. A. (2020). Gated multimodal networks. *Neural Computing and Applications*, 32(14), 10209–10228.
8. Tsai, Y. H. H., Bai, S., Liang, P. P., Kolter, J. Z., Morency, L.-P., & Salakhutdinov, R. (2019). Multimodal transformer for unaligned multimodal language sequences. In Proceedings of the 57th Annual Meeting of the Association for Computational Linguistics, Florence, Italy, (pp. 6558–6569).

9 Vaswani, A., Shazeer, N., Parmar, N., Uszkoreit, J., Jones, L., Gomez, A. N., Kaiser, Ł., & Polosukhin, I. (2017). Attention is all you need. In I. Guyon, U. Von Luxburg, S. Bengio, H. Wallach, R. Fergus, S. Vishwanathan, & R. Garnett (Eds.), *Advances in neural information processing systems* (Vol. 30). Curran Associates, Inc.

10 Zadeh, A., Zellers, R., Pincus, E., & Morency, L. P. (2016). Multimodal sentiment intensity analysis in videos: Facial gestures and verbal messages. *IEEE Intelligent Systems*, 31(6), 82–88.

11 Zadeh, A. B., Liang, P. P., Poria, S., Cambria, E., & Morency, L. P. (2018). Multimodal language analysis in the wild: CMU-MOSEI dataset and interpretable dynamic fusion graph. In Proceedings of the 56th Annual Meeting of the Association for Computational Linguistics (Volume 1: Long Papers), Melbourne, Australia, (pp. 2236–2246).

12 Busso, C., Bulut, M., Lee, C. C., Kazemzadeh, A., Mower, E., Kim, S., Chang, J. N., Lee, S., & Narayanan, S. S. (2008). IEMOCAP: Interactive emotional dyadic motion capture database. *Language Resources and Evaluation*, 42(4), 335–359.

13 Poria, S., Hazarika, D., Majumder, N., Naik, G., Cambria, E., & Mihalcea, R. (2019). MELD: A multimodal multi-party dataset for emotion recognition in conversations. In Proceedings of the 57th Annual Meeting of the Association for Computational Linguistics, Florence, Italy, (pp. 527–536).

6

Application of Attention Mechanisms in Sentiment Analysis

This chapter aims to conduct an in-depth exploration of the core principles of attention mechanisms and systematically elaborate on how they have fundamentally transformed the way sentiment analysis models are constructed. Starting from the origin and basic concepts of attention mechanisms, we will gradually transition to their core role in the Transformer architecture, and then focus on demonstrating their specific applications in text, multimodal, and graph-structured sentiment analysis tasks. Through theoretical explanations, model analysis, and cutting-edge case studies, readers will gain a profound understanding of why attention mechanisms have become an indispensable cornerstone of modern sentiment analysis technology.

6.1 Introduction

6.1.1 Review of Limitations of Traditional Models

Sequence models represented by RNN (recurrent neural network) and LSTM (long short-term memory) have achieved certain success in modeling sequence dependencies. However, their inherent structural flaws limit their further development. The most typical issue is the information bottleneck: after processing the entire sequence, the model only summarizes all information through the final hidden state (or a fixed-length context vector), resulting in the dilution or loss of information input earlier during long-distance transmission. In addition, RNNs are prone to gradient vanishing or explosion during training, making it difficult for the model to capture long-range dependencies.

For example, in the sentence "The food at this restaurant is delicious, but the waiters' attitude is extremely bad," traditional models may struggle to accurately determine that the overall sentiment tendency is negative. This is because they cannot effectively distinguish the relative importance of the two sentiment words "delicious" and "bad" in the sentence, especially when they modify different aspects ("food" and "waiters," respectively). The sequential processing forces the model to compress all historical information into a fixed-size state, which acts as a bottleneck. When the crucial sentiment clue appears early in the sequence, its signal can be overwritten or diluted by subsequent, potentially less relevant tokens. This is not merely a capacity issue but a fundamental architectural constraint.

Another subtle but critical limitation lies in handling negation and scope. In a sentence like "The movie was not very entertaining," the negation word "not" reverses the sentiment of "entertaining." Traditional RNNs and LSTMs, when processing the sequence step-by-step, may fail to robustly capture the precise scope of this negation, especially in longer, more complex sentences, leading to sentiment misclassification, as shown in Figure 6.1. This sequential processing inherently struggles with modeling nonlocal dependencies, a fundamental challenge that becomes more pronounced in nuanced text.

6.1.2 Intuitive Understanding of Attention Mechanisms

Humans achieve information filtering through the attention allocation mechanism, whose core lies in demand-driven resource inclination.

Visually, when looking for a friend in a crowded crowd, humans will automatically focus on key features such as "familiar hairstyle/clothing" and ignore irrelevant backgrounds. Audibly, in a noisy environment, humans can only capture the target conversation sound and block other noises through the cocktail party effect. When reading text, humans will quickly locate transition words and sentiment words; for instance, when reading comments, their attention will first lock onto expressions that determine the core opinion, such as "but" and "terrible." Essentially, the human brain dynamically allocates cognitive resources based on goals and only processes

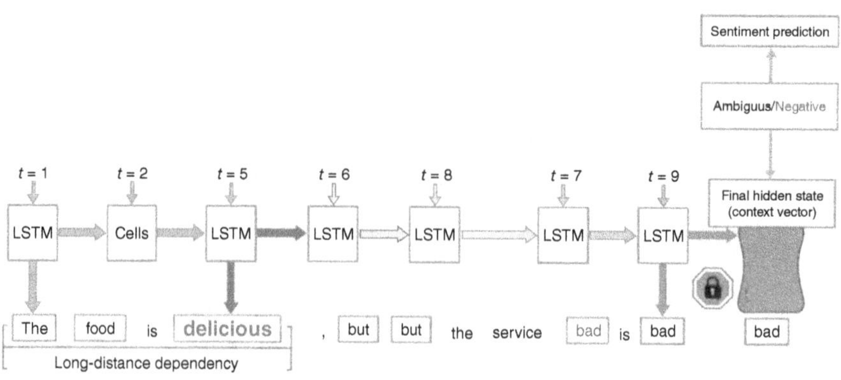

Figure 6.1 Schematic diagram of RNN/LSTM models processing sentiment sentences with transitions.

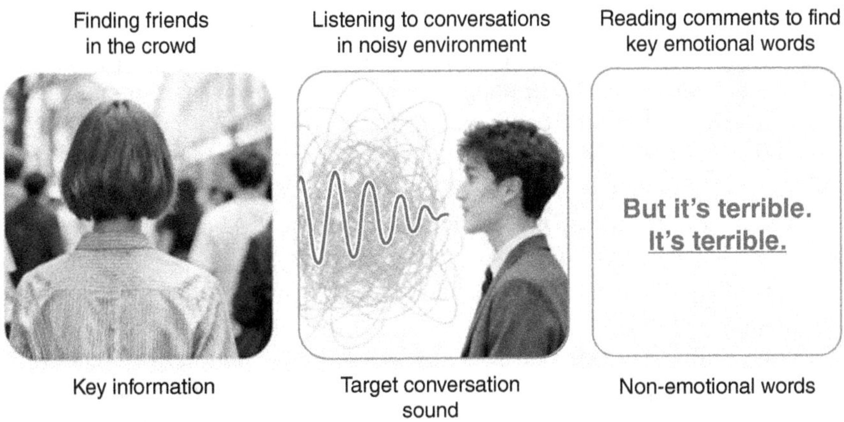

Figure 6.2 Human attention allocation.

high-value information in depth. This cognitive process is highly dynamic and context-dependent; the same visual scene or sentence will be attended to differently based on the current goal or question, as illustrated in Figure 6.2.

To enable models to selectively focus on key input information like humans do, the concept of selective attention in human cognition is introduced into NLP (natural language processing), thus forming the attention mechanism [1]. Its core definition is: when processing sequence data, a technology that enables the model to dynamically and selectively focus on the parts of the input sequence that are more important for the current task (such as sentiment analysis and machine translation), assign higher weights to key information, and reduce the interference of irrelevant information.

This mechanism essentially provides the model with a form of content-based addressing. Unlike fixed architectural priors (like convolution's locality bias), attention allows the model to decide, for each context, which parts of the input are relevant. This flexibility is paramount for language, where the importance of a word is not determined by its position but by its semantic relationship to the current context of understanding. For instance, the importance of the word "slow" depends entirely on what it is describing—it's negative for "service" but potentially positive or neutral for a "slow-paced plot" in a movie review, depending on the viewer's preference. Attention mechanisms provide a data-driven way to learn these complex, context-dependent associations.

6.1.3 Chapter Structure and Learning Path

Starting from the basic principles of attention mechanisms, this chapter will systematically introduce their key role in sentiment analysis. We will first review the general framework and classic models of attention mechanisms, and then conduct an in-depth analysis of their core position in the Transformer architecture. Subsequently, we will explore the applications of attention mechanisms in specific tasks such as text sentiment analysis, aspect-based sentiment analysis (ABSA), and multimodal sentiment analysis, and further introduce advanced variants such as graph attention networks (GATs). Finally, we will present a practical case to demonstrate how to use modern tools to implement ABSA, and discuss the current challenges and future development directions.

The learning path is designed to build knowledge incrementally. We begin by establishing a foundational understanding of why attention was needed, then move to how it works mathematically and structurally, and finally explore what can be achieved by applying it to increasingly complex sentiment analysis scenarios. This progression mirrors the historical development of the field and ensures a solid conceptual grasp.

6.2 Basic Principles and Evolution of Attention Mechanisms

6.2.1 General Framework of Attention Mechanisms

In the attention mechanism, Query, Key, and Value are the core elements, and their relationship can be compared to the working logic of a search engine, as illustrated in Figure 6.3.

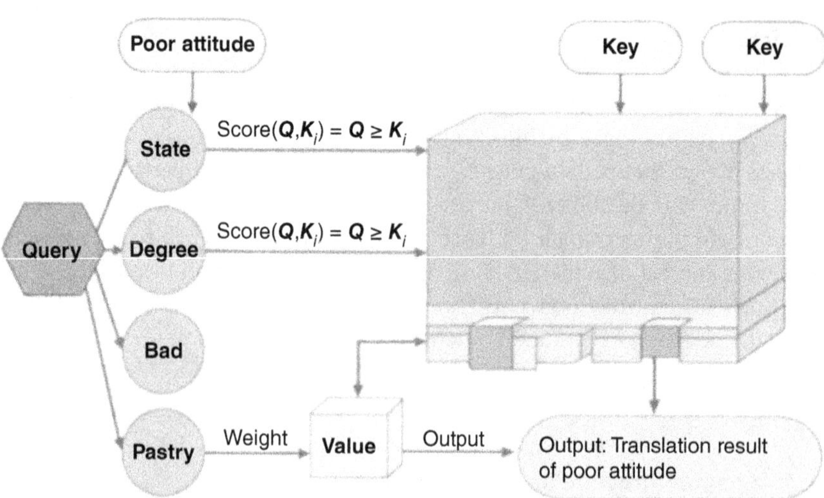

Figure 6.3 Schematic diagram of the interaction between Query, Key, and Value in the attention mechanism.

- Key: Similar to the "label" of each piece of information in the database (e.g., web page title), it is the feature representation of each element in the input sequence. It serves as an identifier that the Query will be matched against.
- Value: Refers to the "specific content" corresponding to the label (e.g., web page text) (i.e., the detailed information of each element). This is the actual information that will be aggregated into the output.
- Query: Represents the user's "retrieval demand" (e.g., search keywords) and stands for the target that the current task needs to focus on. It embodies the current context or goal against which all Keys are compared.

The mathematical workflow of the three is as follows:

1. Calculate the similarity between Query and each Key (e.g., inner product or cosine similarity):

$$\text{score}(Q, K_i) = Q \cdot K_i \tag{6.1}$$

This is similar to matching the relevance between keywords and titles during a search.
2. Normalize the similarity (e.g., using softmax) to obtain attention weights:

$$\alpha_i = \frac{\exp(\text{score }(Q, K_i))}{\sum_j \exp(\text{score }(Q, K_i))} \tag{6.2}$$

A higher weight indicates that the information corresponding to the Key is more important.
3. Perform a weighted sum of Values to obtain the attention output:

$$\text{Attention}(Q, K, V) = \sum_i \alpha_i V_i \tag{6.3}$$

That is, integrate the high-weight content as the final result. For example, when translating attitude is bad, Query is the feature of the target word to be translated, and Key is the feature of each word in the original sentence. By calculating the similarity, the Keys of "bad" and "attitude" will be assigned high weights, and finally, their corresponding Values will be mainly integrated into the translation result.

The choice of similarity function (e.g., dot product and additive) can impact the model's performance and computational efficiency. The softmax normalization ensures that the weights form a probability distribution, focusing the model's "attention" and providing a form of interpretability, as we can inspect which parts of the input received high weights.

6.2.2 Two Classic Attention Models

Additive attention and dot-product attention are two core attention mechanisms in sequence models [2]. The key difference between them lies in how to calculate the similarity between the encoder and decoder states.

Additive attention calculates similarity through a small feed-forward neural network. It concatenates the decoder state and the encoder state, inputs them into a single hidden layer network (usually using tanh activation), and finally outputs a scalar alignment score through a weight vector. This method can effectively learn complex nonlinear relationships between states and does not require the two to have the same dimension. However, it introduces additional model parameters and has high computational costs. The feed-forward network acts as a learned compatibility function, which can be powerful but comes at the expense of increased complexity. The number of parameters in this network grows with the dimensionality of the input states, which can be significant.

Dot-product attention adopts a more efficient calculation method, where the alignment score is directly obtained through the vector dot product of the decoder state and the encoder state. This method does not require introducing new parameters and has extremely high computational efficiency, which is particularly conducive to parallelization. However, when the vector dimension is high, the variance of the dot product result is too large, which will cause the softmax gradient to become smaller and affect the training stability. The high variance arises because the dot product of high-dimensional vectors tends to have large magnitudes. When fed into a softmax function, large input values can lead to extremely peaked distributions where one element has a weight close to 1 and all others are near 0. This results in very small gradients during training, slowing down or stalling learning.

To address this issue, scaled dot-product attention is proposed as a key variant, which divides the dot product result by the square root of the vector dimension. This operation scales the variance of the dot product result back to 1, effectively stabilizing the training process and making it the cornerstone of the multi-head attention mechanism in modern model architectures such as Transformer.

The selection between these two mechanisms often involves a trade-off. Additive attention, with its learned parameters, can be more expressive for smaller-dimensional embeddings or when the relationship between Query and Key is highly nonlinear. In contrast, scaled dot-product attention is the dominant choice in modern architectures due to its computational superiority and proven performance when combined with other components like layer normalization and residual connections. The computational advantage of dot-product attention is massive when implemented on parallel hardware like GPUs, as it can be expressed as large, efficient matrix multiplications, as shown in Figure 6.4.

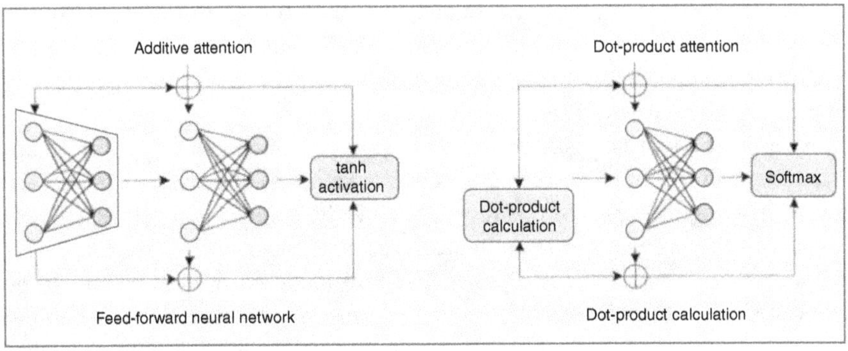

Figure 6.4 Additive attention and dot-product attention.

6.2.3 Self-attention Mechanism

Self-attention is an important evolution of the attention mechanism. Its core lies in the mutual attention between elements within the sequence, enabling the sequence to achieve "self-association and information aggregation." By allowing each element to serve as Query, Key, and Value simultaneously, it calculates the correlation strength between itself and all elements in the sequence. Compared with traditional attention, in self-attention, Query, Key, and Value all come from the same input sequence. This enables the model to directly capture the dependencies within the sequence, such as grammatical structures and anaphora relationships. It's a mechanism for the sequence to "look at itself" and understand the internal relationships between its components.

1. Unified Role Setting: The original embedding vector of each element in the sequence will generate an exclusive Query (used to "query" other elements), Key (used to be "queried" to establish associations), and Value (used to "provide" information to be integrated) through three independent linear layers.
2. Dynamic Calculation of Correlation: For each element's Query, calculate the similarity (e.g., scaled dot product) with the Keys of all elements in the sequence, and then obtain the attention weights through softmax normalization. The level of weight is directly corresponding to the tightness of the association between elements. For example, in the sentence "Xiaoming bought a book, and he likes it very much," the Query of "he" and the Key of "Xiaoming," as well as the Query of "it" and the Key of "book," will generate high weights.
3. Aggregation to Generate New Representations: Perform a weighted sum of the attention weights corresponding to each element and the Values of all elements to generate a new vector that integrates key information of the entire sequence. At this point, the new representations of "he" and "it" have incorporated the information of "Xiaoming" and "book," completing the capture of anaphora relationships.

The core value of the self-attention mechanism for sentiment analysis lies in its ability to directly associate sentiment words with their described objects, effectively solving the problem of long-distance dependencies and significantly improving the accuracy of sentiment polarity judgment.

In sentiment analysis tasks, the sentence structure often has a situation where "sentiment words" and "described objects" are far apart. For example, in the sentence "Although the plot of this movie is slow, the actors' acting skills are very excellent," the positive sentiment word "excellent" needs to be associated with the object "acting skills," and the negative sentiment word "slow" needs to be associated with the object "plot." Traditional models (such as RNNs) rely on the sequential order of the sequence to transmit information step by step. The farther the distance, the greater the information loss, which easily leads to misjudgment of sentiment objects. However, the self-attention mechanism can make "excellent" directly focus on "acting skills" and "slow" directly focus on "plot" by calculating the attention weight between each word and all other words, accurately establishing the corresponding relationship between sentiment and objects. The path length between any two words in a self-attention layer is effectively one, regardless of their positional separation in the sequence. This constant path length for long-range dependencies is a key architectural advantage over RNNs, where the path length grows linearly with distance.

This capability extends beyond simple association. Self-attention can model complex interactions, such as when the sentiment toward an aspect is conditioned on another part of the sentence. For instance, in "The battery life is good for a cheap phone," the positive word "good" is moderated by the clause "for a cheap phone." Self-attention allows the representation of "good" to be influenced by the entire context, enabling a more nuanced sentiment interpretation that considers such qualifiers. The model can learn that "good" has a different meaning and sentiment strength when it co-occurs with "for a cheap phone" compared to when it stands alone. This contextual modulation is a hallmark of human language understanding and is naturally handled by the global receptive field of self-attention.

6.3 Transformer Architecture: A Revolutionary Application of Attention Mechanisms

6.3.1 "Attention Is All You Need": The Birth of Transformer

The core contribution of the paper "Attention Is All You Need" published in 2017 lies in the proposal of the Transformer model [2], which completely abandons cyclic and convolutional structures and is built solely based on the self-attention mechanism. Its specific core contributions are as follows:

1. Introduction of Self-attention Mechanism
   The self-attention mechanism allows each element in the sequence to interact directly with all other elements. By calculating the relationships between the three vectors of Query, Key, and Value, it dynamically determines the weight of each element in different contexts, thereby generating a new representation that integrates global context and effectively captures long-distance dependencies.
2. Proposal of Multi-head Self-attention Mechanism
   The multi-head self-attention mechanism divides the model into multiple heads. Each head independently learns different attention patterns (i.e., the expressive ability of the model).
3. Adoption of Positional Encoding
   Since the self-attention mechanism itself does not consider the posing different representation subspaces. Finally, the outputs of all heads are concatenated and undergo linear transformation to obtain the final result. This enables the model to analyze the sequence from multiple perspectives, capture richer semantic and grammatical information, and improvisational information of elements; the paper introduces positional encoding to make up for this deficiency. Positional encoding is a vector with the same dimension as the word embedding, generated through sine and cosine functions. It contains the order information of each position in the sequence and is directly added to the word embedding vector, enabling the model to utilize both positional information and the relationships between elements.
4. Realization of Fully Parallel Computing: Different from traditional RNNs, both the self-attention mechanism and the feed-forward neural network part in Transformer can be computed in parallel without processing the sequence in chronological order. This greatly improves the training speed and efficiency, and reduces the training time and consumption of computing resources.
5. Construction of Encoder-decoder Architecture: Transformer adopts a classic encoder-decoder architecture. Both the encoder and decoder are formed by stacking multiple identical layers, and each sub-layer uses residual connections and layer normalization to stabilize training. This modular design enables the model to have good generalization ability and provides a basic framework for various subsequent variant models based on Transformer. Such as BERT [3], RoBERTa [8], DeBERTa [15], and T5 [14].

The removal of recurrence was a paradigm shift. It meant that the model was no longer constrained by the sequential nature of processing, allowing for massive parallelization on modern hardware like GPUs and TPUs. This architectural decision, combined with the expressive power of self-attention, directly enabled the training of the large-scale models that define modern NLP today. The ability to train on vastly more data in a reasonable time frame, coupled with the model's capacity to handle long-range context, led to a step change in performance across virtually all NLP tasks.

6.3.2 Multi-head Self-attention Mechanism

To enhance the representational ability of the model, Transformer introduces the multi-head self-attention mechanism. Its basic idea is to split the representation of the input sequence into multiple subspaces, perform attention calculation independently in each subspace, and finally concatenate the results and perform linear transformation. Eventually, the outputs of all heads are concatenated and linearly transformed to integrate into a comprehensive representation. The specific principle is as follows:

1. Linear Projection and Head Splitting
   For the representation matrix X of the input sequence, we use three sets of independent learnable weight matrices W_Q, W_K, and $W_V$for linear transformation respectively to obtain the initial Query, Key, and Value representations:

   $$Q = X\ W^Q, \quad K = X\ W^K, \quad V = X\ W^V \tag{6.4}$$

   Then, the "head splitting" operation equally divides the Q, K, and V matrices into h parts (i.e., h heads) in the feature dimension. For example, if the original feature dimension $d_{\text{model}\}} = 512$ and the number of heads $h = 8$, then the dimension of each head $d_k = d_v = d_{\text{model}}/h = 64$. This step creates an independent subspace projection for each head.
2. Parallel Scaled Dot-product Attention
   Perform scaled dot-product attention calculation independently on each head. For the i-th head:
   Calculate the attention score:

   $$\text{Attention}(Q_i, K_i, V_i) = \text{softmax}\left(\frac{Q_i K_i^T}{\sqrt{d_k}}\right) V_i \tag{6.5}$$

   Among them, $\frac{1}{\sqrt{d_k}}$ is a scaling factor used to prevent the dot product result from being too large, which would cause the softmax gradient to vanish.
3. Concatenation and Final Output
   Concatenate the output matrices $\text{head}_1, \text{head}_2, \ldots, \text{head}_h)$ of the h heads along the feature dimension:

   $$\text{MultiHead}(Q, K, V) = \text{Concat}(\text{head}_1, \ldots, \text{head}_h)\ W^O \tag{6.6}$$

Among them, W^O is a learnable output weight matrix, which is used to map the concatenated high-dimensional features (dimension d_{model}) back to the target dimension and integrate information from different heads.

In sentiment analysis, it can capture features in multiple dimensions such as syntactic dependencies, sentiment associations, and topic information at the same time. This is exactly the great advantage of the multi-head self-attention mechanism in sentiment analysis tasks. It no longer regards sentences as a flat sequence of words but can deconstruct sentences from multiple dimensions in parallel and capture their complex feature interactions. For example, one head may focus on the syntactic structure, another on the sentiment polarity, and the third on the topic keywords, thereby comprehensively improving the accuracy of sentiment judgment.

Empirical studies have shown that different heads do indeed learn specialized functions. Some heads may become adept at attending to the next word for syntactic structure, others to sentence-final words for overall sentiment, and some to adjectives and adverbs, which are strong sentiment carriers. This distributed specialization is a key reason for the model's robustness and high performance.

6.3.3 Overall Architecture of Transformer

Transformer consists of an encoder and a decoder. The encoder stack is composed of N (e.g., 6) identical layers. Each layer contains a multi-head self-attention mechanism and a feed-forward neural network, and each sub-layer is equipped with residual connections and layer normalization to stabilize training. The decoder stack is also formed by stacking N identical layers. Each layer contains three core sub-layers: masked multi-head self-attention (to ensure autoregressive generation and only focus on the generated positions), encoder-decoder attention (also known as cross-attention, whose Key and Value come from the final output of the encoder, and Query comes from the upper layer of the decoder), and a feed-forward network. The detailed definitions, functions and structural comparisons of all core modules above are summarized across Table 6.1. The key components include:

- Residual Connections and Layer Normalization: Residual connections and layer normalization are key technologies to ensure the stable and efficient training of the deep Transformer network. Together, they solve two major problems in deep neural networks: gradient vanishing and unstable training dynamics.

Table 6.1 Main components and functions of the transformer encoder layer.

Component	Function Description	Role in Sentiment Analysis
Multi-head self-attention	Captures dependencies between various elements within the sequence	Associates sentiment words, aspect words, and their modifiers to understand the context
Feed-forward neural network	Performs nonlinear transformation on the representation of each position	Enhances the model's representational ability and extracts high-level semantic features
Residual connection	Adds the input and output of the sub-layer	Alleviates the gradient vanishing problem in deep networks
Layer normalization	Normalizes the features of each sample	Stabilizes the training process and accelerates convergence

- Positional Encoding: Positional encoding is a key innovation of the Transformer model, aiming to solve the inherent permutation invariance problem of its core component, the self-attention mechanism. Since self-attention calculates the context representation through weighted summation, it cannot distinguish the order of elements in the sequence by itself. For example, the input sequences "The cat chases the mouse" and "The mouse chases the cat" will generate exactly the same representation under pure self-attention, which obviously violates the inherent laws of language.
- Feed-forward Neural Network: It is applied after the attention layer to introduce nonlinearity and transformation.

For sentiment analysis, the encoder stack is usually used to generate contextualized representations of the input text. Models like BERT leverage this encoder-only architecture, often adding a special classification token [CLS] at the beginning of the sequence, whose final hidden state is used as the aggregate sequence representation for classification tasks. The idea is that the [CLS] token, through its interactions with all other tokens in the self-attention layers, can accumulate a representation that summarizes the entire sequence's content, which is then fed into a classifier to predict sentiment.

6.4 In-depth Application of Attention Mechanisms in Various Sentiment Analysis Tasks

6.4.1 Enhancement of Text Sentiment Analysis

Regarding how the attention mechanism enhances sentence-level and document-level sentiment classification, its core value lies in that it endows the model with the ability of dynamic focusing and weight allocation, enabling it to ignore redundant information and grasp the key clues for sentiment judgment like humans.

In traditional bag-of-words models or average pooling methods, neutral words like "amazing" and "the" are treated equally, resulting in strong sentiment signals being diluted by a large number of irrelevant words. After introducing the attention mechanism, when processing a sentence, the model calculates an importance score for each word related to the current sentiment judgment task. This is a form of feature weighting, but it's dynamic and context-dependent. The same word (e.g., "good") might receive a high weight in a short, direct review ("Good movie!") but a lower weight in a long, nuanced review where its impact is less decisive among other descriptive words.

Specifically, during the training process, the model learns to identify which lexical features (such as words with strong sentiment polarity, degree adverbs, negative words, etc.) contribute the most to the final sentiment label (such as positive/negative). For a sentence like "The plot was amazingly creative and utterly captivating, though the pacing felt a bit slow.," the attention mechanism will automatically:

1. Focus on Strong Signal Words
   Assign extremely high attention weights to "amazingly" and "utterly captivating" because they carry strong positive sentiment. These are clear, high-intensity sentiment markers.
2. Weaken Neutral Content
   Significantly reduce the weights of structural and neutral words such as "the," "was," "and," and "though." These words are necessary for grammar but carry little to no sentiment information.
3. Handle Complex Situations
   Even if there is slightly negative information like "a bit slow" in the sentence, the model can still make a correct positive judgment because the attention mechanism recognizes the transition word "though" and assigns the main weight to the strong positive content before the transition. The model learns that "though" often signals a contrast, and that the sentiment before the contrast is frequently the dominant one, or at least that the contrast itself needs to be considered. The attention weights would reflect this by potentially down-weighting the negative clause relative to the strong positive ones.

   Visualizing attention weights is an extremely important practical value of the attention mechanism, which greatly improves the interpretability of the model and allows us to "peek into" the "black box" of model decision-making.

   In sentiment analysis tasks, we not only care about the accuracy of the model's judgment but also hope to understand the basis for its decision-making. By overlaying the attention weights calculated by the model on the original text in the form of a heatmap (darker colors indicate higher weights), we can intuitively see which words or phrases the model mainly focuses on when making a "positive" or "negative" judgment. For example, for the sentence "The performance was breathtaking, but the costumes were dull.," if the model gives a negative sentiment, a credible visualization result will show that the highest attention weights are concentrated on "but," "costumes," and "dull." This clearly indicates that:

- The model grasps the key turning point: it correctly identifies that the content after "but" is the focus of sentiment.
- The model understands the association between the evaluation object and the sentiment word: it knows that the aspect of "costumes" is "dull."

This kind of visualization has multiple values:

- Model Diagnosis: If it is found that the model incorrectly assigns high weights to irrelevant words (such as "the" or "and"), it indicates that the model may not have truly learned the task and needs to be adjusted. This could signal overfitting, insufficient training, or problems with the training data.
- Trust Building: When users see that the model's focus is highly consistent with human intuition, they will be more willing to trust and adopt its analysis results. Explainability builds confidence, especially in business applications where decisions have consequences.
- Business Insights: When analyzing user reviews, highlighted sentiment keywords can directly serve as specific starting points for product improvement or service optimization. A product manager can quickly see that many negative reviews focus on "battery life" and "weight," providing clear direction for the next design iteration.

For document-level sentiment analysis, hierarchical attention networks (HANs) [5] extend this idea by first using a word-level attention mechanism to obtain informative word representations for each sentence, and then using a sentence-level attention mechanism to identify key sentences within the document. This two-tiered attention structure effectively handles the varying importance of information at different granularities. In a long product review, not all sentences are equally important for determining the overall sentiment. A sentence like "The delivery was fast" might be positive but less critical than "The product broke after 2 days of use." The sentence-level attention learns to weight the importance of each sentence's representation (which itself is built from attentively weighted words) for the final document-level classification. This hierarchical approach mirrors how humans read long texts, focusing on key sentences and, within those, key phrases.

6.4.2 Breakthrough in ABSA

The core challenge of the "aspect-based" task in sentiment analysis is to accurately associate the general overall sentiment with specific aspects mentioned in the text. This challenge is mainly reflected in the following aspects:

1. Long-distance Dependencies Between Aspect and Opinion Words
   Aspect words and opinion words expressing sentiment may be far apart in the sentence. For example, in "The appetizers we had at the beginning of our long and otherwise enjoyable meal were surprisingly bland," the aspect "appetizers" and the opinion "bland" are separated by many words.
2. Polysemy and Context Dependence of Aspect Words
   The same aspect word may have completely different sentiment polarities in different contexts. The word "size" could be positive ("The size of the apartment is generous"), negative ("The size of the portions is too small"), or neutral depending on the context and user expectations.
3. Intertwined and Conflicting Sentiments of Multiple Aspects
   A sentence may involve multiple aspects, and the sentiments toward these aspects may be conflicting. The classic example is "The food was delicious, but the service was terrible." The model must separate the sentiment for "food" (positive) from the sentiment for "service" (negative) and not let one dominate the overall sentence representation.
4. Implicit Aspects and Sentiment Implications
   Sometimes, aspect words do not appear directly but are implied in the context. For example, "It took forever to get a table" implies the aspect "waiting time" with negative sentiment, and "The pictures are blurry" implies the aspect "camera quality" with negative sentiment.

   The core of the solution lies in the use of the attention mechanism. Through learning, the model focuses more "attention" on the sentiment words and contextual segments related to specific aspects, thereby generating an exclusive and localized sentiment representation for each aspect, and finally achieving an accurate connection between sentiment and aspects. Early work utilized attention mechanisms to associate aspect words with context [4], and subsequent research further refined the attention modeling for aspects [15]. Existing attention-based ABSA models further optimize aspect-aware weight calculation to capture fine-grained sentiment relations [9]. The main ABSA challenges and corresponding attention-based mitigation strategies are systematically summarized in Table 6.2. The attention solutions are as follows:

Table 6.2 Typical challenges and attention solutions in ABSA.

Challenge Type	Example	Attention Solution
Long-distance dependence	"The environment is elegant, but the location is too remote"	Target-dependent attention, using aspect words as Queries to locate opinion words
Aspect polysemy	"The screen is very bright" vs. "The light is too bright"	Context-aware attention weights
Conflicting sentiments of multiple aspects	"The food is delicious, but the service is terrible"	Multi-head attention to focus on different aspects respectively
Implicit aspects	"Waited for half an hour before the food was served" → Aspect: serving speed	Focus on descriptive words in the implicit context through attention

- Target-dependent Attention: Uses aspect words as queries to find relevant sentiment words in the context. The aspect representation serves as the Query, and the sentence context provides the Keys and Values. This forces the attention mechanism to find the parts of the sentence most relevant to the given aspect. For the aspect "service," the Query would be a representation of "service," and the attention mechanism would learn to assign high weights to "terrible" in the sentence "The food was delicious, but the service was terrible."
- Interactive Attention Network (IAN): Encodes the context and aspects separately and realizes bidirectional interaction through cross-attention. It first encodes the context (the whole sentence) and the aspect term separately. Then, it uses the context representation to attend to the aspect (to get an aspect-focused context) and uses the aspect representation to attend to the context (to get a context-aware aspect representation). These two are then combined for prediction. This bidirectional interaction allows for a richer, more nuanced understanding of the relationship.

ABSA models based on BERT and attention mechanisms can refresh the SOTA (state-of-the-art) records. Their success can be attributed to the perfect combination of strong basic semantic understanding and refined attention focusing.

1. BERT

   Provides deep contextualized word representations. Traditional models (such as Word2Vec) or simple RNNs cannot fully understand the complex semantics of words in specific contexts. As a pretrained model, BERT's core advantage lies in generating deep bidirectional context representations through masked language models and self-attention.

2. Attention Mechanism
   Achieves accurate attribute-sentiment alignment. Although BERT has built-in self-attention, sentence-level classification is still relatively rough. To this end, researchers have designed more refined attention architectures:
   - Aspect-specific Attention
     The model will be forced to focus on the context words most relevant to the given aspect term (e.g., "service"). This is usually achieved by calculating the interaction weight between the aspect word representation and the representations of all words in the sentence, ensuring that the sentiment judgment is mainly based on "The service is slow" rather than "The food is great."
   - Hierarchical or Co-attention
     Some advanced models introduce multilayer attention. For example, one layer is responsible for identifying words grammatically related to aspect words (such as "is"), and the other layer focuses on sentiment words (such as "slow"), and they work together through a gating mechanism. HANs have also been applied to document-level sentiment classification [5]. Standard datasets for ABSA, such as those from the SemEval competitions [20], have driven progress in this field.

6.4.3 Cross-modal Attention in Multimodal Sentiment Analysis

Multimodal sentiment analysis aims to integrate information from multiple modalities such as text, images, and audio to understand sentiment content more comprehensively. Early fusion methods include tensor fusion networks [7], while more recent approaches leverage cross-modal transformers [10, 16, 17]. The cross-modal attention mechanism plays a key role in this process.

Cross-modal Attention Mechanism

1. Text-image Attention
   Text-image attention is a key cross-modal interaction mechanism, whose core is to dynamically focus on specific regions of the image under the guidance of text. This mechanism uses each word in the text (such as "puppy" and "cute") as a query vector, and the features of each image patch obtained by encoding the image through CNN (convolutional neural network) or ViT (vision transformer) as keys and values. By calculating the similarity between the text query and all image patch keys, the model generates an attention weight distribution for each word. For example, for the word "puppy," the model will assign an extremely high weight to the area where the dog is located in the image, and a very low weight to irrelevant areas such as the sky and grass. Then, according to these weights, a weighted sum of the values of all image patches is performed, and finally, an enhanced representation integrating relevant visual information is generated for each text word.

2. Text-audio Attention
   The core goal of the text-audio attention mechanism is to achieve fine-grained alignment between the semantic content of the text and the paralinguistic information of the speech. Specifically, this mechanism uses each token in the text sequence as a query, and the audio features (such as Mel-spectrogram frames or extracted prosodic features) as keys and values. By calculating the similarity between queries and keys, the model learns to assign an attention weight distribution for audio features to each text word. For example, when processing sentiment words like "This is so exciting!" in the text, the attention mechanism will automatically find and focus on the corresponding segments in the audio with higher pitch, faster speech rate, and stronger energy. On the contrary, for the word "disappointed" in "I am a bit disappointed," the model will focus on the areas in the audio where the pitch is low, the speech rate slows down, or there are pauses.
3. Transformer-based Multimodal Fusion Models
   Transformer-based multimodal fusion models, such as ViLT (vision-language transformer) and M-BERT (multilingual BERT), represent a paradigm shift: from complex pipelines that rely on external feature extractors to concise designs that perform end-to-end deep fusion within a unified architecture.

   Its core idea is to map the information of different modalities to the same semantic space as early as possible and use the powerful attention mechanism of Transformer for seamless interaction. In ViLT, image patches are linearly projected into embeddings, concatenated with text token embeddings, and fed into a standard Transformer encoder. The self-attention layers then naturally allow every text token to attend to every image patch and vice versa, learning the complex cross-modal interactions directly from data. This approach simplifies the architecture and has been shown to be highly effective, demonstrating that the attention mechanism is a universal primitive for modeling intramodal and intermodal dependencies. There is no longer a need for separate, pretrained feature extractors whose representations might be in incompatible spaces; the model learns to align and fuse the modalities jointly from raw or lightly processed inputs.

6.5 Advanced Attention Variants and GATs

6.5.1 Born for Efficiency: Sparse Attention Mechanism

The core operation of the standard self-attention mechanism is to calculate the correlation between all pairs of input positions, which requires generating an attention score matrix. For a sequence of length n, the size of this matrix is $n * n$, and its computational complexity is $O(n^2)$. This quadratic complexity has become a major bottleneck when processing long sequences. To break this limitation, researchers have proposed a variety of efficient attention mechanisms, such as sparse attention (only calculating scores between some pairs of positions), local attention (limiting the attention range of each position), and linear attention (reducing the complexity to linear through kernel function approximation), aiming to maintain model performance while significantly improving computational efficiency. The memory requirement also scales as $O(n^2)$, which quickly becomes prohibitive for long documents, books, or high-resolution images when split into patches.

To address the $O(n^2)$ computational bottleneck of standard self-attention, models such as Longformer [11] and BigBird [12] have successfully reduced the computational complexity to the linear level $O(n)$ by introducing the sparse attention mechanism while maintaining strong performance. Another line of work focuses on linear-time attention variants [18]. Its core idea is: not all token pairs need to undergo intensive attention calculation, and we can design a more efficient attention pattern. The intuition is that in a long sequence, a token's meaning is primarily determined by its local context and a few key global tokens, rather than by every single other token.

These models usually combine three key sparse attention patterns:

1. Sliding Window Attention
   Similar to CNNs, each token only focuses on the tokens within a fixed window nearby (e.g., 512 tokens on the left and right). This captures local context information, and its computational cost is linear with the sequence length. This is based on the linguistic principle of locality—words are often most strongly related to their immediate neighbors for syntactic and short-range semantic relationships.
2. Global Attention
   Pre-specify a small number of special tokens (such as the [CLS] token or keywords in the question), allowing them to focus on all tokens in the sequence and be focused on by all tokens. This ensures that the model has a global perspective and can integrate summary information of the entire sequence. These global tokens act as "hubs" that collect information from the entire sequence and can then broadcast it back. The [CLS] token is a natural candidate for this.
3. Random Attention
   Each token randomly focuses on a small number of other positions in the sequence. This is equivalent to adding random connections to the attention graph, which helps to discover and capture those crucial long-range dependencies beyond the sliding window range. This is inspired by random graph theory and ensures that the graph connecting all tokens has a small diameter, allowing information to flow between any two tokens in a small number of steps, even if they are far apart in the sequence.

Taking the BigBird model as an example, it combines the above three patterns (sliding window, random attention, and global attention) to form a sparse attention mechanism that approximates a fully connected graph. Theoretical proofs show that this structure can well simulate the function of standard self-attention, but the computational efficiency is greatly improved, so it can process documents with thousands or even tens of thousands of tokens, solving the core pain point of traditional Transformer in long-text applications.

This capability is crucial for document-level sentiment analysis, where understanding the overall sentiment requires integrating information from across a long document, such as a product manual or a lengthy review. Sparse attention makes it feasible to apply powerful Transformer models to such tasks without prohibitive computational cost.

6.5.2 Graph Attention Networks

GATs have a wide range of application scenarios in graph-structured data [6]. Their core value lies in their ability to model the importance between nodes in a graph differently. When data has a natural graph structure, GAT no longer treats each neighbor node as equally important but dynamically assigns weights to different neighbors through the attention mechanism, thereby capturing complex relationship dependencies. They have been applied to tasks such as multimodal sentiment analysis using social graphs [7] and visual question answering [19]. The following are several typical application scenarios:

1. Social Network Analysis
   In a social graph, each user is a node, and the following relationship is an edge. GAT can be used for user profiling or influence prediction. For sentiment analysis, a user's sentiment might be influenced more by their close friends or opinion leaders than by casual acquaintances. GAT can learn these influence patterns.
2. Dialogue Systems and Interaction Modeling
   Model a conversation as a graph, where each utterance is a node, and edges can represent reply relationships or temporal relationships. GAT can be used for sentiment analysis or reply generation. The sentiment of an utterance is not independent; it's influenced by previous utterances, the speaker's role, and the conversational context. GAT can model these dependencies more flexibly than a sequential model.
3. Knowledge Graph-enhanced NLP Tasks
   In a knowledge graph, entities are nodes and relationships are edges. Applying GAT to knowledge graphs can help learn high-quality embeddings for entities. These embeddings can then be used to enhance sentiment

analysis by providing external world knowledge. For example, knowing that a product is "made by Apple" might carry a prior positive sentiment bias that the model can leverage if it sees the entity "iPhone" in a text.

6.5.2.1 Working Principles

The workflow of GAT can be systematically decomposed into the following three steps:

1. Calculate Attention Coefficients
   For each neighbor of the central node, calculate an unnormalized attention coefficient through a learnable attention function to measure the importance of the neighbor to the central node.
2. Normalize Attention Weights
   Use the softmax function to normalize the attention coefficients of all neighbors, converting them into a probability distribution with a sum of 1.
3. Aggregate Weighted Information
   Use the normalized attention weights as coefficients to perform a weighted sum of the feature vectors of the neighbor nodes, thereby obtaining the updated representation of the central node.

6.5.2.2 Application in Sentiment Analysis

1. Dialogue Sentiment Analysis
   To overcome the limitations of traditional sequence models in analyzing dialogue sentiment, we use GATs for processing. This method models the dialogue as a graph structure, where nodes are utterances and edges define their associations (such as temporal relationships and speakers). Through its attention mechanism, GAT allows each utterance node to dynamically assign weights to different neighbor nodes (such as other speakers) when aggregating information, thereby accurately capturing the social influence between speakers and long-distance context dependencies, and achieving a more delicate understanding of sentiment.
2. Knowledge Graph-based Sentiment Analysis
   Knowledge graph-based sentiment analysis aims to use external structured knowledge to enhance the understanding of the sentiment of entities and concepts in the text. Its core idea is that the rich association relationships (such as attributes, categories, and co-occurrence relationships) of entities themselves in the knowledge graph carry potential and transferable sentiment signals. In this framework, we align the entities mentioned in the text with the knowledge graph to construct a subgraph containing text entities and external knowledge entities. Subsequently, a GAT is applied to perform

information propagation and aggregation on this graph. For instance, if a review mentions "iPhone," the knowledge graph can provide related entities like "Apple Inc." (typically viewed positively) and "high price" (potentially negative). GAT can learn to weigh the influence of these related concepts from the knowledge graph to form a more informed sentiment representation for "iPhone" in the given textual context.

6.6 Practical Cases and Code Implementation

6.6.1 Case Study

The goal is to automatically and accurately extract customer feedback on each specific aspect from a large number of reviews, just like a professional restaurant manager.

The task requires the model to not only identify various aspects mentioned in the reviews (such as "lobster pasta," "serving speed," and "environment") but also associate the correct sentiment polarity (positive/negative/neutral) with each aspect. The challenge is that a review often contains multiple aspects and mixed sentiments. For example, in the review "The lobster pasta is fresh and chewy, but the waiters have a cold attitude and the serving is slow," the model must accurately decouple:

- "Lobster pasta": Positive
- "Waiters' attitude": Negative
- "Serving speed": Negative

This is a fine-grained classification task that goes beyond assigning a single label to the whole text. It requires a nuanced understanding of the relationship between specific entities (aspects) and the descriptive language surrounding them.

6.6.1.1 Common Datasets

- SemEval-2014 Task 4: Restaurant reviews, including aspect words and sentiment polarity.
- Laptop-14: Laptop review dataset
- Restaurant-14/16: Restaurant review datasets
- Twitter ABSA: Social media data

These datasets provide annotations in the form of (sentence, aspect, and sentiment) triplets, which are essential for supervised training.

6.6.1.2 Technical Implementation Path

Modern deep learning-based solutions, such as target-dependent attention mechanisms, are ideal for handling this task. The model will use each aspect word (such as "lobster pasta") as a Query to find descriptive words related to it (such as "fresh and chewy") in the context of the entire review, and calculate attention weights to focus on these key opinion words. Finally, based on this "aspect-context" pair, the sentiment polarity is classified. In this way, the model can achieve fine-grained sentiment attribution and provide accurate data insights for business decisions.

For the ABSA task of restaurant reviews, the optimal technical selection is to use a pretrained BERT model as the basic encoder and customize an ABSA task head for it.

The specific implementation is as follows: we use BERT to encode the entire review and obtain the contextual representation of each token. The key lies in the design of the downstream task head: for each aspect word identified in the review (such as "lobster pasta"), we take its hidden state corresponding to the BERT output layer as the query vector. Then, through a target-dependent attention layer, calculate the correlation weight between this aspect word and all other words in the review, thereby generating an enhanced representation for this aspect that integrates key contextual information. Finally, this aspect-specific representation is fed into a simple softmax classifier to output the sentiment polarity of "positive/negative/neutral." This approach is often more effective than simply using the [CLS] token or the aspect token's own embedding, as it dynamically constructs a representation tailored to the interaction between the aspect and its context.

```
Key Code
def prepare_training_data():
    # Sample data - should be loaded from files in practice
    sentences = [
        "The food was excellent but the service was terrible.",
        "Great ambiance and friendly staff.",
        "The laptop has good battery life but poor screen quality.",
        "The pizza was delicious and the beer was cold.",
        "Slow service and overpriced food."
    ]
    aspects = ["food", "service", "ambiance", "staff", "battery life",
               "screen quality", "pizza", "beer", "service", "food"]
    labels = ["positive", "negative", "positive", "positive", "positive",
             "negative", "positive", "positive", "negative", "negative"]

    processor = ABSADataProcessor()
    encoded_data = processor.encode_sentence_aspect_pair(sentences, aspects,
labels)

    dataset = Dataset.from_dict({
        'input_ids': encoded_data['input_ids'],
        'attention_mask': encoded_data['attention_mask'],
        'labels': encoded_data['labels']
    })

    return dataset.train_test_split(test_size=0.2, seed=42)

# Train the model
```

```
def main():
    # Prepare data
    datasets = prepare_training_data()

    # Initialize model
    absa_model = ABSAModel("bert-base-uncased")

    # Train
    trainer = absa_model.train(
        train_dataset=datasets["train"],
        eval_dataset=datasets["test"]
    )

    # Evaluate
    eval_results = trainer.evaluate()
    print(f"Evaluation results: {eval_results}")
```

6.6.1.3 Result Analysis

After training the model, we can analyze the attention weights to understand how the model makes decisions. For the sentence "The food was excellent, but the service was slow," we can visualize the attention distribution when focusing on the aspect "food." We will find that the model assigns high weights to "excellent," which is the key opinion word for this aspect. Similarly, when focusing on "service," the model will focus on "slow." This visualization not only verifies the effectiveness of the model but also provides interpretability for the results.

6.6.2 Considerations in Practice

In practical applications, it is necessary to comprehensively consider model performance and resource consumption. Lightweight models (such as DistilBERT) are suitable for scenarios with limited resources, while large models (such as RoBERTa and DeBERTa) perform better in tasks with high accuracy requirements. In addition, during model deployment, factors such as inference speed, memory usage, and hardware compatibility also need to be considered. The choice involves a trade-off, and systematic guidance for selecting ABSA models under different constraints is summarized in Table 6.3. DistilBERT, for example, is a distilled version of BERT that is 40% smaller and 60% faster while retaining 97% of its language understanding capabilities. This might be sufficient for many production sentiment analysis systems. RoBERTa, which is BERT with more robust training procedures (more data, longer training, and dynamic masking), often provides a small but consistent performance boost. DeBERTa, with its disentangled attention and enhanced mask decoder, has shown SOTA performance on many benchmarks but is also more complex. The decision should be driven by the specific constraints of the deployment environment (e.g., cloud API vs. edge device) and the business cost of prediction errors.

Table 6.3 Recommendations for ABSA model selection.

Model Type	Representative Models	Advantages	Disadvantages	Applicable Scenarios
Lightweight models	DistilBERT and TinyBERT	Fast inference and low resource consumption	Slightly lower accuracy	Mobile terminals and real-time scenarios
General-purpose models	BERT and RoBERTa	High accuracy and strong versatility	High computational resource requirements	Most ABSA tasks
Latest large models	DeBERTa and T5	SOTA performance and strong multitask capability	Extremely high training and deployment costs	Tasks with high accuracy requirements and research-oriented tasks

Computational resources and deployment are core challenges faced by modern NLP models, especially large-scale Transformer models.

The challenges in the training phase are mainly reflected in hardware costs. Training a BERT-base model may require hundreds or even thousands of GPU hours, while the training cost of a model with 100 billion parameters can reach millions of dollars, accompanied by huge energy consumption. This leads to technical barriers and the centralization of research resources. This has led to a trend where only large tech companies and well-funded research labs can afford to pretrain such models from scratch, while the wider community fine-tunes existing pretrained models.

The challenges in the inference phase are concentrated on latency, throughput, and cost. Large models have numerous parameters, resulting in high memory usage and slow inference speed. To meet the requirement of millisecond-level response for online services, it is usually necessary to deploy expensive GPU clusters, which sharply increases the operation and maintenance costs. Techniques like model quantization (reducing the precision of the numbers used, e.g., from 32-bit to 8-bit), pruning (removing less important weights), and knowledge distillation (training a smaller "student" model to mimic a larger "teacher" model) are essential to make these models viable for real-time applications. Serving frameworks like TensorFlow Serving, TorchServe, and ONNX Runtime are optimized for low-latency model inference.

6.7 Challenges, Limitations, and Future Outlook

6.7.1 Current Challenges and Limitations

Computational Costs: Although sparse attention mechanisms (such as those used in Longformer and BigBird) reduce the computational complexity from quadratic to linear, the requirements for computational resources are still demanding. Training these models still requires a large amount of GPU memory and computing power, and the inference phase also faces challenges. The optimization of sparse operations on hardware is not as mature as that of dense computing, making it difficult to give full play to the parallel advantages of GPUs, resulting in still high actual deployment costs. Sparse matrix operations are less optimized on standard deep learning frameworks and hardware, which are primarily designed for dense matrix multiplications. This means that even though the theoretical FLOPs are lower, the wall-clock time and memory bandwidth usage might not improve as much as expected. Research into specialized hardware and kernels for sparse attention is ongoing.

The Debate on "Attention Is Not Explanation": The pioneering research by Jain and Wallace (2019) triggered a profound debate on "attention is not explanation [13]." Through experiments, they revealed that there is not always a reliable causal relationship between neurons with high attention weights and the model's prediction results. Different attention heads may learn different weight distributions but draw the same prediction results; conversely, sometimes perturbing the attention weights through adversarial methods may not change the final output. We must view the visualization results critically and regard them as one of the auxiliary tools for understanding the model, rather than the only "explanation" gold standard. Attention weights show where the model is looking, but they don't necessarily explain why that led to a particular prediction. The model's decision could be based on complex, nonlinear interactions that are not fully captured by the simple weighted average of value vectors. Furthermore, high attention to a word doesn't mean the model is using it in the same way a human would; it might be attending to it for syntactic rather than sentiment-related reasons.

Learning of Spurious Correlations: Models may learn spurious correlations in the data during training instead of real causal relationships. For example, if in a dataset, the word "Russian" frequently co-occurs with negative reviews (e.g., in a political context), the model might learn to associate "Russian" with negative sentiment, which is a spurious correlation that does not hold generally. Attention mechanisms can sometimes amplify these biases by focusing on these surface-level cues. If the model learns to heavily attend to the word "Russian" whenever it appears and then predicts negative sentiment, the attention visualization might misleadingly make the model's decision look "reasonable" (it's focusing on a specific word), when in fact it's based on a bias. This highlights the importance of using diverse training data and techniques for debiasing models.

6.7.2 Future Research Directions

To address the above challenges, future research may develop in the following directions:

1. More Efficient Attention Mechanisms
   To break through the $O(n^2)$ computational bottleneck of standard attention, researchers have proposed attention variants with linear time complexity, such as Performer and Linear Transformer [18]. Their core idea is to mathematically reconstruct the standard softmax attention. Through methods such as random feature mapping or kernel function approximation, the complexity is successfully reduced to $O(n)$. Future work will focus on making these linear attention models both efficient and as expressive as their softmax-based counterparts, especially on a wider range of tasks. The goal is to find approximations that do not sacrifice significant performance while gaining massive scalability. This will be crucial for applying Transformer models to even longer sequences, such as entire books, code repositories, or long-term historical data.
2. In-depth Integration with Large Language Models (LLMs)
   As the core of LLMs, the attention mechanism endows them with strong contextual learning capabilities. Using this feature, we can implement complex zero-shot/few-shot sentiment analysis. For ABSA, we can list a small number of examples in the prompt. The attention mechanism of LLMs can quickly capture the task pattern and accurately associate aspects with sentiments without fine-tuning, which significantly reduces the cost of data annotation and the difficulty of domain adaptation. Future research will explore more effective prompting strategies and how to best leverage the internal attention mechanisms of LLMs for interpretable and controllable sentiment analysis. This includes techniques like chain-of-thought prompting, where the model is asked to reason step-by-step, potentially allowing us to better understand its "thought process" for sentiment judgment.
3. Trustworthy and Controllable Attention
   Trustworthy and controllable attention aims to integrate human prior knowledge into the model to improve its robustness and fairness. For example, we can design attention constraints to force the model to pay attention to specific aspects or to ignore known spurious features. Another direction is to develop methods to better calibrate attention weights with feature importance, making them more reliable as explanations. Research in model editing and causal intervention will also contribute to making attention-based models more trustworthy. This might involve training models so that their attention distributions are more aligned with human judgments of importance or developing methods to audit and correct attention patterns that lead to biased or incorrect predictions. The ultimate goal is to build models whose decision-making process is not only accurate but also transparent, fair, and aligned with human values.

6.8 Chapter Summary

This chapter systematically expounds on the core role and development context of attention mechanisms in sentiment analysis. From initially being an auxiliary tool for RNN to becoming the cornerstone of the Transformer architecture, attention mechanisms have not only significantly improved the accuracy and interpretability of sentiment analysis but also promoted the research on sentiment analysis in complex scenarios such as multimodality and graph structures.

We reviewed the specific applications of attention mechanisms in tasks such as text sentiment classification, aspect-based analysis, and multimodal fusion, and introduced advanced variants such as sparse attention and graph attention. Through practical cases, we demonstrated how to use modern tools to quickly build a sentiment analysis system with attention mechanisms.

Although challenges such as computational costs and interpretability still exist, as a core idea of modern NLP, attention mechanisms will continue to promote the development of sentiment analysis technology. In the next chapter, we will further explore the latest progress and application prospects of Transformer-based LLMs (such as BERT and GPT) in sentiment analysis. The journey from simple weighted averaging to sophisticated context-aware feature extraction represents a paradigm shift in NLP, and attention has been the driving force behind it. Its ability to dynamically focus on relevant information has brought us closer to building models that understand language with human-like context sensitivity.

References

1 Bahdanau, D. (2014). Neural machine translation by jointly learning to align and translate. arXiv preprint arXiv:1409.0473.

2 Vaswani, A., Shazeer, N., Parmar, N., Uszkoreit, J., Jones, L., Gomez, A.N., Kaiser, Ł., & Polosukhin, I. (2017). Attention is all you need. In I. Guyon, U. Von Luxburg, S. Bengio, H. Wallach, R. Fergus, S. Vishwanathan, & R. Garnett (Eds.), *Advances in neural information processing systems*, vol. 30. Curran Associates, Inc.

3 Devlin, J., Chang, M. W., Lee, K., & Toutanova, K. (2019). BERT: Pre-training of deep bidirectional transformers for language understanding. In Proceedings of the 2019 Conference of the North American Chapter of the Association for Computational Linguistics: Human Language Technologies, Volume 1 (Long and Short Papers), Minneapolis, USA, (pp. 4171–4186).

4 Wang, Y., Huang, M., Zhu, X., & Zhao, L. (2016). Attention-based LSTM for aspect-level sentiment classification. In Proceedings of the 2016 Conference on Empirical Methods in Natural Language Processing, Austin, USA, (pp. 606–615).

5 Yang, Z., Yang, D., Dyer, C., He, X., Smola, A., & Hovy, E. (2016). Hierarchical attention networks for document classification. In Proceedings of the 2016 Conference of the North American Chapter of the Association for Computational Linguistics: Human Language Technologies, San Diego, USA, (pp. 1480–1489).

6 Veličković, P., Cucurull, G., Casanova, A., Romero, A., Liò, P., & Bengio, Y. (2018). Graph attention networks. In International Conference on Learning Representations. Vancouver, Canada.

7 Zadeh, A., Chen, M., Poria, S., Cambria, E., & Morency, L. P. (2017). Tensor fusion network for multimodal sentiment analysis. In Proceedings of the 2017 Conference on Empirical Methods in Natural Language Processing, Copenhagen, Denmark, (pp. 1103–1114).

8 Liu, Y., Ott, M., Goyal, N., Du, J., Joshi, M., Chen, D., Levy, O., Lewis, M., Zettlemoyer, L., & Stoyanov, V. (2019). RoBERTa: A robustly optimized BERT pretraining approach. arXiv preprint arXiv:1907.11692.

9 Nguyen, H. T., & Le Nguyen, M. (2018). Effective attention networks for aspect-level sentiment classification. In 10th International Conference on Knowledge and Systems Engineering (KSE), Ho Chi Minh City, Vietnam, (pp. 25–30). IEEE.

10 Kim, W., Son, B., & Kim, I. (2021). ViLT: Vision-and-language transformer without convolution or region supervision. In International Conference on Machine Learning, Virtual, (pp. 5583–5594). PMLR.

11 Beltagy, I., Peters, M. E., & Cohan, A. (2020). Longformer: The long-document transformer. arXiv preprint arXiv:2004.05150.

12 Zaheer, M., Guruganesh, G., Dubey, K. A., Ainslie, J., Alberti, C., Ontanon, S., Pham, P., Ravula, A., Wang, Q., Yang, L., & Ahmed, A. (2020). Big Bird: Transformers for longer sequences. *Advances in Neural Information Processing Systems*, 33, 17283–17297.

13 Jain, S., & Wallace, B. C. (2019). Attention is not explanation. arXiv preprint arXiv:1902.10186.

14 Raffel, C., Shazeer, N., Roberts, A., Lee, K., Narang, S., Matena, M., Zhou, Y., Li, W., & Liu, P. J. (2020). Exploring the limits of transfer learning with a unified text-to-text transformer. *Journal of Machine Learning Research*, 21(140), 1–67.

15 He, P., Liu, X., Gao, J., & Chen, W. (2020). DeBERTa: Decoding-enhanced BERT with disentangled attention. arXiv preprint arXiv:2006.03654.

16 Yu, W., Xu, H., Yuan, Z., & Wu, J. (2021). Learning modality-specific representations with self-supervised multi-task learning for multimodal sentiment analysis. *Proceedings of the AAAI Conference on Artificial Intelligence*, 35(12), 10790–10797.

17 Tsai, Y. H. H., Bai, S., Liang, P. P., Kolter, J. Z., Morency, L. P., & Salakhutdinov, R. (2019). Multimodal transformer for unaligned multimodal language sequences. In Proceedings of the 57th Annual Meeting of the Association for Computational Linguistics, Florence, Italy, (p. 6558).

18 Katharopoulos, A., Vyas, A., Pappas, N., & Fleuret, F. (2020). Transformers are RNNs: Fast autoregressive transformers with linear attention. In International Conference on Machine Learning, Virtual, (pp. 5156–5165). PMLR.

19 Shao, B., Gong, Y., Qi, W., Cao, G., Ji, J., & Lin, X. (2020). Graph-based transformer with cross-candidate verification for semantic parsing. *Proceedings of the AAAI Conference on Artificial Intelligence*, 34(5), 8807–8814.

20 Pontiki, M., Galanis, D., Papageorgiou, H., Androutsopoulos, I., Manandhar, S., Al-Smadi, M., Al-Ayyoub, M., Zhao, Y., Qin, B., De Clercq, O., & Hoste, V. (2016). Semeval-2016 task 5: Aspect based sentiment analysis. In International Workshop on Semantic Evaluation, San Diego, USA, (pp. 19–30).

7

Advanced Technologies and Future Trends

The field of sentiment analysis is undergoing a paradigm shift driven by large language models (LLMs). With the emergence of advanced models like BERT and GPT, we have moved beyond traditional lexical statistics and feature engineering approaches, entering a new era of deep contextual understanding and latent semantic processing. These models not only significantly improve sentiment classification accuracy but, more importantly, are redefining the boundaries of sentiment analysis tasks and their practical applications.

This chapter systematically explores the latest advancements in technological transformation. First, we will analyze the pivotal role of LLMs in sentiment analysis, demonstrating how their pretraining and fine-tuning mechanisms enable deeper semantic understanding. Second, we will examine innovative applications of generative artificial intelligence (AI) in sentiment analysis, highlighting breakthroughs in data augmentation and model interpretability. Regarding cross-linguistic and cross-cultural analysis, the chapter delves into current challenges such as linguistic differences and cultural biases, while introducing cutting-edge solutions and technical approaches.

Of particular note is that with the rapid advancement of technology, sentiment analysis is confronting unprecedented ethical challenges. Issues such as data privacy protection, algorithmic fairness, and model transparency have become increasingly prominent, necessitating the establishment of corresponding governance frameworks alongside technological progress. Moreover, emerging fields like real-time sentiment analysis and multimodal fusion demonstrate tremendous potential for development.

7.1 The Role of LLMs: From BERT to GPT

7.1.1 Introduction: Paradigm Shift from Traditional Models to LLMs

Traditional models exhibit fundamental limitations in three key aspects. First, they heavily rely on large-scale, high-quality labeled data. Both support vector machines (SVMs) and recurrent neural networks (RNNs) require collecting massive datasets for specific domains (e.g., movie reviews and product evaluations), a process that is costly and inflexible. Second, their contextual understanding remains limited. While RNNs can process sequences, they struggle with long-distance dependencies. Convolutional neural networks (CNNs) excel at capturing local features but fail to grasp global semantic coherence. This makes them ineffective at handling complex linguistic phenomena like irony, double negation, or context-dependent implicit emotions (e.g., "This phone is 'so fast' I don't have time to charge"). Essentially, these models operate more like pattern recognition systems than true semantic interpreters.

The emergence of LLMs [1] was specifically designed to address these limitations, with their core driving force being the "pretraining and fine-tuning" paradigm. This paradigm divides model training into two distinct yet closely interconnected phases:

During the pretraining phase, the model learns universal language patterns from massive text data to build foundational linguistic capabilities. In the fine-tuning phase, it undergoes targeted adjustments using limited task-specific data to rapidly adapt to specific tasks. This approach maintains a deep understanding of language structures while enabling efficient task transfer, effectively addressing the limitations of traditional methods that rely on large-scale labeled data and limited contextual comprehension.

This paradigm shift has led to a revolutionary breakthrough, with three key points:

Deep Contextual Understanding: Transformer-based LLMs like BERT [2] leverage self-attention mechanisms to simultaneously evaluate relationships among all words in a sentence, enabling precise capture of long-range semantic dependencies and complex linguistic structures. This capability allows the model to accurately interpret the negative connotation of "too light" in a sentence such as "For a camera, it's too light" within specific contextual contexts.

The Groundbreaking Zero-shot and Few-shot Learning Capabilities: This is the defining feature that distinguishes LLMs from traditional models. Through sophisticated prompt engineering, LLMs can perform sentiment analysis tasks directly without any task-specific labeled data (zero-shot) or with only minimal examples (few-shot). For instance, when given the instruction: "Please determine the sentiment polarity of the following review: 'The plot twist in this movie caught me off guard.'" The model can leverage its pretrained knowledge to make inferences and judgments. This capability unlocks new possibilities for rapid deployment in new domains and low-resource language scenarios.

In summary, the evolution from traditional models to LLMs marks a paradigm shift from "task-specific, data-driven" pattern matching to "general-purpose, knowledge-driven" semantic understanding. LLMs have not only significantly elevated the technical ceiling of sentiment analysis but, more importantly, redefined human-computer interaction. By transforming this once highly specialized task into a flexible tool that can be guided and controlled through natural language, they have created a lasting impact across the entire field.

7.1.2 Transformer Architecture and Self-attention Mechanism Essentials

As the cornerstone of LLMs, the Transformer model has revolutionized the technical paradigm of natural language processing. Its core design abandons traditional RNN and CNN architectures, instead relying entirely on self-attention mechanisms [3, 4] to construct a powerful encoder-decoder architecture. This framework not only serves as the blueprint for encoder models like BERT and decoder models like GPT but also provides a fundamental understanding of how LLMs operate (Figure 7.1).

Attentional Mechanism: capturing the key to deep emotional dependence.

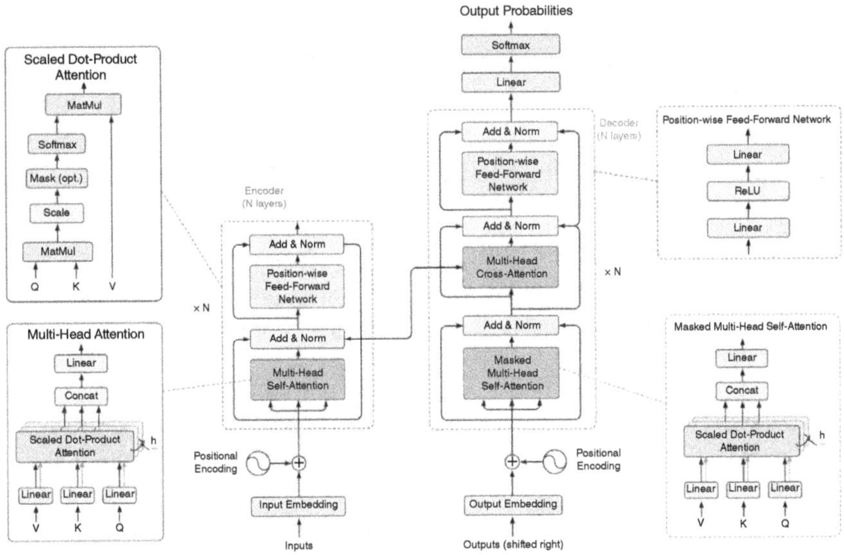

Figure 7.1 Transformer architecture diagram.

In sentiment analysis, a sentence's emotional tendency is not determined by isolated emotional words, but rather by complex interactions between lexical elements and their long-distance modifying relationships. The core concept of self-attention mechanisms lies in granting each word in a sequence the ability to "engage in dialogue" with all other words within the sequence. This enables dynamic calculation of each word's importance based on global contextual information.

Unlike traditional RNNs, which require the gradual transmission of hidden states (where information decays or is forgotten as distance increases), the self-attention mechanism inherently possesses a global perspective.

One-step Direct Connection: When processing the representation of a "topic," it doesn't require sequential processing through "I," "like," "this," "film," "of," and "profound" as in RNNs to capture the "profound" information. In the self-attention layer, "topic" and "profound" are directly connected regardless of the number of words separating them. This mechanism completely resolves the gradient vanishing or information bottleneck issues in long-distance dependencies.

Dynamic Focus: The weights of self-attention are dynamically calculated. In different contexts, the same word may focus on different neighbors. For example, in the sentence "Although the special effects are terrible, the film's profound theme saves it," when processing "theme," the model highly emphasizes "profound" and "saves" while downplaying the impact of "terrible."

The attention mechanism empowers the model to comprehend sentence-level semantic structures through its global, dynamic, and context-dependent interactions. This enables the model to not merely "see" words but to "read" the intricate web of relationships between them—precisely the key to accurately decoding complex human emotional expressions.

7.1.3 BERT and Its Variants: Applications of Deep Bidirectional Contextual Understanding

The core breakthrough of the BERT model lies in its achievement of deep bidirectional language representation through unique pretraining tasks. Unlike previous approaches based on unidirectional language models, BERT utilizes the Transformer encoder architecture and is pretrained via two key tasks: masked language modeling (MLM) and next sentence prediction (NSP).

In the MLM task, 15% of the tokens in the input sequence are randomly masked, and the model is required to predict the original masked words based on all the unmasked context. This design forces the model to move beyond unidirectional context and instead integrate the full contextual information from both the left and right sides of the target word, enabling it to grasp the precise meaning of words in specific contexts. To mitigate the inconsistency between the "[MASK]" token used during pretraining and its absence in downstream tasks, BERT does not always replace masked words with the special token. Instead, it sometimes replaces them with random words or leaves them unchanged, which enhances the robustness of the model's representations.

Simultaneously, the NSP task aims to help the model understand the relationships between sentences. During training, the model must determine whether two given sentences are consecutive in the original text. This task compels the model to learn logical and coherent connections between sentences, such as identifying contrast, cause-and-effect, or parallel relationships.

Through the joint training of MLM and NSP, BERT [5] not only masters fine-grained differences at the lexical and syntactic levels but also builds an understanding of sentence-level semantics and discourse logic. This comprehensive foundation in language understanding allows BERT to far surpass previous models in tasks such as sentiment analysis, which require insight into implicit contextual meanings and complex linguistic phenomena. Essentially, BERT learns a universal, deep language representation model from massive amounts of data and can be easily fine-tuned to adapt to various downstream tasks.

BERT's bidirectional encoding capability [6] enables it to capture contextual information from both sides of the target vocabulary simultaneously. When analyzing expressions like "so good it's unbelievable" and "so bad it's unbelievable," the model establishes strong associations between the degree adverb "unbelievable" and its modifying core adjectives "good" or "bad" through self-attention mechanisms. This allows it to accurately determine that the former conveys extreme praise while the latter expresses strong criticism. This global contextual understanding mechanism enables BERT to transcend local semantic limitations, precisely identify emotional polarity based on complete context, and significantly improve accuracy in judging complex emotional expressions.

Fine-tuning the pretrained BERT model is a critical process that efficiently transfers its extensive general language knowledge to specific tasks. This process does not involve training a new model from scratch but rather performs a "precision refinement" and "directional guidance" based on the powerful language representations already formed by BERT, using a relatively small amount of task-specific labeled data. The core idea is to leverage the general language patterns acquired during pretraining (such as grammar and common semantic relationships) and, through fine-tuning, enable the model to learn how to apply these patterns to specific scenarios (such as determining the sentiment tendency of a review).

Specifically, for sentiment classification tasks, a brand-new, randomly initialized classifier (typically a simple fully connected layer) is added on top of the final output layer of the BERT model (i.e., the output vector corresponding to the [CLS] token). After processing by the self-attention mechanism, the vector of this [CLS] token is considered to encapsulate aggregated semantic information of the entire input sequence. Subsequently, using review data labeled with positive, negative, or neutral sentiments, the entire model (including both BERT itself and the newly added classifier) is trained end-to-end with a relatively low learning rate.

At this stage, the model parameters undergo subtle adjustments: the lower-layer parameters of BERT may change minimally, primarily learning high-level feature combinations relevant to the task, while the top-layer parameters and the classifier undergo more significant changes to learn how to accurately map the information in the [CLS] vector to specific sentiment categories.

For more fine-grained tasks such as aspect-level sentiment analysis, the fine-tuning strategy differs. In this case, instead of relying solely on the [CLS] token, the output vectors corresponding to each word in the sequence are utilized. For example, in the sentence "The restaurant's ambiance was great, but the service was too slow," to determine the sentiment toward the aspect term "service," the output vector corresponding to that word is extracted and fed into a classifier. Similarly, through end-to-end fine-tuning, the model learns to focus more on the modifier "too slow" to the right of "service" and downplays the influence of "great" on the left when encoding the word "service," thereby accurately outputting a negative sentiment judgment specific to that aspect.

In summary, fine-tuning acts like an efficient "recalibration" process. It fully leverages the bidirectional understanding capabilities and world knowledge acquired during BERT's pretraining, requiring only a small amount of data and computational resources to transform its powerful general potential into exceptional performance on specific sentiment analysis tasks.

Following the groundbreaking work of BERT, researchers quickly proposed various improved variants [7, 8] aimed at enhancing its performance, efficiency, or both. Among them, RoBERTa, ALBERT, and DistilBERT represent three distinct directions of development, whose core advantages, parameter scales and application scenarios are systematically compared in Table 7.1.

RoBERTa [9] can be seen as a "more robust" BERT. It does not introduce fundamental architectural changes but instead unleashes the full potential of the BERT architecture through more refined training strategies. Key improvements include: removing the NSP task, which was considered potentially ineffective or even harmful; and using larger batch sizes, training on larger datasets with dynamic masking for longer periods. These optimizations enabled RoBERTa to significantly surpass the original BERT on multiple natural language understanding benchmarks, establishing the performance ceiling achievable with "more data, longer training, and better strategies," while maintaining computational cost and model size comparable to BERT.

In contrast to RoBERTa's pursuit of ultimate performance, ALBERT [10] focuses primarily on parameter efficiency. It drastically reduces the number of

Table 7.1 Comparison of BERT and its major variant models.

Model Name	Core Features	Parameter Quantity (Base Version)	Key Advantages
BERT	Transformer encoder with bidirectional attention; MLM and NSP pretraining	110 M	Strong bidirectional contextual understanding; high generalization ability of pretraining and fine-tuning
RoBERTa	Remove NSP and keep only MLM; dynamic masking; increase data volume	110 M	The training strategy is efficient, delivering better performance than BERT with the same parameters
ALBERT	Cross-layer parameter sharing; SOP replaces NSP; word embedding matrix factorization	12 M (BERT only 1/9)	The parameter count drops sharply; the training inference speed is fast; the generalization is strong
DistilBERT	Knowledge distillation reduces BERT size while retaining 70% of parameters, with cosine loss optimization	77 M (BERT 70%)	Reasoning speed increased by 60%; VRAM decreased by 40%; performance loss is minimal

model parameters through two key techniques: first, factorizing the word embedding matrix by decomposing the large vocabulary projection matrix into two smaller matrices, thereby addressing the issue of excessive parameters occupied by word embeddings in BERT; second, cross-layer parameter sharing, where all Transformer encoder layers share the same set of parameters, greatly reducing the total parameter count. Although ALBERT has far fewer parameters than BERT, by maintaining or even increasing the hidden layer dimension, its performance on various tasks remains comparable to BERT, even surpassing it after longer training steps, achieving significant memory efficiency while preserving performance.

DistilBERT, on the other hand, takes a distinctly different path of "model compression," aiming to create a smaller and faster model with minimal performance loss. It employs knowledge distillation, where a pretrained large BERT model (the "teacher model") guides the training of a smaller model (the "student model"). The student model's learning objective is not only to fit the original data but also to mimic the output probability distribution generated by the teacher model. Through this approach, DistilBERT captures the rich knowledge embedded in the teacher model, ultimately achieving a 40% reduction in model size, a 60% increase in inference speed, while retaining 97% of the original BERT's performance, making it an ideal choice for deployment in resource-constrained environments.

In summary, these variants reflect different trade-offs in the development of NLP models: RoBERTa represents the achievements in the pursuit of ultimate performance regardless of cost; ALBERT finds an elegant balance between parameter efficiency and model performance; while DistilBERT vividly demonstrates how sacrificing a small amount of performance can yield significant efficiency gains for practical application scenarios.

7.1.4 GPT Series and Generative Sentiment Analysis

The GPT series models (from GPT-1 to GPT-4) are fundamentally based on their autoregressive generation paradigm, which is rooted in the pure decoder Transformer architecture. Unlike BERT, which treats the entire sentence as a bidirectional encoder, GPT strictly follows a left-to-right unidirectional sequence during both training and generation. During pretraining, its task is to predict the next most likely word based on all preceding words. This "next-word prediction" objective enables GPT to develop robust language generation capabilities.

In contrast, BERT [11], as a bidirectional encoder, leverages the MLM to utilize the complete context on both sides of the target word during pretraining, thereby achieving a deep understanding of sentence-level structures. This bidirectional architecture enables it to excel in tasks requiring holistic semantic comprehension, such as sentiment analysis and text classification.

The fundamental differences between BERT and GPT lead to distinct application domains: BERT functions as a scholarly "analyst" excelling in deep text analysis and classification, while GPT operates as a creative "writer" adept at generating content through prompts. In sentiment analysis practice, this distinction manifests as follows: BERT can directly encode sentences into holistic vectors for sentiment classification through fine-tuning, whereas GPT requires designing prompts (e.g., "Classify the sentiment of the following comment: 'This movie is fantastic!' → Sentiment: Positive") to guide it in generating specific label words (e.g., "Positive") for classification tasks.

In the realm of sentiment analysis, GPT serves as a meticulous "commentary analyst." Unlike traditional classification models that merely assign "positive" or "negative" labels, GPT can conduct in-depth text analysis through instructions like "Analyze the following review, identify its emotional orientation, and list key supporting reasons." For instance, when processing the review "The restaurant boasts an elegant ambiance but the service is unbearably slow," GPT not only determines a "mixed sentiment" or "overall negative" evaluation, but also generates contextual explanations: "This review expresses complex emotions. While the 'elegant ambiance' represents positive elements, the predominant negative factor—'service being unbearably slow'—outweighs environmental advantages in shaping the customer experience." This approach provides businesses with actionable insights that far surpass the value of simplistic labels.

Second, GPT excels at crafting nuanced emotional rewriting. When given tasks like "Rewrite the positive review below as a negative one while preserving its key factual elements," it demonstrates remarkable control over linguistic emotional nuances.

Prompt engineering is pivotal for activating GPT's sentiment analysis capabilities. By crafting precise instructions (e.g., "Classify sentiment: positive/negative/neutral"), we can steer the model's generative power toward classification tasks. Well-crafted prompts define task boundaries, control output formats, and enable rapid adaptation to new domains through few-shot examples, ultimately achieving efficient and accurate sentiment analysis without additional training.

7.1.5 Challenges and Limitations of LLMs

While LLMs demonstrate exceptional performance in sentiment analysis tasks, they still face several severe challenges during practical deployment and application.

First, computational resource consumption poses a major obstacle. Models with billions of parameters require enormous memory bandwidth and computing power for inference, leading to three specific issues: (1) relatively high inference latency, which makes it difficult to meet the demands of real-time analysis; (2) high deployment costs, as dedicated GPU server clusters are necessary; and (3) substantial energy consumption, which is inconsistent with the development concept of green computing. These limitations are particularly prominent in online application scenarios that need to handle a large number of concurrent requests.

Second, the issue of model bias remains an unresolved problem. The training data for LLMs is mainly sourced from the internet, and such data inherently contains various biases and stereotypes existing in human society. In the specific application of sentiment analysis, this bias may manifest in the following ways: discrepancies in recognition accuracy for specific dialects or regional expressions; differential treatment of language usage among different social groups; and misunderstandings of emotional expression styles in minority cultural contexts. For instance, models may exhibit systematic misjudgments of informal writing styles or the linguistic characteristics of specific communities. When amplified, such biases can pose hidden risks to social equity.

Third, result instability is another concern worthy of attention. LLMs are highly sensitive to prompt engineering—minor changes in prompts, including wording, the order of examples, and even the use of punctuation marks—can lead to significantly different analysis results. This instability presents enormous challenges to quality control in production environments. Meanwhile, models exhibit obvious inconsistencies when handling complex linguistic phenomena: they may provide contradictory judgments for texts that convey the same emotion but use different expressions; and their recognition accuracy fluctuates drastically when processing texts containing rhetorical devices such as irony and metaphor.

Addressing these challenges requires a multifaceted approach: reducing resource consumption through model compression and optimization technologies; enhancing model fairness via data cleaning and debiasing algorithms; and improving result stability by developing standardized prompt frameworks and calibration techniques. Only when substantial progress is made in these areas can the application of LLMs in sentiment analysis truly move toward maturity.

7.2 Application of Generative AI in Sentiment Analysis

7.2.1 Synthetic Data Generation and Data Augmentation

In the practical application of sentiment analysis, the scarcity of high-quality annotated data has become a key bottleneck restricting model performance, which is particularly prominent in specific domains and fine-grained tasks.

The challenges of domain adaptation are particularly evident in specialized fields such as finance, healthcare, and legal professions. These domains not only contain extensive technical terminology and specific expressions but also often involve more nuanced and complex emotional communication. For instance, in finance, professional terms like "liquidity crunch" and "valuation correction" carry profound negative connotations, yet general sentiment analysis models struggle to accurately identify such emotional tendencies due to the lack of domain-specific labeled data. Similarly, in healthcare, patient descriptions of "drug tolerance" or "mild adverse reactions" require professional expertise to properly interpret their emotional undertones.

The challenges in fine-grained analysis are particularly evident in tasks such as implicit sentiment recognition and aspect-level sentiment analysis [12]. Traditional sentiment analysis models primarily rely on explicit sentiment lexicons, yet often struggle with implicit expressions that depend on contextual cues and common sense. In aspect-level sentiment analysis, the data scarcity issue becomes even more complex, as it requires fine-grained labeling of sentiment tendencies across different aspects within the same text. For instance, comments like "The camera quality is excellent, but the battery life is insufficient" demand separate sentiment labeling for both "image quality" and "battery life" aspects.

In the face of these data challenges, generative AI offers innovative solutions. Through carefully designed prompt engineering, LLMs can generate high-quality synthetic data, effectively expanding training samples for specific domains and fine-grained tasks. This approach not only maintains domain expertise but also ensures consistent labeling, opening up new possibilities for improving the performance of sentiment analysis models in scenarios with scarce data.

Generative AI effectively addresses data scarcity in sentiment analysis through systematic data generation processes, whose complete technical flow is illustrated in Figure 7.2. The process begins with carefully designed prompts that explicitly define text themes, emotional polarity, language style, and output formats to ensure the synthesized data's goal-oriented nature. During the generation and filtering phase, preset prompts are used to batch-produce candidate texts, followed by rigorous quality control including automated rule checks and manual sampling verification to eliminate low-quality or mislabeled samples, ensuring data accuracy and diversity. Ultimately, the filtered high-quality synthetic data is blended with the original labeled data in proportion to form an augmented training set. This strategy significantly enhances the generalization ability and robustness of sentiment analysis models in specific domains and fine-grained tasks, while effectively mitigating overfitting issues caused by insufficient data.

Enhancing training datasets through high-quality synthetic data generation [13] significantly improves model performance and generalization capabilities in low-resource scenarios. This approach demonstrates effectiveness in three key aspects: first, synthetic data directly expands the scale and diversity of training samples, enabling models to learn richer linguistic patterns and emotional features while effectively mitigating overfitting caused by data scarcity. Second, precise control over generated content allows targeted supplementation of rare categories or domain-specific samples, addressing data distribution imbalances and enhancing models' ability to recognize edge cases. Most importantly, this method exposes

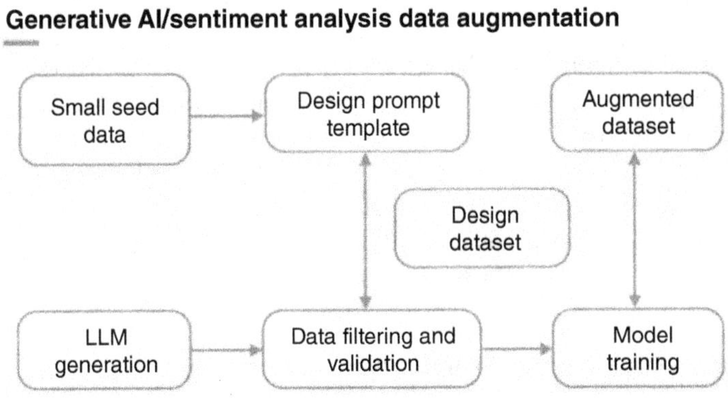

Figure 7.2 Workflow diagram of generative AI for sentiment analysis data augmentation.

models to broader linguistic variations and contextual scenarios during training, thereby improving their adaptability to unseen data and generalization capabilities, ultimately ensuring more robust performance in practical applications.

7.2.2 Enhancing Model Robustness and Explainability

Generative AI can efficiently produce adversarial samples by applying subtle yet carefully designed perturbations to original texts. These samples maintain the original syntax and semantics while introducing specific adverbs, synonym substitutions, or structural adjustments to generate text that appears indistinguishable to humans but significantly disrupts model predictions. For instance, in sentiment analysis tasks, generative models can transform statements like "This camera has excellent image quality" into potentially misleading expressions such as "It must be said that this camera's image quality is truly outstanding." Such adversarial samples expose decision blind spots in the original model. When these carefully crafted samples are incorporated into training datasets, the model is compelled to learn fundamental emotional characteristics rather than superficial lexical associations. This approach significantly enhances its discriminative robustness in handling complex linguistic phenomena and improves resistance to real-world noise data and malicious attacks.

The use of generative AI to provide interpretable reports for sentiment analysis models represents a significant advancement in model transparency. When traditional models produce classification results, we can input both the original text and prediction results into generative models. By designing prompts such as "Please analyze the following review, explain why its sentiment is judged as negative, and list key evidence," we can trigger the model's explanatory generation capability. Through analyzing emotional cues, contextual relationships, and semantic focus in the text, generative models can produce structured analyses like "The main reasons for judging this review as negative are: (1) explicitly pointing out the functional flaw of 'extremely poor battery life'; (2) using strong negative emotion words like 'disappointing'; (3) generating negative evaluations by comparing expectations with reality." This approach not only transforms the decision-making process of black-box models into intuitive natural language descriptions but also helps developers validate the rationality of model decision logic. Simultaneously, it provides end-users with more persuasive judgment bases, effectively building a cognitive bridge between machine learning models and human understanding.

7.2.3 Potential Risks and Future Exploration

While synthetic data effectively alleviates data scarcity issues, its application carries significant risks. The foremost risk lies in the entrenchment and amplification of biases: When learning from raw data, generative models inevitably absorb existing sociocultural biases and stereotypes. When generating new samples based on these biased datasets, the models may further reinforce and propagate these biases, resulting in systematic distortions in gender, racial, or cultural dimensions. Another critical risk is distributional shift—generative models may produce "falsified" data patterns that appear plausible but deviate from real-world distributions. Once such patterns infiltrate the training set, the model learns incorrect feature associations, leading to performance degradation in real-world applications.

The application of generative AI [14] in sentiment analysis is transitioning from static analysis to dynamic interaction and creative generation. At the task level, its potential first manifests in emotional dialogue simulation: Through carefully crafted prompts, generative AI can act as virtual users with specific emotional states or personality traits, engaging in multi-round dialogues with real systems. This capability enables enterprises to extensively test the responsiveness of customer service systems, psychological counseling robots, and similar applications when interacting with users experiencing emotions like anger, anxiety, or joy, providing rich data support for optimizing human-machine interaction experiences.

Furthermore, generative AI demonstrates unique value in emotional creative generation. It not only analyzes emotions but also actively creates specific emotional elements in creative texts like poetry, stories, and advertising copy based on instructions. For instance, in marketing, the model can generate a series of social media tweets for a brand using the emotional tones of "nostalgia" and "warmth." In game development, it can dynamically generate dialogues that match the emotional states of non-player characters (NPCs).

These advanced applications demonstrate the evolution of affective computing from a passive tool for understanding and categorization to an active emotional agent capable of expression, interaction, and creation. While challenges remain in emotional consistency, long-term memory, and deep comprehension, generative AI is undoubtedly reshaping the boundaries of how we use machines to understand and express human emotions.

7.3 Cross-language and Cross-cultural Sentiment Analysis

7.3.1 Definitions and Importance

Cross-lingual sentiment analysis utilizes linguistic knowledge or data from resource-rich source languages (e.g., English) to interpret the emotional tone of texts in resource-constrained target languages. The core challenge lies in structural differences across languages, including variations in grammar, vocabulary, and sentence patterns. Its primary objective is to address the lack of high-quality annotated data in most of the thousands of languages worldwide, enabling technology transfer from high-resource to low-resource languages. For instance, applying a model trained on English movie reviews to directly analyze the sentiment in French or Chinese movie reviews exemplifies cross-lingual sentiment analysis.

Cross-cultural sentiment analysis examines how people from different cultural backgrounds express emotions differently within the same language. The core challenge lies in cultural context and value differences. Even when using the same language, people from different cultural backgrounds may interpret the same words, emojis, or topics with completely different emotional meanings.

In international brand reputation management, cross-lingual sentiment analysis enables companies to break down language barriers and achieve comprehensive monitoring of global social media, news websites, and review platforms. A brand can instantly understand how it is being discussed in markets such as China, Japan, Brazil, or Arabic-speaking regions, allowing it to promptly detect and respond to potential PR crises. Meanwhile, cross-cultural analysis provides deeper insights: for example, while North American users might express satisfaction with "awesome!," Chinese users may use "我认为非常好" ("I think it's good"), which carries a more reserved emotional intensity. Failure to understand such cultural nuances could lead brands to misinterpret user sentiment, resulting in missed opportunities or overreactions.

In global market research, these two analytical approaches together offer companies unprecedented macro-level perspectives and micro-level insights. Cross-lingual analysis can consolidate feedback on a new product from users across multiple countries, quickly identifying common strengths (e.g., "battery life") and weaknesses (e.g., "fragile screen"). Cross-cultural analysis, on the other hand, reveals differences in product acceptance across cultural contexts. For instance, a minimalist product design might be praised as "sleek and premium" in Western markets, while in some emerging markets, it could be perceived as "plain and lacking distinctive features." Such insights are indispensable for developing effective localized marketing and product strategies.

The social value of this technology in fostering cross-cultural communication is equally significant. For government agencies, international organizations, and non-profits, cross-lingual sentiment analysis helps gauge global public sentiment toward specific policies or social events. More importantly, cross-cultural analysis can uncover patterns and underlying reasons for different groups' emotional reactions to the same event, identifying potential misunderstandings and conflict points. This provides data-driven support for building a more harmonious and mutually understanding global dialogue environment.

In summary, cross-lingual and cross-cultural sentiment analysis have elevated global corporate operations and international communication from "relying on educated guesses" to a new era of "understanding through data." They are not only powerful tools for enhancing business competitiveness but also vital bridges connecting diverse linguistic and cultural worlds, fostering global collaboration.

7.3.2 Key Challenges: Language and Cultural Barriers

In a globalized context, cross-lingual sentiment analysis faces the formidable challenge of dual barriers—linguistic and cultural. These challenges exist not only at the technical level but are deeply rooted in the intrinsic characteristics of human language and culture, requiring in-depth analysis from multiple dimensions, with representative cross-cultural emotional expression discrepancies summarized in Table 7.2.

Table 7.2 Cross-cultural differences in emotional expression.

Phrase/Symbol	East Asian Culture	North American Culture	Middle Eastern Culture
Smile	May convey awkwardness, compliance, or politeness, not just pleasure	It is usually equivalent to positive emotions, which are expressions of friendliness and happiness	It generally represents positive emotions, but the meaning may be more complex than in North America, and may also contain a certain element of humility
Eye contact	Prolonged eye contact may be seen as rude or provocative, and appropriate eye contact is a sign of respect, but short	Long eye contact is seen as a sign of confidence, focus, and respect for the other person	A long stare is a sign of respect, showing that you care about the other person
Thumb-up gesture	Express agreement, approval, or encouragement	Expresses agreement or approval	In some Middle Eastern countries, this gesture may have an insulting meaning
White	Related to funerals, representing grief and mourning	Symbolizes purity, happiness, and holiness	In some Middle Eastern countries, white has a meaning of purity and sanctity, but in some contexts it may also be associated with mourning

(Continued)

Table 7.2 (Continued)

Phrase/Symbol	East Asian Culture	North American Culture	Middle Eastern Culture
Red	Symbolizes joy, good luck, and enthusiasm	It is usually associated with love, passion, and energy, but in some cases, it can also mean danger and anger	Red is considered unlucky in Nigeria and Germany, but in countries like Denmark, Romania, and Argentina, it's considered a lucky color

1. Linguistic Barriers

   First, the linguistic barrier manifests in the incommensurability at the lexical level. Emotion words often lack perfect equivalents across languages, forming unique affective semantic fields. For example, the Chinese term "怅然" blends a dual sentiment of loss and nostalgia, while the Russian word "тоска" conveys a kind of spiritual anguish that is difficult to alleviate—nuances that are hard to capture precisely in English. Such lexical gaps complicate feature extraction in sentiment analysis, making it difficult for models to accurately capture subtle emotional distinctions in specific languages.

   Grammar also poses an obstacle by shaping how emotions are expressed. Word order rules in different languages directly influence the organization of emotional information. For instance, the German verb-second rule and frame structures often require readers to wait until the end of a sentence to determine its sentiment. Similarly, Japanese expresses emotional tone through sentence-final particles, a structure starkly different from the subject-verb-object pattern of English. These structural differences demand that sentiment analysis models adapt to the grammatical characteristics of each language, rather than simply applying architectures designed for English.

   Slang and idioms, being the most vivid carriers of emotion, also present some of the toughest comprehension challenges. From the Chinese internet catchphrase "YYDS" (short for "永恒的神," meaning "undisputed champion" or "eternal idol") to the Spanish expression "estar en la luna" (literally "to be on the moon," figuratively "to be absent-minded"), such phrases carry strong temporal and regional cultural connotations. Their meanings often extend far beyond literal interpretation, requiring models to possess deep cultural background knowledge for accurate understanding.

2. Cultural Barriers

   The existence of cultural barriers further complicates cross-cultural sentiment analysis [15]. Emotional expression varies significantly across cultures, particularly in terms of directness. East Asian cultures, for example, tend toward indirect and implicit expression—a phrase like "This proposal could use more consideration" may actually signal strong disapproval. In contrast, Western cultures often favor straightforward expression, as in the explicit statement, "This is completely unacceptable." Such differences necessitate that sentiment analysis models understand cultural context rather than relying solely on literal analysis.

Some culture-specific emotional concepts deepen this divide. Examples include the German "Schadenfreude" (malicious joy at another's misfortune) and the Portuguese "Saudade" (a profound, melancholic longing for something or someone that may never return). These emotion concepts, which lack direct equivalents in other languages, reflect unique emotional experiences shaped by specific cultural backgrounds. Accurately interpreting them requires models to grasp the underlying cultural psychology and philosophical foundations.

Cultural symbols and historical events can also evoke completely opposite emotional associations in different cultural contexts, representing one of the most challenging aspects of cross-cultural sentiment analysis. For instance, the dragon symbolizes authority and good fortune in Chinese culture but often represents evil in Western traditions. Similarly, while white wedding dresses signify purity in the West, in some Asian countries, the color white is associated with mourning. Such deep-seated cultural differences mean that the same symbol can trigger entirely opposite emotional reactions depending on the cultural setting.

3. Toward a Solution

Breaking through these barriers requires the construction of cognitive models capable of deeply integrating linguistic knowledge and cultural context. This means sentiment analysis systems must not only understand the surface meaning of language but also grasp the cultural logic and emotional expression norms behind it. Current research directions include building cross-cultural sentiment lexicons, developing culturally adaptive algorithms, and constructing training datasets that incorporate diverse cultural backgrounds. Only by placing cultural understanding at the core of sentiment analysis can we achieve accurate and fair cross-cultural sentiment analysis, providing reliable technical support for global digital communication.

7.3.3 Mainstream Technical Methods

The two mainstream technical frameworks for cross-lingual sentiment analysis are systematically compared in Figure 7.3, including their core logic, advantages and inherent limitations.

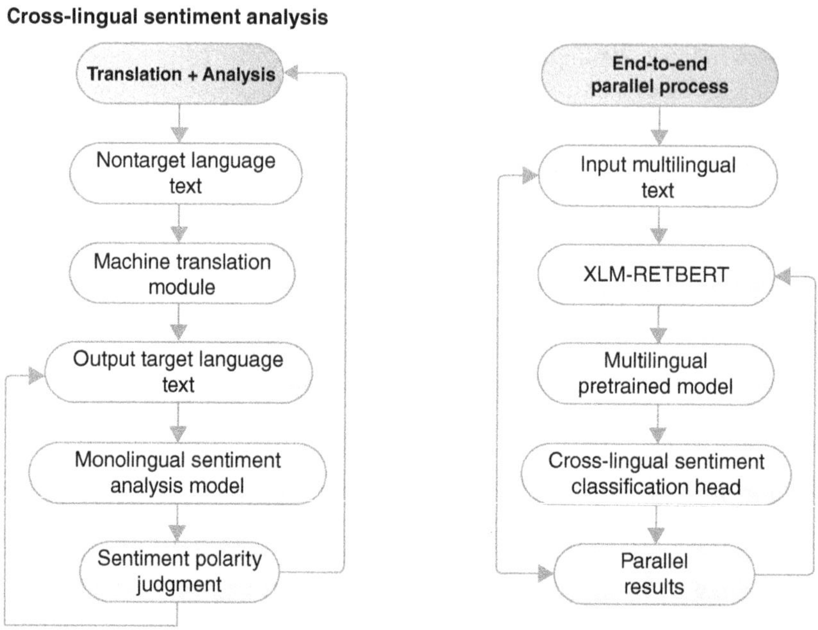

Figure 7.3 Comparison of two mainstream technical approaches for cross-language sentiment analysis.

1. Translation-based Approach
   The translation-based sequential approach is a relatively traditional and straightforward technical pathway in cross-lingual sentiment analysis [16]. This method adopts a step-by-step processing workflow: first, all nontarget language texts to be analyzed (such as Chinese, Japanese, or Arabic) are uniformly converted into the target language (usually English) via a machine translation system; then, the translated texts are input into a well-trained sentiment analysis model based on the target language for analysis; finally, sentiment judgment results are obtained. The core idea of this approach is to build a "language conversion bridge" through machine translation, unifying and simplifying sentiment analysis tasks across multiple languages into an analysis task for a single target language.

   The advantages of this method are mainly reflected in its technical simplicity and resource reusability. From the implementation perspective, developers do not need to build a separate sentiment analysis system for each language; instead, they can directly utilize existing high-quality machine translation engines (such as Google Translate, OpenAI Translator, etc.) and fully validated English sentiment analysis models (such as fine-tuned models based on BERT and RoBERTa). This strategy significantly lowers the technical threshold and development costs for multilingual support, making it particularly suitable for basic application scenarios that require rapid deployment. Meanwhile, since only a single-language sentiment analysis pipeline needs to be maintained, the system's maintenance costs and update complexity are also effectively controlled.

However, the fundamental flaw of this method lies in the fact that its performance is entirely dependent on the quality of machine translation. During the translation process, the emotional information in the text may be lost at multiple levels: at the lexical level, the imbalance of emotional words between different languages (for example, the Chinese word "窝心" can mean either "comforting" or "distressing") easily leads to misjudgment of emotional polarity; at the syntactic level, differences in language structures may alter emotional modification relationships—for instance, the subtle emotions expressed through sentence-final particles in Japanese often disappear completely when translated into English; at the cultural level, expressions rich in cultural characteristics (such as the Chinese internet slang "破防" [meaning "to be deeply moved or emotionally overwhelmed"] and the English slang "salt in the wound" [meaning "to make a bad situation worse"]) are most likely to lose their essential emotional connotations during cross-lingual conversion. In addition, issues such as semantic bias and context loss that may be introduced during translation will all be amplified into final sentiment judgment errors through a cascading effect.

Despite these limitations, the translation-based approach still has application value in specific scenarios: when the target language lacks sufficient labeled data to train a dedicated model, or when the emotional texts to be processed are relatively standardized and straightforward, this method can still provide a feasible solution. However, with the development of new technologies such as cross-lingual pretrained models, it is gradually being replaced by more advanced methods in scenarios with high accuracy requirements.

2. A Multi-language Pretraining Model-based Approach
These models (e.g., mBERT and XLM-RoBERTa) were originally designed for cross-lingual tasks. They undergo pretraining on large-scale mixed corpora encompassing hundreds of languages, such as MLM. Their core objective is to learn a shared, cross-lingual semantic representation space. Within this space, semantically similar sentences or words across languages (e.g., the Chinese "hao" and the English "good") share comparable vector representations, despite their different surface forms.

Zero-shot Cross-lingual Transfer: This application best demonstrates the method's advantages. Researchers first fine-tune multilingual models (e.g., XLM-RoBERTa) using abundant English sentiment-annotated data, enabling the model to map semantic representations from English sentences to sentiment labels. Subsequently, without requiring any annotated data in target languages (e.g., Swahili), the fine-tuned model is directly applied to analyze texts in that language. Since the model has already "seen" and understood the intrinsic connections between multiple languages during pretraining, it can effectively transfer the "sentiment concepts" learned in English to semantic representations of other languages, thereby achieving cross-lingual sentiment analysis.

Sample-efficient Learning: When target languages have limited labeled data (e.g., dozens to hundreds of samples), performance can be significantly improved. In this approach, the model is first fine-tuned on English data, then further fine-tuned using a small number of target language samples. This effectively enables the model to quickly adapt to local linguistic expressions at minimal cost, yielding more reliable and accurate analytical results compared to zero-shot transfer.

Multilingual pretraining models achieve more end-to-end and robust cross-lingual sentiment analysis through their inherent cross-lingual representation capabilities. By avoiding information loss during translation, they represent the future direction of technological development in this field. Meanwhile, translation-based approaches still hold practical value in scenarios requiring rapid verification where precision is not a top priority.

7.3.4 Future Research Directions

Building sentiment analysis models with genuine cultural awareness is an inevitable requirement for advancing AI technology to a higher level. From the perspective of technological evolution, current models trained on single-cultural datasets have already shown obvious performance bottlenecks. When processing texts in cross-cultural scenarios, the accuracy of these models often declines significantly. This limitation not only undermines the universal application of the technology but also restricts the practical value of sentiment analysis in globalized contexts. Therefore, breaking through cultural barriers has become a key breakthrough point for improving model performance.

From the perspective of social development, the lack of cultural awareness may lead to serious ethical issues in technology. In the digital space where diverse cultures coexist, if a sentiment analysis system fails to understand the expression habits and values of different cultural groups, it may produce systematic analytical biases. When applied in high-risk fields such as healthcare, judicial evaluation, and credit rating, such biases may result in unfair treatment of groups with specific cultural backgrounds. For instance, in mental health assessment, misclassifying normal emotional expressions in certain cultures as abnormal could lead to severe consequences.

From the perspective of commercial applications, the lack of cultural awareness will directly constrain enterprises' global development. In scenarios such as cross-border e-commerce, international marketing, and global customer service, accurately understanding the emotional needs of consumers from different cultural backgrounds has become a core factor in enhancing commercial competitiveness. A sentiment analysis system capable of perceiving cultural differences can help enterprises better grasp market dynamics and develop marketing strategies that align with local cultural characteristics, thereby gaining an advantage in global competition.

From the perspective of human-machine collaboration, sentiment analysis models with cultural awareness will open up new possibilities for human-machine interaction. In application scenarios such as virtual assistants, intelligent customer service, and online education, if the system can understand users' cultural backgrounds and expression habits, it can provide more personalized and appropriate services. This in-depth understanding helps establish more natural and harmonious human-machine relationships, enabling AI technology to better serve human society.

Therefore, developing culturally aware sentiment analysis is not merely a technical issue but also a crucial topic related to technological inclusiveness, social equity, and commercial value. This requires us to integrate a multicultural perspective into technological research and development, consider the characteristics of different cultural groups in model design, and focus on evaluating cultural adaptability during application deployment—ultimately achieving the coordinated development of technology and culture.

The integration of knowledge graphs with multilingual LLMs represents a pivotal approach for achieving cultural-aware sentiment analysis. Future research will focus on constructing cross-cultural knowledge graphs that incorporate cultural common sense, social norms, and symbolic semantics, while deeply integrating dynamic retrieval mechanisms with LLMs. When processing texts, the model can dynamically access relevant cultural context information for joint reasoning, enabling accurate interpretation of culturally specific emotional expressions. This technical framework not only addresses the cultural hallucination issues inherent in LLMs but also establishes context-based emotional understanding capabilities, laying the foundation for truly credible cross-cultural AI.

7.4 Future Development Direction

7.4.1 Real-time Sentiment Analysis: Opportunities and Technical Requirements

The value of real-time sentiment analysis lies in its ability to translate public sentiment into actionable strategic intelligence, providing organizations with unprecedented speed and insight into decision-making.

In brand public opinion crisis early warning, real-time sentiment analysis is like a 24/7 sentry. It can immediately identify and alert when negative comments are emerging on social media, news sites, or forums.

In real-time monitoring of financial market sentiment, it functions as a market pulse monitor. By analyzing the emotional trends in financial news, analyst reports, and social media discussions, it captures early emotional signals that influence market fluctuations. Traders and algorithms can swiftly make investment decisions based on public optimism or pessimism toward specific companies, policies, or economic events, thereby seizing the initiative in rapidly changing markets.

Although real-time sentiment analysis is of great value, it faces severe performance challenges in terms of technical implementation, and its core lies in the fact that the system must meet the demanding requirements of high speed, high concurrency, and high efficiency at the same time.

Low latency is the lifeblood of real-time systems. It requires the sentiment analysis model to complete a single reasoning in milliseconds, ensuring that the sentiment judgment is completed immediately after a social media post or a live broadcast bullet is generated. Otherwise, the analysis results will lose the value of early warning and immediate intervention.

High throughput is related to the system's processing capacity. When facing the massive information flow generated by the concurrent users of social media platforms, the system architecture must be able to process thousands of data streams in parallel, avoid analysis delays or system crashes caused by data accumulation, and ensure the comprehensiveness and continuity of public opinion monitoring.

To address these challenges, model lightweighting has emerged as a critical technical pathway. Directly deploying large pretrained models often fails to meet real-time requirements, necessitating a series of compression techniques to balance performance and efficiency. These include knowledge distillation, where a lightweight "student model" learns from a large "teacher model"; quantization techniques that reduce the numerical precision of model weights to minimize computational and storage costs; and pruning, which removes redundant weights or connections to create leaner, more efficient architectures. These technologies collectively aim to significantly enhance inference speed and reduce resource consumption while maintaining model accuracy, enabling deployment in resource-constrained edge environments or cloud services requiring rapid response.

In real-time sentiment analysis systems [17], the integration of stream processing frameworks with lightweight models forms the core technical architecture. The system begins with data acquisition, continuously collecting data streams from social media, news sources, and other channels. Stream processing frameworks (such as Apache Flink or Spark Streaming) act as the system's engine, handling high-speed data streams through preprocessing operations, including cleaning, deduplication, and windowing.

The preprocessed text data is distributed to the model service layer, which hosts lightweight sentiment analysis models optimized through techniques like knowledge distillation [18] and quantization. These models are compact and fast in inference, enabling sentiment judgment with millisecond-level latency. The stream processing framework concurrently schedules multiple model instances to handle high-concurrency requests, ensuring system throughput.

Ultimately, analytical outputs (including sentiment tags and confidence levels) are delivered in real time to monitoring dashboards or alert systems, enabling operations teams to instantly track public sentiment trends. This architecture achieves low-latency, high-throughput real-time data analysis through the efficient orchestration of stream processing frameworks and the rapid inference capabilities of lightweight models.

7.4.2 Ethical Considerations in Sentiment Analysis

The hidden long-term risks including social bias amplification and malicious misuse of sentiment analysis models are systematically summarized in Table 7.3. The process by which sentiment analysis models learn and amplify social biases from training data is a hidden yet far-reaching issue. The root cause lies in the fact that the network texts, reviews, and social media data used to train these models inherently contain various explicit and implicit biases present in human society.

The mechanism of bias acquisition and amplification primarily manifests in the following ways: when processing massive datasets, models statistically learn correlations between vocabulary and emotional labels. If training data frequently associates specific genders with certain occupations or traits (e.g., women being more often described as "emotional" while men are predominantly labeled as "leadership-oriented"), or if particular regions or accents are consistently paired with negative evaluations, these statistical patterns become internalized as the model's "worldview." More critically, during training, such recurring bias patterns are reinforced through their "statistical significance," causing systematic prediction biases when encountering relevant groups. This amplifies biases inherent in the original data.

Table 7.3 Main ethical risks and mitigation strategies of sentiment analysis.

Ethical Risk	Embody	Potential Mitigation Strategies
Data bias risk	Uneven coverage of training data with missing samples of minority groups Data contains discriminatory content that reinforces model bias Insufficient adaptation of cross-cultural emotional expressions	Conduct dataset auditing and supplement niche samples Use adversarial debiasing algorithm to reduce bias
Privacy risk	The data contains user names, consumption habits, and other privacy The sensitive data is not desensitized and is easy to be stolen and abused The privacy protection of cross-institutional collaboration is insufficient	Data anonymization/differential privacy desensitization Adopt federated learning to reduce data transmission
Algorithm opacity risk	The model becomes a "black box," resulting in no basis for decision-making The responsibility for model errors is unclear. Overreliance on the model and lack of manual review	Visualize decision logic with LIME/SHAP Establish accountability system and traceability process Implement manual review for high-risk scenarios
Technology abuse risk	Companies manipulate reviews to mislead consumers Malicious actors manipulate public opinion and spread rumors Model results are overinterpreted	Establish industry ethics norms and delineate usage boundaries Establish a model-based filing system Strengthen user education and alert to result errors
Emotion manipulation risk	Pushing single emotional content, exacerbating information cocoon Using fragile emotions to induce consumption Targeted communication content manipulation of cognition	Establish a content diversity push mechanism Review emotional marketing and prohibit malicious inducement Release technical guidelines

Sentiment analysis technology carries significant risks of malicious exploitation. In the business sector, companies may use this technology to implement differential pricing against consumers demonstrating strong purchasing intent or dissatisfaction, constituting price discrimination. In the job market, employers might analyze job seekers' social media histories to conduct unfair screening based on emotional characteristics. In the public sphere, malicious actors could leverage sentiment analysis to monitor public sentiment vulnerabilities in real-time, strategically disseminating disinformation and manipulating public opinion. More alarmingly, cybercriminals can automate the identification of emotionally vulnerable individuals online, enabling targeted emotional fraud and psychological manipulation. These potential abuses not only infringe on personal rights but may also undermine the foundation of social trust, urgently requiring the establishment of corresponding ethical guidelines and legal regulatory frameworks.

Explaining model decisions and establishing accountability mechanisms are key pillars to ensure the responsible development of sentiment analysis technologies.

The importance of decision explanation manifests in three key aspects. First, when a model classifies a review as negative, understanding the rationale behind this judgment is crucial—whether it's triggered by keyword patterns or contextual reasoning. Clear explanations help developers verify if the model's decisions are based on sound logic rather than bias. Second, in high-risk scenarios like recruitment screening and credit assessment, transparent decision-making forms the foundation for maintaining user trust, as affected individuals have the right to understand the basis of machine judgments. Most importantly, by analyzing decision paths in erroneous cases, we can precisely identify model weaknesses and make targeted improvements to the model.

Establishing accountability mechanisms serves as the institutional safeguard for technology implementation. When model errors cause actual harm (such as rejecting loan applications due to flawed sentiment analysis), there must be a clear path for tracing responsibility. This requires defining the respective boundaries of duties among development entities, deployment entities, and regulatory authorities, thereby encouraging all parties to adopt more prudent approaches during model design, validation, and deployment phases. The absence of accountability would enable technology abuse and hinder the healthy development of the industry.

7.4.3 Data Privacy and Security Challenges

When handling publicly available data such as social media, strict compliance with data protection regulations like the GDPR and CCPA is essential. First, data being "publicly available" does not equate to unlimited commercial analysis use. Under the GDPR's "purpose limitation" principle, companies must clearly inform users of the intended use (e.g., sentiment analysis) during data collection and obtain valid legal grounds (such as explicit consent or legitimate interests). For California residents covered by the CCPA, businesses must provide opt-out rights for data sales.

Secondly, strict data minimization measures must be implemented. During data processing, directly identifiable identifiers (such as names and phone numbers) and indirectly identifiable identifiers (such as IP addresses and device IDs) should be immediately removed or anonymized. Even when conducting sentiment analysis, it should be performed at the aggregated data level to avoid linking to identifiable individuals. Additionally, enterprises need to establish comprehensive data governance frameworks, including data retention policies (ensuring data is securely deleted after specified periods) and security safeguards to prevent unauthorized access. Finally, data subject rights must be respected, with mechanisms in place to respond to users' requests for access, correction, or deletion of their personal information. Only within such a compliance framework can sentiment analysis technology develop healthily without infringing on personal privacy.

Against the backdrop of increasingly stringent data regulations, protecting user privacy [19] has become a core issue in the development of sentiment analysis models. Differential privacy addresses this by adding precisely calibrated noise to the training data, preventing the model from inferring individual information while maintaining overall statistical accuracy. Federated learning adopts a distributed training architecture where original user data remains on local devices, and only encrypted model parameter updates are uploaded, eliminating the risk of data leakage at the source. Homomorphic encryption enables direct model inference on encrypted data, ensuring that sensitive information remains ciphertext throughout the entire processing cycle. Meanwhile, generative synthetic data technology creates simulated datasets that replicate the statistical properties of real data but contain no personally identifiable information, offering a fundamental privacy-preserving solution for model training. These cutting-edge technologies are driving the transformation of sentiment analysis systems from traditional data protection models toward a "privacy-first" architectural paradigm, providing a solid technical foundation for balancing data value extraction with personal privacy protection.

7.4.4 Summary and Outlook

This paper systematically explores the cutting-edge developments and future directions in the field of sentiment analysis [20]. Technologically, LLMs and generative AI have brought about paradigm shifts, not only significantly improving analytical accuracy but also addressing core challenges such as data scarcity and model robustness through features like synthetic data generation and adversarial sample construction. Meanwhile, advancements in multimodal analysis, attention mechanisms, and real-time processing technologies have greatly expanded the application boundaries of sentiment analysis.

However, the rapid advancement of technology also brings profound challenges. The complexity of cross-linguistic and cultural differences, the importance of model bias and privacy protection, and the risks of malicious technology use all highlight that sentiment analysis is no longer a purely technical subject. It is evolving into a comprehensive field requiring coordinated efforts in technological development, ethical standards, legal regulation, and social impact. Future development must balance technical capabilities with social responsibility. While pursuing analytical accuracy, we must ensure algorithmic fairness, transparency, and inclusivity toward multiculturalism to truly realize this technology's potential in empowering social progress.

The field of sentiment analysis is entering a new phase of development, with its future shaped by four key dimensions: precision, real-time processing, multimodal integration, and responsible development. As LLMs integrate with interdisciplinary knowledge from neuroscience, sentiment analysis will transcend current text comprehension limitations, enabling nuanced capture and accurate interpretation of complex human emotions. Advances in real-time stream processing and lightweight models will make millisecond-level sentiment insights possible, providing unprecedented immediacy for decision-making. Meanwhile, the multimodal fusion of text, voice, visual, and physiological signals will establish a comprehensive emotional perception capability, completely breaking down information barriers between single-modal data.

However, the rapid advancement of technology must go hand in hand with robust ethical frameworks. The future development of sentiment analysis urgently requires researchers, developers, and users to collaborate in establishing consensus on algorithmic fairness, privacy protection, cultural sensitivity, and technical transparency. Only when technological progress is balanced with humanistic considerations can we ensure that this powerful tool truly serves social welfare. In diverse fields such as commerce, healthcare, and education, sentiment analysis should become a beneficial force that enhances communication and improves well-being, laying a solid foundation for achieving a future of harmonious coexistence between humans and machines.

References

1 Wang, Y., Li, Q., Dai, Z., & Xu, Y. (2024). Current status and trends in large language modeling research. *Chinese Journal of Engineering*, 46(8), 1411–1425.

2 Chunxia, Y., Yu, H., Qigang, C., & Wenwen, M. (2023). Aspect-based implicit sentiment analysis model based on BERT and attention mechanism. *Nanjing Xinxi Gongcheng Daxue Xuebao*, 15(5), 551–560.

3 Shi, L., Wang, Y., Cheng, Y., & Wei, R. (2020). Review of attention mechanism in natural language processing. *Data Analysis and Knowledge Discovery*, 4(5), 1–14.
4 Lyu, X., Tian, C., Zhang, L., Du, Y., Zhang, X., & Cai, Z. (2024). A multimodal sentiment analysis model incorporating multi-feature and attention mechanisms. *Data Analysis and Knowledge Discovery*, 8(5), 91–101.
5 Yan, C., & He, L. (2022). Research on text sentiment analysis based on a BERT-based dual-channel neural network model. *Intelligent Computer and Applications*, 12(5), 16–22.
6 Xie, R., & Li, Y. (2020). A text sentiment classification model based on BERT and dual-channel attention mechanism. *Journal of Data Acquisition and Processing*, 35(4), 642–652.
7 Sun, R., & Zhou, Y. (2023). Sentiment prediction based on machine learning and advanced transformer models. *Advances in Applied Mathematics*, 12, 1090–1099.
8 Bashiri, H., & Naderi, H. (2024). Comprehensive review and comparative analysis of transformer models in sentiment analysis. *Knowledge and Information Systems*, 66(12), 7305–7361.
9 Chen, Y., Zheng, G., & Xiao, W. (2023). Sentiment analysis of Chinese film reviews based on RoBERTa and syntactic information. *Science Technology and Engineering*, 23(18), 7844–7851.
10 Zeng, C., Wen, C., Sun, Y., Pan, L., & He, P. (2021). Sentiment analysis of bullet screen texts based on ALBERT-CRNN. *Journal of Zhengzhou University (Natural Science Edition)*, 53(3), 1–8.
11 Hoang, M., Bihorac, O. A., & Rouces, J. (2019). Aspect-based sentiment analysis using BERT. In Proceedings of the 22nd Nordic Conference on Computational Linguistics, Turku, Finland, (pp. 187–196).
12 Birjali, M., Kasri, M., & Beni-Hssane, A. (2021). A comprehensive survey on sentiment analysis: Approaches, challenges and trends. *Knowledge-Based Systems*, 226, 107134.
13 Collado-Montañez, J., Martín-Valdivia, M. T., & Martínez-Cámara, E. (2025). Data augmentation based on large language models for radiological report classification. *Knowledge-Based Systems*, 308, 112745.
14 Fui-Hoon Nah, F., Zheng, R., Cai, J., Siau, K., & Chen, L. (2023). Generative AI and ChatGPT: Applications, challenges, and AI-human collaboration. *Journal of Information Technology Case and Application Research*, 25(3), 277–304.
15 Imran, A. S., Daudpota, S. M., Kastrati, Z., & Batra, R. (2020). Cross-cultural polarity and emotion detection using sentiment analysis and deep learning on COVID-19 related tweets. *IEEE Access*, 8, 181074–181090.
16 Xu, Y., Cao, H., Du, W., & Wang, W. (2022). A survey of cross-lingual sentiment analysis: Methodologies, models and evaluations. *Data Science and Engineering*, 7(3), 279–299.

17 Rani, S., & Kumar, P. (2017). A sentiment analysis system to improve teaching and learning. *Computer*, 50(5), 36–43.
18 Wang, Q., Wang, X., Yang, J., & Bi, Y. (2024). Multimodal sentiment analysis method based on knowledge distillation for imbalanced data. SSRN 5066846.
19 Feng, D., Zhang, M., & Li, H. (2014). Big data security and privacy protection. *Chinese Journal of Computers*, 37(1), 246–258.
20 Kumar, A., & Sebastian, T. M. (2012). Sentiment analysis: A perspective on its past, present and future. *International Journal of Intelligent Systems and Applications*, 4(10), 1–14.

8

Practical Applications of Sentiment Analysis

As the culmination of this book, this chapter is dedicated to building a bridge between cutting-edge technology and real-world applications. Going beyond theoretical discussions, we will delve into how sentiment analysis serves as a core driver of decision-making and innovation across three key domains: business intelligence, public safety and governance, and public health.

We begin with business intelligence, uncovering how sentiment analysis decodes massive volumes of user reviews and social media feedback. This enables enterprises to accurately grasp market trends, optimize product strategies, enhance customer experience (CX), and safeguard brand reputation. An in-depth case study on new product launches will vividly illustrate the entire process from public opinion early warning to strategy adjustment.

Next, our perspective expands to the field of public safety and governance. This section explores how sentiment analysis acts as a "barometer" of social emotions, assisting government agencies in guiding public opinion, providing early warnings of crises, evaluating policy effectiveness, and even contributing to the fight against cybercrime. Real-world cases will demonstrate its potential to improve the efficiency of social governance.

Finally, we focus on public health, where the application of sentiment analysis is particularly profound. From tracking public emotional attitudes toward vaccination to monitoring public panic and needs during public health incidents such as pandemics, cases will prove that it is an indispensable tool for achieving precise public health interventions.

To address core challenges in practice, this chapter features a "Technical Deep Dive: Conquering Social Media Data" module. It specifically analyzes key technical difficulties unique to processing social media information, such as noise filtering, dialect recognition, and sarcasm detection.

The chapter concludes with a highly practical practitioner's guide. It systematically compares the advantages and disadvantages of mainstream open-source tools and commercial platforms, and provides clear selection recommendations and implementation roadmaps. The aim is to empower readers, regardless of their background, to successfully deploy sentiment analysis capabilities in their own work scenarios, truly transforming knowledge into value.

8.1 Business Intelligence: From VoC to Strategic Advantage

In the era of "customer-centricity," an enterprise's ability to understand and respond to customer needs has increasingly become a key determinant of its core competitiveness. This section focuses on how enterprises leverage sentiment analysis to transform massive and disorganized customer feedback data into core assets that drive growth, foster innovation, and enhance brand loyalty.

8.1.1 Core Issue: The "VoC" Drowned Out

In the digital age, the sheer volume and fragmentation of customer feedback—spanning social media, e-commerce reviews, customer service tickets, and survey responses—have created a critical challenge: the "voice of the customer" (VoC) is often drowned out. This data deluge is predominantly unstructured, comprising nuanced sentiments, casual complaints, and spontaneous praise, making it inherently resistant to simple categorization. Traditional manual analysis methods, reliant on human reading, spreadsheets, and basic keyword searches, are too slow, limited in scope, and subject to cognitive bias to process this flood of information in a timely or comprehensive manner.

The consequence of this analytical bottleneck is a significant lag in corporate insight. Enterprises are left unable to quickly identify emerging customer pain points, spot subtle market trends, or detect the early warning signals of a potential brand crisis. A product flaw repeatedly mentioned in forum posts, a nascent competitor gaining traction in app store reviews, or a wave of frustration building in social media comments can easily go unnoticed until it escalates. This intelligence gap forces decision-making into a reactive posture; strategies are formulated in response to problems that have already gained momentum, rather than being shaped by proactive, forward-looking insight.

As a result, invaluable opportunities to enhance customer satisfaction, foster loyalty, and drive strategic innovation are routinely missed. The inability to listen at scale and in real time means that product development roadmaps may not align with actual user needs, marketing campaigns might miss the mark, and customer service resources can be misallocated. Over time, this erodes brand trust and competitive advantage, as customers increasingly gravitate toward brands that demonstrate they are listening and responding empathetically.

Therefore, navigating this complexity requires a paradigm shift from periodic listening to continuous, intelligent sense-making. The solution lies in leveraging advanced technologies like natural language processing (NLP), sentiment analysis, and machine learning. These AI-driven systems can automatically ingest, structure, and analyze millions of data points from across the entire customer journey. They can identify not just explicit topics, but also underlying emotions, intent, and emerging themes, transforming raw, chaotic feedback into a structured, quantifiable, and actionable strategic asset.

By building a centralized, intelligent VoC program powered by such technology, enterprises can finally move beyond mere data collection to genuine customer understanding. This enables them to transition from being reactive firefighters to proactive partners, anticipating needs, mitigating risks before they escalate, and consistently delivering experiences that resonate. In an economy where CX is a primary battleground, mastering this ability to decipher the true "VoC" is no longer a luxury—it is a fundamental imperative for sustainable growth and resilience.

8.1.2 Solution: Building an Emotion-driven Decision-making Loop

To address the issue of the "VoC" being drowned out, enterprises need to build an intelligent, data-driven decision-making loop centered on sentiment analysis, which runs through the entire processes of brand management, product innovation, and marketing.

8.1.2.1 Loop 1: Omnichannel Listening and Brand Reputation Management

Brand reputation is the lifeline of enterprises in the digital age, and emotion is a core indicator for measuring brand health. Enterprises need to establish a unified "sentiment analysis hub" to integrate text data from various channels, and the visualized data presentation of the whole monitoring process is shown in Figure 8.1.

Technology Application: Enterprises first need to break down data silos and integrate text data from all channels—such as social media, news websites, e-commerce platforms, customer service tickets, and survey responses—through technical means [1]. Social media sentiment analysis can be optimized via vortex search-based adaptive boosting algorithms [2]. Subsequently, an optimized

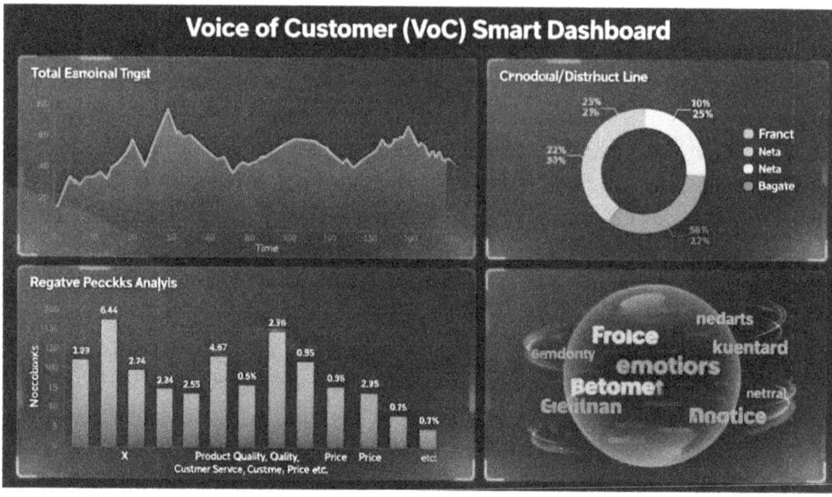

Figure 8.1 Schematic diagram of VoC smart dashboard.

real-time sentiment classification model is used to automatically and continuously score the sentiment (positive, negative, neutral) of massive texts, thereby enabling macro-monitoring of the overall health of the brand. More importantly, the system needs to establish an intelligent early warning mechanism: when the volume or intensity of negative discussions on a particular topic surges in a short period, or when the proportion of negative sentiment exceeds a preset threshold, the system will automatically issue alerts to the public relations, customer service, and product teams, along with key original feedback samples. This enables enterprises to shift their crisis public relations response model from post-event remediation to in-event or even pre-event intervention. For example, when the issue of "battery overheating" of a new mobile phone is first mentioned on a few tech forums with negative sentiment, the brand can immediately become aware of it. This provides an opportunity to launch an internal investigation and prepare communication scripts before the issue trends on social media, thereby seizing the initiative in public opinion.

8.1.2.2 Loop 2: Product Innovation and Competitor Analysis

Customer reviews are a valuable "goldmine of demands" for product managers, and aspect-based sentiment analysis (ABSA) makes it possible to efficiently extract value from them.

Technology Application: ABSA technology goes beyond the simplistic model of classifying an entire review as "positive" or "negative." It can accurately identify the various aspects mentioned in a review and determine the sentiment toward each aspect [3]. For example, for the review "The camera quality of this phone is amazing, but the battery life is terrible," the ABSA model can automatically extract two sentiment pairs: ("camera quality," positive) and ("battery life," negative).

When this analysis is applied to a large number of historical reviews of a company's own products, the product team can obtain a data-driven "health check report." The system can automatically summarize all users' positive praise and negative complaints about dozens or even hundreds of specific features, such as "battery life," "screen display," "system fluency," "design," and "camera." This enables product iteration decisions to be based on objective data from all user feedback, rather than relying on the subjective intuition of senior management or the opinions of a small number of vocal users. Which functions are core strengths that need to be maintained? Which are shortcomings that need to be urgently addressed? Priorities become clear at a glance.

Furthermore, by comparing the sentiment scores of their own products with those of key competitors across various aspects, enterprises can create a "product competitiveness map." This provides a clear understanding of their core advantages, critical shortcomings, as well as the competitive advantages and pain points of their rivals. It serves as a data support for prioritizing product iterations, developing new features, and positioning products differently in the market.

8.1.2.3 Loop 3: Precision Marketing and Sales Enablement

Sentiment analysis can quantify the emotional impact of marketing campaigns and provide sales teams with signals of potential customer intent.

Technology Application:

- **Marketing Campaign Evaluation:** During marketing campaigns such as new product launches, advertising placements, and KOL collaborations, real-time analysis of the emotional response to related discussions on social media is conducted. This not only focuses on changes in the volume of discussions but also pays close attention to shifts in sentiment polarity. It helps the marketing team evaluate the true ROI (return on investment) of the campaign and adjust the communication strategy in a timely manner.
- **KOL Selection:** Analyze the emotional tendencies of KOLs' historical content and the emotional resonance of their fans' interactions. This helps identify opinion leaders in specific fields (such as beauty and digital products) who can trigger strong positive emotional responses from their audiences, thereby improving the efficiency of marketing collaborations.
- **Sales Lead Generation:** Analyze the remarks of potential customers on public platforms such as social media and forums. When signals of purchase

intent or dissatisfaction with competitors are captured—such as "I want to change my phone" or "The XX brand computer keeps crashing"—they are marked as high-value sales leads, helping the sales team reach out to potential customers with precision.

8.1.3 Case Deep Dive: Product Launch Monitoring for a Global Consumer Electronics Company

8.1.3.1 Background

A global consumer electronics company launched a new flagship smartphone. Facing fierce market competition and short public attention spans, the management needed to quickly and accurately grasp the initial response of the global market within the 72-hour golden window after the launch to adjust strategies in a timely manner.

8.1.3.2 Data Sources

- Twitter: To capture real-time public sentiment and topic spread.
- Reddit: To gain in-depth discussions from tech-savvy users in the technology section.
- Comment Sections of Major Tech Media: To understand the opinions of professional media readers.
- Major E-commerce Platforms: To collect direct feedback from early preorder users.

8.1.3.3 Analysis Process

1. **Real-time Data Collection and Multilingual Processing:** Real-time data crawling of over 1,000 pieces of data per second was achieved through API interfaces and web crawler technology. To address the multilingual challenge, the XLM-R multilingual pretrained model was adopted, which can accurately process low-resource languages (such as Southeast Asian minority languages) and avoid sentiment misjudgment caused by translation errors. Ultimately, the accuracy of sentiment recognition for non-English feedback was increased to 92% [4].
2. **Overall Sentiment Trend Analysis:** An "emotion index model" was built, where each piece of feedback was labeled as "positive (+1)," "neutral (0)," or "negative (–1)." The overall hourly sentiment index (ranging from −100 to 100) was calculated through weighting, and a real-time trend curve was plotted. Meanwhile, historical data from the launch of the previous generation flagship phone was integrated to form a "Same Period Comparison View." For example, 12 hours after the launch, the sentiment index of the new phone

was 68, which was 30.8% higher than that of the previous generation during the same period, initially verifying higher overall market recognition.

3. **In-depth Aspect-based Sentiment Mining:** Different from the traditional "overall sentiment analysis," the project adopted an "aspect-based sentiment recognition model" to automatically extract the core dimensions of user discussions from massive feedback [5]. Finally, four high-heat discussion aspects were identified, ranked by the frequency of mentions as follows: "camera system" (38% mention rate), "screen refresh rate" (22%), "battery life" (20%), and "pricing strategy" (15%). Further analysis of the sentiment tendency of each aspect provided a precise direction for subsequent actions.

8.1.3.4 Key Insights and Business Actions

Findings:

- **Camera System:** Received overwhelming praise, with "night mode" and "telephoto lens" frequently mentioned with positive sentiment.
- **Battery Life:** Reviews were polarized. Ordinary users were satisfied, but some heavy mobile game users and users who spent long hours on video calls complained that the battery life "did not meet expectations."
- **Pricing Strategy:** Received a normal response in European and American markets but triggered a high concentration of negative sentiment in some key emerging markets. Words such as "too expensive" and "not worth it" appeared frequently in discussions.

Actions:

- **Marketing Team:** Immediately adjusted the global promotional materials and social media advertisements for the next week. The marketing focus was shifted to the well-received "camera night shooting" feature, and comparative samples and short videos were produced for viral dissemination.
- **Public Relations and Product Teams:** Within 24 hours of the escalation of negative discussions about battery life, a technical explanation was released through official channels. It explained the differences between the battery life laboratory test standards and actual usage scenarios, and promised to launch a "high-performance mode" in the next software update to optimize power consumption, thereby reassuring the core user group.
- **Sales and Pricing Department:** Based on the insights, an urgent assessment was conducted on early promotion plans (such as bundled gifts and interest-free installments) for specific emerging markets to alleviate price resistance.

8.1.3.5 Outcomes

Through this practice, the company successfully transformed sentiment analysis from a "post-event summary" into a "decision-making guide." It not only amplified the product's advantages in a timely manner but also took effective measures to address negative public opinions before they escalated [6]. This case proves that real-time sentiment analysis can help enterprises during the critical period of new product launches: quickly verify market reactions, promptly identify potential risks, and accurately guide the allocation of marketing resources, ultimately converting the voice of customers into a competitive advantage.

In today's fast-paced market environment, the ability to understand the voice of customers in real time has become a core capability of enterprises. Sentiment analysis is precisely the key tool for transforming massive user feedback into actionable insights, allowing enterprises to capture the critical signals that determine success or failure amid the data deluge.

8.2 Public Safety and Governance: Sensing the Pulse of Society

The application of sentiment analysis is not limited to the commercial field; in public services and governance, it is emerging as a powerful tool. It assists governments and social institutions in more keenly sensing social emotions, providing early warnings of potential risks, and responding efficiently during crises.

8.2.1 Challenges: Understanding Complex Public Opinion and Responding to Emergencies

In the digital age, governments face increasingly complex challenges in public opinion governance during policy formulation and emergency management. Traditional governance models are difficult to adapt to the massive, fragmented, and dynamically changing public opinion feedback. These challenges can be summarized into three core pain points.

Firstly, there is a lag in public opinion feedback, leading to a disconnect between policy adjustments and public needs. Currently, some public opinion collection still relies on traditional methods, such as offline surveys and letters and visits, which have long processes and a "time lag" in information transmission. For example, when a local government promoted the old community renovation policy, it initially collected opinions through resident representative forums and decided on a "unified elevator installation" plan. However, when the policy was implemented, it was discovered that a large number of elderly residents were resistant due to concerns about cost sharing, while young people were more concerned about the optimization of parking facilities. Such segmented demands were not taken seriously until the policy implementation was hindered due to poor feedback channels. This not only increased administrative costs but also raised public doubts about the scientific nature of the policy.

Secondly, the information overload dilemma dilutes effective public opinion signals. With the popularization of channels, such as social platforms and government message boards, governments need to process massive amounts of public opinion information every day, which is mixed with repeated demands, emotional expressions, and even false information. Taking the emergency response to an extreme weather event as an example, the local government hotline and social media received tens of thousands of messages, including urgent requests for help such as "vehicles trapped due to road waterlogging" and irrelevant remarks such as "complaints about inaccurate weather forecasts." Staff had to spend a lot of energy screening effective information, resulting in delays in handling some urgent requests due to information being drowned out.

Finally, it is difficult to identify key contradictions and emergency information, making it hard to accurately grasp the core of public opinion. Under complex social issues, public opinion presents the characteristics of "diversification and circularization," with significant differences in demands among different groups. Moreover, in emergency events, help-seeking information is often accompanied by a large amount of redundant content, making it difficult to locate core contradictions in a timely manner. For example, when a local government formulated supporting policies for the "double reduction" (reduction of homework and after-school tutoring) in education, among parents, there were voices of "worrying about the quality of after-school services" and demands of "hoping to increase art courses," along with expressions related to the interests of training institutions. The government needed to strip out interference from massive information to identify the key contradiction of "insufficient teachers for after-school services." In emergency events such as epidemic prevention and control, if emergency information such as "requests for help due to material shortages" and "medical needs of special groups" cannot be quickly extracted from the complex feedback, it will directly affect the efficiency of emergency response and even trigger people's livelihood risks.

8.2.2 Solution: A New Paradigm of Data-driven Social Governance

Sentiment analysis provides a new path to address the above challenges, promoting social governance toward a more refined and forward-looking model.

8.2.2.1 Public Opinion and Policy Evaluation

1. **Dynamically Evaluate Policy Acceptance and Social Impact:** With the help of NLP technology, feedback from multiple channels such as government platform messages, social media discussions, and news comment sections can be captured in real time to quantitatively analyze the public's attitude toward policy drafts or implemented policies. For example, when a local government promoted the "mandatory waste classification policy," monitoring through the public opinion system found that: in the early stage of policy release, the overall acceptance rate was only 42%, and the opposition mainly focused on "complex classification standards (38% mention rate)" and "insufficient recycling facilities (29%)." Three months after implementation, the acceptance rate increased to 68%, and the reasons for approval shifted to "obvious environmental improvement effect (45%)" and "good community guidance services (32%)." This dynamic data can not only intuitively present the effect of policy implementation but also identify differentiated needs through the breakdown of regions and groups. For example, the elderly are more concerned about "simplified classification teaching," while young people call for "popularization of intelligent recycling equipment," providing a segmented direction for policy adjustments.
2. **Accurately Identify Core Reasons for Approval and Opposition:** Different from the traditional "vague" summary of public opinion, AI models can automatically extract "key viewpoints" and "sentiment tendencies" from policy discussions, and even locate specific details of controversial focal points. Taking the "public transportation fare increase policy" in a certain city as an example, the public opinion system identified from 50,000 pieces of feedback that: the core reason for approval was "fares have not been adjusted for many years and need to support route expansion (61% share)," while the opposition was concentrated on "increased travel costs for low-income groups (43%)" and "mismatch between service quality and fares on some routes (35%)." Based on this, the government not only clarified the optimization direction of "needing to launch subsidy policies for low-income groups" but also initiated special rectification of bus punctuality rate and carriage environment in response to "service quality disputes." In the end, the policy adjustment gained 75% public support, achieving a win-win situation of "policy optimization" and "satisfaction of public opinion."

8.2.2.2 Early Warning of Social Risks

The outbreak of mass incidents or social contradictions is often accompanied by early signals of "abnormal emotional agglomeration" and "accelerated topic spread." A data-driven risk early warning system can identify risk signs in advance by monitoring the "emotional intensity" and "spread trend" of specific social issues, gaining time for managers to handle them. Its core logic is to build a "social emotion monitoring index system," including key dimensions such as "proportion of negative emotions," "topic spread speed," "growth rate of participants in discussions," and "frequency of extreme remarks." A "risk early warning index" (ranging from 0 to 100, with 60 and above as the early warning threshold) is generated through real-time data modeling. For example, in a certain region, there were local complaints about "enterprises defaulting on employees' wages." Initially, there were only sporadic discussions on local forums (with a negative emotion proportion of 25% and a spread speed of 0.5 posts per minute). However, 3 days later, the relevant topic broke out on short video platforms (with the negative emotion proportion rising to 82%, the spread speed reaching 50 posts per minute, and the risk early warning index exceeding 75), and the system immediately triggered an early warning. After receiving the signal, the local human resources and social security department intervened in the enterprise coordination in advance, promoted the implementation of the salary payment plan, and avoided the contradiction from escalating into a mass rights protection incident. This "data-first" early warning model breaks the limitation of traditional "post-event disposal" and moves the risk resolution node from "after the contradiction breaks out" to "in the early stage of emotional agglomeration," significantly reducing the cost of social governance.

8.2.2.3 Smart Emergency Response and Disaster Management

Technology Application: After a disaster occurs, the system can use "sentiment analysis + named entity recognition" technology to intelligently process real-time feedback from social media (such as Weibo and Douyin), government hotlines, and rescue platforms. On one hand, through sentiment analysis, it identifies information with high-intensity negative emotions such as "panic" and "urgency," and prioritizes marking emergency help-seeking content. On the other hand, through named entity recognition, it extracts key information such as "location (e.g., XX community, XX road section)," "needs (e.g., water, medicine, and electricity)," and "number of trapped people," and automatically filters redundant content such as "irrelevant complaints" and "repeated help-seeking." For example, when a certain region was hit by a rainstorm disaster in 2023, the system screened out 1,200 valid help-seeking messages from 200,000 pieces of information within one hour. Key information such as "3 people trapped in the basement of XX community due to waterlogging" and "XX hospital urgently needs generators" was directly synchronized to the rescue command center, saving a lot of time for information screening in rescue operations.

Emotion and Demand Geographic Heat Map: A visual map based on a geographic information system, where different regions are displayed in different colors (from light yellow to dark red) according to the emotional intensity (such as panic and urgency) of help-seeking information on social media. At the same time, clear icons (water droplets, crosses, and lightning) are used to mark specific material needs (water, medicine, electricity, etc.) extracted from the text. The rescue command center can intuitively grasp the overall emotional situation of the disaster area and the areas in urgent need of assistance, realizing the precise and efficient deployment of rescue forces, as shown in Figure 8.2.

8.2.3 Ethical Spotlight: Power, Bias, and Privacy

Although data-driven social governance has greatly improved decision-making efficiency, the boundaries of technological application and ethical risks cannot be ignored. When the government uses tools such as sentiment analysis and big data monitoring to engage in social management, three major ethical propositions—"the balance between power expansion and public rights protection," "the risk of discrimination caused by algorithmic bias," and "the boundary between personal privacy and public safety"—have become increasingly prominent. It is necessary to establish clear ethical guidelines and restraint mechanisms to prevent technology from becoming an "unjust governance tool" [7].

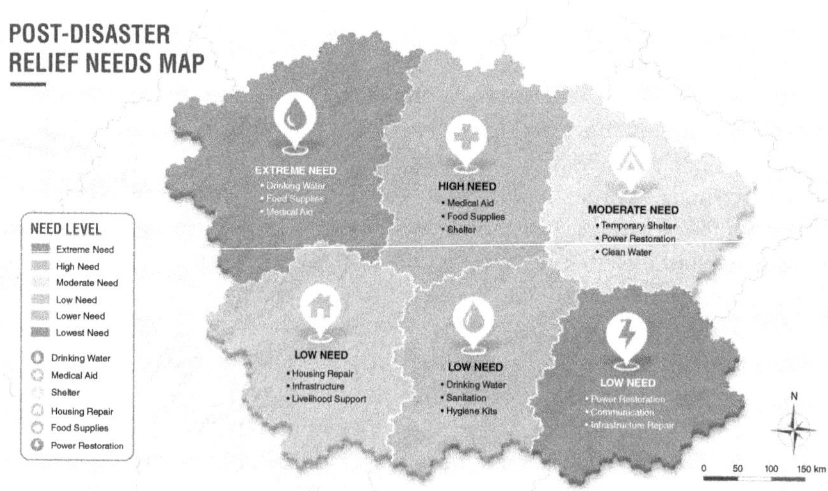

Figure 8.2 Schematic diagram of "emotion and demand geographic heat map" in disaster response.

8.2.3.1 Power Balance and Monitoring Risks

When the government uses sentiment analysis technology for social governance, without boundary constraints, it is prone to the risk of slipping from "public opinion perception" to "excessive monitoring," breaking the balance between "public power" and "citizen rights." For example, some regions have attempted to conduct "all-time, indiscriminate" monitoring of social media remarks, and even marked "neutral complaints" as "negative emotions" and included them in the key focus scope. This expanded monitoring model not only violates the original intention of "governance for the people" but also may inhibit the public's freedom of speech, leading to a "chilling effect." To avoid this risk, the core lies in establishing a "transparency principle" and a "public supervision mechanism." On one hand, the government needs to disclose the scope and boundaries of technological application: clearly inform the public "which issues will be monitored," "what channels are used for data collection," and "for which governance scenarios the analysis results will only be used." For example, it is restricted to "only targeting content related to public interests such as public policy discussions and disaster emergency help-seeking," and the use of technology for monitoring in the field of private life is prohibited. On the other hand, third-party supervision institutions (such as university research teams and public welfare organizations) should be introduced to conduct regular audits of the data usage process, verify whether there are problems such as "over-range monitoring" and "data abuse," and ensure that public power operates "in the sun" to prevent technology from becoming a tool for power expansion.

8.2.3.2 Harm of Algorithmic Bias

As mentioned in Chapter 7, social biases inherent in training data are not merely incidental—they become deeply integrated into the fabric of AI models during the learning process. This integration poses significant risks when models are trained primarily on language data from mainstream demographic groups. Such data often overrepresents the linguistic patterns, cultural references, and emotional expressions of dominant social groups, while sidelining those of ethnic minorities, communities in specific dialect regions, and other marginalized populations.

The consequence is a critical gap in the model's ability to accurately interpret speech emotions from these underrepresented groups. For instance, phrases or tones that carry neutral or positive connotations within a minority community may be misclassified as negative or even threatening by the model, due to a lack of contextual and cultural understanding in its training data. This is not a random error but a systematic bias that can label entire groups' remarks with unwarranted negativity [8].

When such biased judgments are deployed in high-stakes public decision-making—such as in law enforcement risk assessments, social service allocations, or hiring screening systems—they do more than produce incorrect outputs. They can directly trigger discriminatory consequences: limiting opportunities for marginalized individuals, reinforcing harmful stereotypes, and exacerbating existing social inequalities. These outcomes undermine the fairness and legitimacy of AI-driven public policies. Therefore, continuous bias audits—regular evaluations to identify and quantify such disparities—and ongoing model optimization—adjusting training data and algorithms to center underrepresented voices—are not just technical best practices but crucial safeguards for ensuring AI serves all members of society equitably.

8.2.3.3 Bottom Line of Privacy Protection

In all public safety applications, the strictest data privacy protection standards must be adopted. Anonymous data should be used as much as possible in the data collection stage, and technologies such as differential privacy should be used in the analysis process to ensure that the analysis results cannot be traced back to specific individuals. The final reports and insights released must be highly aggregated and de-identified, and any form of violation of citizens' personal privacy must be resolutely prevented. This principle is consistent with the ethical discussions in Chapter 7 and subsequent Chapter 9, and is the foundation for the healthy application of technology.

8.3 Public Health: A New Window into Community Well-being

Sentiment analysis has opened up a new perspective in the field of public health, enabling health institutions to break through traditional and lagging survey methods. It allows them to gain insights into group health trends and public emotions at a lower cost and with higher timeliness.

8.3.1 Challenges: Lagging Health Data and Overlooked Psychological Signals

In the field of public health, the timely perception of health trends and the early identification of mental health issues are key prerequisites for formulating effective intervention strategies. However, under the traditional public health management model, two major pain points—"lagging health data" and "hidden psychological signals"—have long existed. These not only restrict the accuracy of public health decision-making but also may delay the optimal timing for disease prevention and control and psychological intervention.

Traditional public health surveys rely on methods such as offline questionnaires and medical institution case statistics, which have obvious problems of "long cycles, high costs, and narrow coverage." They are difficult to capture rapidly changing health trends. For example, a certain region conducted a "survey on risk factors of chronic diseases among residents." The entire process, from designing the questionnaire, organizing the research team, to conducting home visits and summarizing and analyzing the data, took 3–6 months. When the survey results were finally presented, the living habits of local residents (such as diet structure and exercise frequency) may have changed due to seasonal changes and policy adjustments (such as new takeaway supervision regulations). This leads to the data failing to reflect the current real health risks. In addition, such surveys often require a large investment of human and material resources, and the number of people covered in a single survey is limited. It is difficult to reach groups such as remote rural areas and mobile populations, resulting in "fragmented" health data and the inability to form a comprehensive judgment of health trends. In the event of a public health emergency, the impact of data lag is even more significant—if dynamic data such as population infection symptoms and transmission paths cannot be quickly grasped, it will directly affect the efficiency of adjusting prevention and control measures.

Compared with the lag of physical health data, mental health issues are more likely to fall into the dilemma of "difficult to detect and late intervention" due to the "hidden nature of signals." The manifestations of mental health problems often do not have the typical symptoms of physical diseases (such as fever and pain) but mostly exist in hidden forms such as "low mood," "sleep disorders," and "social withdrawal." Moreover, due to the "stigma" of mental illness, the public is often unwilling to take the initiative to disclose their mental state to medical institutions or communities [9]. In the traditional public health system, mental health screening mostly relies on the "active consultation" model, meaning that individuals are only included in management when their mental problems are severe enough to affect their normal lives and they take the initiative to seek help. This results in a large number of people in a state of "mental sub-health" or early mental illness being missed. For example, anxiety among teenagers due to academic pressure may gradually develop into depression if not identified in a timely manner. Long-term occupational burnout among workplace groups may also evolve into more serious mental disorders due to the lack of early intervention. This not only harms individual health but also increases the difficulty and cost of subsequent public health interventions.

8.3.2 Solution: Using Digital Footprints to Gain Insights into Group Health

By analyzing the "digital footprints" left by people on social media and online communities, sentiment analysis can provide supplementary and real-time data on the health status of groups.

8.3.2.1 Mental Health Trend Monitoring (Group Level)

Language expressions on social media often imply an individual's mental state. By analyzing large-scale anonymized social media data, it is possible to capture mental health trends at the group level, breaking the limitation of traditional screening that "relies on active consultation" and providing a scientific basis for the allocation of public health resources. In terms of technical implementation, research teams can build a "mental health language model" that uses machine learning to identify characteristic language related to depression and anxiety. For example, frequent use of words such as "insomnia," "meaningless," and "loneliness," or expressions of emotions such as "loss of interest in social activities" and "self-denial" will all be marked as "potential mental risk signals." Based on this model, analyzing social media data in different regions and seasons can reveal significant differences in mental health trends. For example, the mention rate of "depression-related language" in northern regions in winter is 32% higher than that in summer, which is presumably related to "short sunshine hours and reduced outdoor activities." In cities with a high concentration of universities, "anxiety-related expressions" surge by 45% every graduation season, focusing on "employment pressure" and "confusion about the future." These macro trend data can directly guide the allocation of public health resources: for northern regions in winter, health departments can increase the opening frequency of community psychological service stations and organize "sunshine psychology lectures"; before the graduation season, additional temporary psychological counseling points are set up around universities, and a 24-hour psychological assistance hotline is opened. Compared with the traditional "passive waiting for help" model, this "advance prediction and precise delivery" method of resource allocation can make mental health services cover more people with potential needs, significantly improving the efficiency of public health services.

8.3.2.2 Epidemiological Intelligence

This concept, known as informatics in epidemiology, bridges data science and public health by leveraging informatics methods to extract actionable insights from large-scale data—especially critical during public health crises like the COVID-19 pandemic. Among its key applications, sentiment analysis stands out as a powerful tool for real-time public sentiment monitoring: it can systematically gauge fluctuations in the public's panic levels regarding a disease (e.g., spikes in anxiety during infection surges) and track shifting attitudes toward core prevention and control measures, such as mask-wearing compliance, lockdown policies, and vaccination willingness [10]. This real-time visibility allows public health authorities to adjust communication strategies promptly—for instance, addressing vaccine hesitancy by tailoring messages to counter specific concerns identified in sentiment data.

Moreover, pairing sentiment analysis with topic recognition elevates its impact by transforming unstructured text (from social media, news comments, or forums) into targeted intelligence. This combination enables rapid localization and tracking of health-related rumors: it can pinpoint the emergence of misinformation (such as conspiracy theories about "virus origins" or exaggerated claims about "vaccine side effects"), map its spread path across platforms, and quantify its impact by analyzing associated sentiment (e.g., anger or fear driving rumor sharing). By identifying these misinformation hotspots early, public health teams can deploy fact-checking efforts strategically, curbing the spread of harmful narratives before they erode trust in public health guidelines or disrupt crisis response.

8.3.2.3 Improving Patient Experience

Hospitals and medical institutions now have the capability to proactively and automatically analyze patient feedback scattered across diverse online platforms, including dedicated healthcare review websites, social media channels, and even hospital-specific feedback portals. This shift from manual, time-consuming feedback sorting to automated analysis allows institutions to capture a broader, more real-time view of patient experiences, unearthing insights that might otherwise be lost in large volumes of unstructured text.

At the core of this process is ABSA, an advanced NLP technique that goes beyond general positive/negative sentiment classification. Instead, it precisely extracts targeted emotional evaluations tied to specific service dimensions critical to patient satisfaction: "doctor's attitude" (e.g., empathy and communication clarity), "nurse care" (e.g., responsiveness and professionalism), "waiting time" (e.g., for appointments and test results), "hospital environment" (e.g., cleanliness and comfort), "treatment effect" (e.g., symptom improvement and recovery speed), and "cost transparency" (e.g., clarity on billing and explanation of charges).

This granular breakdown delivers tangible value to hospital managers: it replaces vague, overall satisfaction scores with actionable, dimension-specific data. For example, if ABSA reveals consistent negative sentiment around "waiting time for diagnostic tests," managers can directly optimize scheduling systems or allocate more resources to that area. By addressing these specific pain points—rather than making broad, unfocused changes—hospitals can streamline service processes more efficiently, tailor improvements to patient needs, and ultimately drive meaningful enhancements in patient satisfaction and loyalty.

8.3.3 Case Deep Dive: Analysis of the "Infodemic" During the COVID-19 Vaccination Campaign

8.3.3.1 Background

During the global promotion of COVID-19 vaccines, the "infodemic" spread in parallel with the viral pandemic. A large amount of misinformation, rumors, and public hesitation and skepticism about vaccines seriously hindered the progress of vaccination. To effectively address this dilemma, the primary task of public health institutions was to accurately grasp the sources and specific contents of negative emotions, providing a scientific basis for the subsequent formulation of response strategies.

8.3.3.2 Methods

This study adopted a combination of "large-scale data collection + advanced technical modeling" to ensure the comprehensiveness and accuracy of the analysis results.

Data Collection: The research team extensively collected millions of public tweets related to COVID-19 vaccines. These data covered multiple countries and regions around the world, with a time span that ran through the critical stages of vaccine promotion, providing a rich material foundation for subsequent analysis.

Technical Analysis: The BERT model was used to classify the sentiment of the collected tweets, accurately distinguishing between positive, neutral, and negative emotions in the text. At the same time, combined with topic modeling technology, the specific concerns behind negative emotions were deeply explored, achieving a breakthrough from "sentiment identification" to "problem location," as shown in Figure 8.3.

8.3.3.3 Findings and Countermeasures

Findings:

1. **Temporal Evolution of Concern Topics:** In the early phases of widespread vaccine rollouts, public negative emotions centered predominantly on two practical, experience-driven concerns: "excessively fast vaccine development speed" and "mild side effects." These worries stemmed from tangible uncertainties about the balance between expediency and safety—many individuals

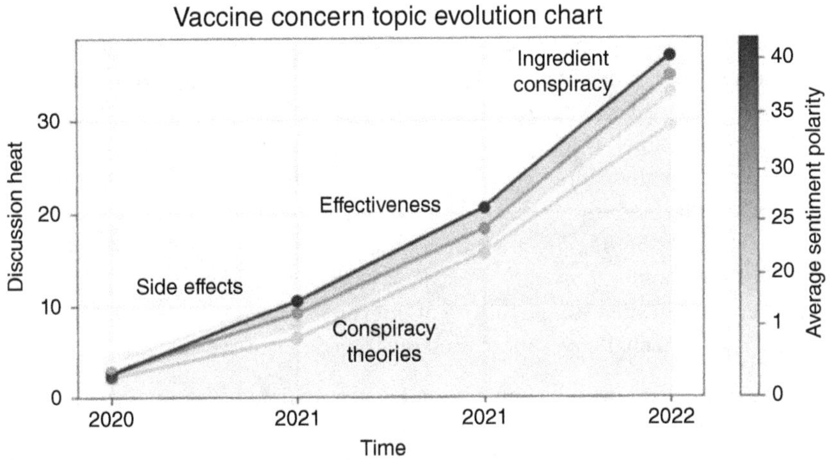

Figure 8.3 Vaccine concern topic evolution chart.

feared that the accelerated development timelines, often compressed to address urgent public health crises, might bypass rigorous safety checks or compromise thorough testing, leaving unforeseen risks. Parallel to this, there was widespread anxiety about mild postvaccination discomfort: people expressed unease about common, temporary reactions like fatigue, low-grade fever, or soreness at the injection site, with some worrying these symptoms might signal broader health impacts, even when public health authorities clarified their typicality. As time progressed, however, the nature of negative sentiment shifted markedly from these grounded, specific concerns toward more extreme, unsubstantiated "conspiracy theories." This shift was often fueled by misinformation spreading rapidly across social media and unregulated online platforms. Public discourse increasingly fixated on unfounded claims: some questioned whether vaccine ingredients harbored "special purposes," such as hidden tracking mechanisms or substances alleged to alter bodily functions, while others suspected that vaccine administration itself served "ulterior motives"—ranging from unfounded claims of population control to baseless links between vaccination and long-term, severe health issues. Unlike the early concerns, which could be addressed with data on safety trials or transparent explanations of side effects, these conspiracy-driven negative emotions were far more resistant to factual correction, as they often rooted in distrust of institutions rather than gaps in information.

2. **Regional Differences in Concern Topics:** The public's core concerns about vaccines exhibit striking variations across different countries and regions, shaped largely by local socioeconomic conditions, healthcare infrastructure,

and information ecosystems. In regions where medical resources are relatively scarce—such as remote rural areas in low- and middle-income countries, or underserved communities with limited healthcare facilities—public worries center primarily on vaccine accessibility and vaccination convenience. For these populations, the key barriers to acceptance are practical rather than ideological: many express anxiety about whether they can easily obtain vaccines (e.g., limited supply reaching rural clinics, long distances to vaccination sites) and whether the process will fit their daily lives (e.g., inflexible appointment times conflicting with work, lack of transportation to clinics). These concerns often stem from a history of uneven healthcare access, making tangible logistical challenges more pressing than debates over vaccine safety.

In contrast, in regions with more complex, unregulated information dissemination—such as areas with high social media penetration but weak fact-checking systems, or societies with deep distrust of official institutions—the impact of extreme negative information, particularly "ingredient conspiracy theories," is far more prominent. Here, public concerns shift from practical access to unfounded fears: rumors about vaccines containing "hidden tracking devices," "harmful toxins," or "substances that alter DNA" spread rapidly through peer networks and viral posts. Unlike resource-scarce regions, where skepticism often fades with improved access, these conspiracy-driven worries are amplified by echo chambers online, where misinformation is rarely challenged. Even in regions with robust vaccine supply, this type of extreme negative information can erode public trust, leading to low vaccination rates despite the absence of practical barriers.

Countermeasures:

- Based on precise insights, public health institutions abandoned the "one-size-fits-all" publicity model and formulated targeted information communication strategies.
- To address concerns about "side effects," a large number of popular science videos and graphics on the principles, commonness, and safety of vaccine side effects were released in collaboration with medical experts.
- For persistent "conspiracy theories," efforts were shifted to collaborating with trusted leaders in local communities (religious leaders, community doctors, and sports stars) to refute rumors through them, which was far more effective than official direct statements.
- In different regions, the focus of publicity was adjusted according to the main concern topics to achieve localized publicity.

Through the combination of sentiment analysis and topic modeling, public health decision-makers were able to track the evolution of the "infodemic" like tracking a virus and conduct precise “prevention and control” of it for the first time.

8.4 Technical Deep Dive: Unique Challenges and Strategies in Social Media Sentiment Analysis

All the applications mentioned earlier are based on the effective processing of social media, a complex data source. This section will delve into the unique challenges faced in social media sentiment analysis and introduce advanced strategies and techniques to address these challenges.

8.4.1 The “Unstructured” Nature of Data

Social media text is the most free and creative field of natural language expression, posing significant difficulties for sentiment analysis [11].

8.4.1.1 Creativity and Informality of Language

- **Internet Slang and Abbreviations:** Such as “yyds” (an internet slang in Chinese meaning “the best of all time”), “AWSL” (an internet slang in Chinese meaning “I’m dying of excitement/admiration”), and “LOL” (laugh out loud). Their emotional meanings are highly context-dependent.
- **Spelling Variations:** Deliberate spelling mistakes (e.g., “coooooool”) and homophonic words.
- **Emojis and Kaomojis:** Such as “😂,” “🐮 🍺” (a combination of emoji and character in Chinese meaning “awesome”), and “(╯'□')╯︵┴──┴” (a kaomoji representing anger). They carry rich emotions, but some symbols have multiple meanings (e.g., “😂” can express extreme joy or helplessness and a forced smile).
- **Countermeasures:** Building and maintaining a dedicated dictionary for specific fields and platforms is fundamental. At the same time, the official sentiment tendency descriptions provided by the Unicode Consortium for emojis can be used as initial labels, followed by fine-tuning based on contextual learning.

8.4.1.2 Lack of Context and Fragmentation

Challenge: Character limits on platforms like Twitter result in extremely concise texts and a lack of sufficient contextual information, making it extremely difficult to understand rhetorical devices such as sarcasm and irony. For example, the sentence “This phone is really ‘smooth’—it takes ten seconds to open an app" may be misjudged as positive sentiment by the model without context and common sense.

Solution: Models based on Transformer (such as BERT) have significant advantages over traditional models due to their strong contextual understanding capabilities. Their attention mechanism can capture the relationships between words that are far apart in the sentence, better understanding the contradiction between "smooth" and "10 seconds," thereby identifying the sarcastic meaning.

8.4.1.3 Integration of Multimodal Information

Challenge: On platforms such as Instagram and TikTok, text is often accompanied by images or videos, and there are many cases of "inconsistency between images and text." For example, the accompanying image is a crying face, but the text says "I'm so happy today." Analyzing only the text will lead to completely wrong sentiment judgments.

Solution: This requires multimodal sentiment analysis, where the model needs to process both text and visual features simultaneously and learn the complex relationships between them to make accurate sentiment judgments.

8.4.2 Platform Characteristics and Analysis Strategies

Different social media platforms have unique characteristics and corresponding sentiment analysis strategies also need to be differentiated [12]. The following is a comparison of the characteristics and analysis strategies of major platforms, as shown in Table 8.1.

Strategy differentiation is reflected in the following aspects: on Twitter, more emphasis is placed on real-time performance and the analysis of topic trigger points; Reddit is suitable for in-depth community opinion and long-text analysis; for Instagram/TikTok, visual sentiment analysis must be introduced to make comprehensive and accurate sentiment judgments.

8.4.3 Advanced Technique Examples

8.4.3.1 Handling Emojis

Advanced models do not simply equate "😂" with "happiness" but judge it based on the context. For example, in the sentence "This joke made me laugh to death 😂," "😂" expresses positive sentiment (amusement); in the sentence "My phone crashed again, I really don't know what to do with it 😂," "😂" expresses negative sentiment (helplessness and self-mockery). Usually, it is necessary to fine-tune the pretrained model on massive social media data to achieve this precise judgment.

Table 8.1 Comparison of sentiment analysis characteristics of mainstream social media platforms.

Platform	Main Content Form	Data API Openness	Typical User Behavior	Main Challenges and Opportunities in Sentiment Analysis
Twitter/Weibo	Short text, hashtags, reposts, and comments	High	Real-time interaction, topic participation, and rapid information dissemination	Challenges: Concise text with limited context; Opportunities: High real-time performance, enabling quick capture of public opinion hotspots and sentiment changes
Reddit	Long text discussions and subreddit classification	Medium	In-depth discussions, professional exchanges, and strong sense of community belonging	Challenges: Large text volume, requiring accurate extraction of core viewpoints; Opportunities: Enabling in-depth community opinion mining and long-text sentiment analysis
Facebook	Image-text combination, friend interaction content, and group discussions	Low	Social interaction, content sharing, and strict privacy settings	Challenges: Difficult data acquisition with many private contents; Opportunities: Access to more personal and authentic emotional content, suitable for analyzing the emotions of small groups
Instagram/ TikTok	Mainly images and short videos, with short accompanying text	Low	Visual content consumption, creative sharing, and high interactivity	Challenges: Limited text information, requiring reliance on visual information; Opportunities: Combining visual sentiment analysis to more comprehensively understand users' emotional expressions

8.4.3.2 Identifying Sarcasm

By learning a large number of example sentences containing sarcasm, the model can identify typical signals, including:

- **Lexical Signals:** Overuse of exaggerated positive words (such as "too," "perfect," and "extremely").
- **Contextual Contradictions:** Such as the contradiction between "smooth" and "10 seconds" mentioned earlier.
- **Punctuation Marks:** Using quotation marks to indicate special meanings or repeated use of exclamation marks and question marks.
- **General Knowledge:** Combining with external knowledge bases (such as the common sense that "it takes ten seconds to open an app" is slow).

8.4.3.3 Utilizing Metadata

Sentiment judgment should not be based solely on the text itself; rich metadata can provide powerful auxiliary signals:

- **User Tags:** The identity of the publisher (such as whether they are a well-known "Apple hater" or "Mi fan") will affect the credibility of their remarks.
- **Hashtags:** Hashtags like #FailedProduct inherently carry strong negative sentiment.
- **Repost Chains and Citations:** If a neutral tweet is reposted and commented on by a large number of angry users, its overall emotional impact may be negative. Analyzing the communication network can enhance the accuracy of sentiment judgment.

8.5 Practitioner's Guide: Tools, Platforms, and Selection Methods

This section focuses on the practical application scenarios of sentiment analysis, aiming to build a clear and operable tool selection and evaluation framework for readers with implementation needs. Whether you are an operator in the marketing department of an enterprise who needs to gain insights into user feedback on products through sentiment analysis, a practitioner in the public affairs field who wants to sort out the public's attitude toward policies with the help of tools, or a researcher who needs to process text sentiment data in a specific field, you can systematically master the entire process from "clarifying needs" to "selecting tools" and then to "verifying results" through the content of this section. This avoids deviations between sentiment analysis results and actual needs due to insufficient tool adaptability or missing evaluation dimensions, and ultimately helps you more efficiently transform sentiment analysis technology into practical capabilities to solve work problems [13].

8.5.1 Core Choice: Build Versus Buy

Before starting a project, it is necessary to clarify whether to choose to build a sentiment analysis solution in-house or purchase one.

8.5.1.1 Build (In-house Development)

Advantages: Enterprises can develop tailored sentiment analysis models that are deeply aligned with their unique business scenarios, rather than relying on generic, one-size-fits-all solutions. This customization starts with integrating industry-specific terms and defining business-unique emotional dimensions—two elements critical to ensuring analysis results directly serve operational goals. For instance, e-commerce platforms, which focus heavily on CX touchpoints, can train models to prioritize exclusive evaluation dimensions like "logistics experience" (e.g., delivery speed and package condition) and "after-sales service" (e.g., return efficiency and customer support responsiveness). Unlike off-the-shelf models that might overlook these niche metrics or misinterpret industry jargon (such as "FBA delay" or "size exchange"), these customized tools generate insights that directly map to the platform's core concerns, like optimizing fulfillment processes or improving post-purchase support.

Beyond better alignment with business needs, self-built sentiment analysis tools also offer significant advantages in data security and privacy protection. When enterprises build their own systems, all data storage and processing—from collecting customer reviews and social media feedback to running model training and analysis—takes place within the enterprise's internal infrastructure. This eliminates the risks associated with third-party platforms, such as data breaches during transmission or unauthorized access to sensitive information (like customer contact details or proprietary business metrics). By keeping data within their own secure environments, enterprises can more easily comply with strict data protection regulations (such as GDPR or CCPA) and build greater trust with customers, who increasingly value control over their personal information.

Disadvantages: Building and maintaining an effective AI-driven sentiment analysis system demands substantial, multifaceted investments—starting with a robust internal technical team. This team cannot rely on a single role but requires a diverse mix of specialists: data scientists to clean, analyze, and derive insights from unstructured text data; NLP engineers to design and implement core sentiment classification and topic recognition models; and MLOps engineers to ensure the system runs reliably at scale, manage model deployment, and monitor performance over time. Beyond these technical roles, additional professional teams are essential: algorithm engineers to refine model accuracy (e.g., reducing bias in sentiment judgments) and data annotators to create high-quality labeled datasets—critical for training models to distinguish nuanced emotions and context-specific phrases.

Equally significant are the ongoing resource commitments. Continuous investment in computing resources is nonnegotiable: processing large volumes of real-time data (from social media, review platforms, or public forums) requires powerful cloud servers, GPU clusters, and storage solutions, all of which incur recurring costs. There are also ongoing model iteration costs: as language patterns, public sentiment trends, and user needs evolve, models must be regularly retrained, tested, and updated to avoid becoming obsolete.

Compounding these challenges is the extended timeline from development to launch. Building such a system involves multiple time-intensive stages—data collection and annotation, model design and training, rigorous testing to ensure accuracy and fairness, and integration with existing hospital or public health systems. This long cycle makes it difficult to quickly adapt to short-term, urgent needs—such as addressing a sudden surge in vaccine misinformation or responding to a spike in patient complaints about a specific hospital service.

8.5.1.2 Buy (Purchasing Commercial Solutions)

Advantages: Fast deployment with out-of-the-box functionality; no need to focus on underlying technology and infrastructure maintenance; commercial platforms usually come with mature visual dashboards and reporting functions.

Disadvantages: Low flexibility, and the model may not be well-suited to professional fields; cumulative costs of continuous subscriptions may be high; data needs to be uploaded to third-party cloud servers, posing risks to data security and privacy compliance.

8.5.2 Build Path: Open-source Ecosystem

If you choose or tend to build in-house, the open-source ecosystem provides various tools from entry-level to professional.

8.5.2.1 Entry-level Libraries

- **NLTK:** Known as the "encyclopedia" of Python NLP, it provides rich text processing tools (such as word segmentation and part-of-speech tagging) and basic sentiment analysis modules. Its VADER (Valence Aware Dictionary and sEntiment Reasoner) library is particularly worth trying. It is a dictionary and rule-based sentiment analysis tool with an excellent ability to recognize informal language, abbreviations, and emojis commonly found in social media texts [14].

- **TextBlob:** Built on NLTK, it provides a more concise and user-friendly API. Its built-in pattern recognizer can quickly assign a polarity and subjectivity score to the text, allowing developers to implement basic sentiment analysis functions with just one or two lines of code.

8.5.2.2 Professional-level Frameworks

- **Hugging Face Transformers:** Currently, the industry's common standard, it has a large model library containing thousands of pretrained models (such as BERT and RoBERTa), which can be easily downloaded for sentiment analysis tasks.
- **Code Example:** Using Hugging Face for Sentiment Analysis

```
from transformers import pipeline
# Create a sentiment analysis pipeline and automatically  download the
pre-trained model
classifier = pipeline("sentiment-analysis")
# Perform sentiment analysis on the text
result = classifier("I love this product! The quality is amazing.")
print(result)
# Output: [{'label': 'POSITIVE', 'score': 0.9998}]
# It can also handle
Chineseresult_
chinese = classifier("The quality of this product is terrible,
very disappointing.")
print(result_chinese)
# Output: [{'label': 'NEGATIVE', 'score': 0.995}]
```

- For production environments, it is necessary to annotate your own data and fine-tune the pretrained model to achieve the best domain performance.

8.5.2.3 Ecosystem Tools

- **spaCy:** A benchmark for industrial-grade NLP processing. It provides basic NLP functions such as word segmentation, lemmatization, and named entity recognition with extremely high speed and accuracy. Using spaCy for data cleaning and preprocessing before feeding text into large models such as BERT is a best practice for building efficient and stable production pipelines.
- **Scikit-learn:** Despite the popularity of deep learning, traditional machine learning models (such as logistic regression and support vector machines) still have their value in specific scenarios, especially when labeled data is limited or computing resources are tight. Scikit-learn provides a complete machine learning toolchain, facilitating feature engineering (such as TF-IDF), model training, and evaluation. It is an excellent platform for conducting algorithm comparison experiments.

8.5.3 Buy Path: Overview of Commercial SaaS Platforms

If purchasing is more in line with your needs, there are several main types of commercial SaaS platforms available on the market:

8.5.3.1 Social Listening Platforms

Leading third-party public opinion analysis platforms—represented by industry leaders like Brandwatch and Sprinklr—boast a core advantage: preconfigured, extensively covered data sources, with social media data as their cornerstone. These platforms aggregate data from a vast array of channels, including major social networks, forums, news sites, and review platforms, eliminating the need for enterprises to handle tedious, resource-heavy preprocessing tasks. Teams no longer have to manage data collection, clean messy unstructured text, or remove duplicate entries; instead, they can directly access real-time public opinion dynamics, saving significant time and labor costs.

Another key strength of these platforms is their powerful visual dashboards. These interfaces intuitively present critical metrics: brand mention volume (showing how often a brand is discussed), sentiment trends (tracking shifts between positive, negative, and neutral opinions), emerging hot topics (highlighting what audiences care about most), and profiles of influential figures (identifying key voices driving conversations). This makes them ideal for marketing, public relations, and brand teams: they support macro reputation monitoring (keeping tabs on overall brand perception), competitor comparison (benchmarking against rivals' public sentiment), and marketing campaign effect evaluation (measuring how campaigns influence audience opinions)—all enabling "out-of-the-box use" without requiring deep technical expertise [15].

8.5.3.2 CX Management Platforms

Leading CX management platforms—such as Medallia and Qualtrics—stand out by embedding sentiment analysis deeply into the entire CX lifecycle, rather than treating it as a standalone tool. Their core strength lies in seamless integration: they automatically pull in customer feedback from a multitude of touchpoints, unifying data that often exists in silos. These touchpoints span both public and private channels, including structured surveys, real-time customer service chat logs, app store reviews, social media comments, and even post-purchase follow-up emails.

By consolidating this feedback, these platforms create a unified customer view—a holistic picture of how customers feel across every interaction with a brand. This goes far beyond just analyzing public social media remarks: it unlocks insights from private, often more candid channels (like one-on-one support conversations), where customers may share unfiltered opinions about pain points or satisfaction. Armed with this comprehensive data, enterprises can move beyond surface-level sentiment tracking to drive closed-loop optimization: they can identify gaps in products (e.g., app usability issues from reviews), refine services (e.g., slow support response times from chat logs), and enhance support processes—directly addressing the root causes of positive or negative sentiment to improve overall CX.

8.5.3.3 Cloud Vendor API Services

Including Google Cloud Natural Language API, Amazon Comprehend, and Microsoft Azure Text Analytics. Such services are mainly oriented to developers and provide ready-to-use standardized NLP capabilities. Developers only need a few lines of code to call a RESTful API to assign sentiment labels to text. This approach has flexibility between the previous two: it does not provide ready-made data and dashboards like social listening platforms but allows developers to seamlessly integrate its sentiment analysis capabilities into their own business systems, data pipelines, or mobile applications. It is very suitable for scenarios where intelligent text analysis functions need to be added to internal tools.

8.5.4 How to Make an Informed Choice: Decision Framework and Evaluation Criteria

8.5.4.1 Sentiment Analysis Solution Selection Matrix

Enterprises face diverse sentiment analysis demands across different business scenarios, and there are obvious gaps in performance, cost, deployment difficulty, and compliance among mainstream implementation schemes, including open-source libraries, cloud vendor APIs, and SaaS platforms. To facilitate rapid quantitative screening and targeted decision-making for business practitioners, this subsection constructs a multi-dimensional evaluation matrix covering accuracy customization, resource cost, data compatibility, deployment cycle, and model interpretability, as shown in Table 8.2.

8.5.4.2 Final Evaluation Recommendations

Before making the final decision, it is recommended to follow these steps:

1. **Clarify Core Needs:** Return to business goals and determine the type of data to be analyzed (such as tweets and customer service tickets), the expected accuracy, the budget, and the project timeline.
2. **Create a Shortlist:** Based on the above matrix, select 2–3 solutions that best fit your situation.
3. **Conduct a Proof of Concept:** This is a key step. Prepare a small sample set containing hundreds of pieces of real business data, use it to test each

candidate solution, check whether the output results meet expectations, the accuracy, and whether it can identify the granular aspects of concern.

4. **Make a Decision:** Based on the objective results of the proof of concept, combined with factors such as cost and integration difficulty, finally select the most suitable tool or path.

Through this systematic method, you can avoid being misled by exaggerated marketing promotions and ensure that the selected sentiment analysis solution truly meets business needs, converting the "VoC" and "Pulse of Society" into actual strategic advantages.

Table 8.2 Sentiment analysis solution selection matrix.

Evaluation Dimension	Open-source Libraries	Cloud Vendor APIs	SaaS Platforms
Accuracy and customization needs	High, can be deeply customized for specific fields	Medium, partial fine-tuning available, limited customization	Low, mainly general models, difficult to deeply customize
Development resources and budget	High, requires professional technical team, high initial investment	Medium, requires certain development capabilities, pay-as-you-go	Low, no professional development team required, subscription-based payment
Data sources and language support	Flexible, can independently connect to various data sources, multi-language support needs to be handled by oneself	Relatively flexible, supports common data sources and multi-languages	Fixed, mostly connected to mainstream public data sources, limited language support
Deployment speed requirement	Slow, needs to complete model development, training, and deployment	Relatively fast, API integration is relatively simple	Fast, out-of-the-box
Interpretability and compliance	High, can independently control model logic, easy to meet compliance requirements	Medium, some provide interpretation functions, compliance depends on the vendor	Low, model logic is opaque, compliance depends on vendor commitments

References

1 Huang, D., Gao, R., Zhang, G., & Yu, J. (2026). SG-DTAM: Joint staged generation and dynamic time alignment for missing and unaligned modalities in sentiment analysis. *Expert Systems with Applications*, 299(PA), 129750.

2 Ye, F., & Zhao, Z. (2025). Scalable vortex search-tuned intelligent adaptive boosting for sentiment analysis of social media data using natural language processing. *Systems and Soft Computing*, 7, 200403.

3 Gnanapriya, S., & Anandan, K. (2025). Sentiment analysis of microblog text based on sentiment dictionary. *E-Learning and Digital Media*, 22(6), 505–522.

4 Jahanbin, K., & Chahooki, Z. A. M. (2025). Aspect-level sentiment analysis in social media using a hybrid deep transfer learning approach. *Knowledge-Based Systems*, 330(PA), 114125.

5 Arunmozhi, M., Sunitha, R., & Rajalakshmi, D. (2025). MADTRAS: Dataset for aspect-based sentiment analysis of movie reviews in Tamil. *Data in Brief*, 63, 112073.

6 Li, Z., & Zhao, K. (2026). RL-DFN: A reinforcement learning-driven dual-view feature fusion network for aspect-based sentiment analysis in online public opinion. *Expert Systems with Applications*, 298(PD), 129850.

7 Zhang, J., & Xiang, Y. (2025). Simplified syntax-guided domain-shared representation learning for cross-domain aspect-based sentiment analysis. *Engineering Applications of Artificial Intelligence*, 160(PB), 111934.

8 Yang, Z., He, Q., Yu, M., Du, N., & Lu, Y. (2026). TCTR: Text-guided contrastive learning with token-level reconstruction network for missing modalities in multimodal sentiment analysis. *Information Fusion*, 126(PA), 103571.

9 Lei, X., Ma, M., & Li, Y. (2025). DRLCCI: A hybrid fusion network leveraging disentangled representation learning and cross-modal collaborative interaction for multi-modal sentiment analysis. *Neurocomputing*, 658, 131733.

10 Omojowo, A. F. (2025). Hybrid data mining for pandemic public opinion analysis: Integrating sentiment, topic, and geolocation data. *Journal of Electrical Systems and Information Technology*, 12(1), 88.

11 Luo, Y., Liu, J., & Wu, R. (2025). Mitigating modality imbalance in multimodal sentiment analysis via emotion-enriched visual encoding and pyramid gated fusion. *Neurocomputing*, 658, 131746.

12 Dubey, K. A., & Saraswat, M. (2025). Adaptive BERT-assisted feature vector representation and ensemble deep learning approach for sentiment analysis with heuristic improvement. *Signal, Image and Video Processing*, 19(15), 1294.

13 Askarizade, M., & Davoodijam, E. (2025). Analyzing public sentiment in Iranian presidential elections on Twitter using large language models. *Journal of Computational Social Science*, 8(4), 102.

14 Charitha, B. S. N. B., & Radhika, R. (2025). Stacking based ensemble learning and BERT with FHO approach for analysing sentiment in Twitter big data. In *Progress in artificial intelligence* (pp. 1–18).

15 Annan, A., Eiden, L. A., Wang, D., Du, J., Rastegar-Mojarad, M., Nomula, V. K., & Wang, X. (2025). Evaluating large language models for sentiment analysis and hesitancy analysis on vaccine posts from social media: Qualitative study. *JMIR Formative Research*, 9, e64723.

9

Conclusion and Outlook

This final chapter serves as the culmination and synthesis of the exploration into sentiment analysis undertaken throughout this book. It is designed to consolidate the established knowledge, critically reflect on the field's broader implications, and chart a course for its future development.

The chapter commences with a comprehensive review, systematically retracing the technological trajectory of sentiment analysis and distilling the core value of its diverse applications to synthesize the book's primary findings. Building upon this retrospective foundation, the discussion pivots to a critical and extensive examination of the salient ethical dilemmas inherent in the technology. A significant portion of the chapter is devoted to a systematic analysis of multifaceted risks, from algorithmic bias and the potential for social manipulation to the emergent challenges of emotional privacy. In response, a structured framework for responsible AI governance is proposed.

Subsequently, the focus shifts toward the horizon of the field, outlining promising future research directions. This forward-looking section investigates the profound integration of sentiment analysis with causal inference, explainable AI, and the synergistic capabilities of generative AI. Crucially, it highlights the necessity of establishing a new paradigm centered on human-computer collaboration. The overarching aim of this chapter is to equip the reader with a perspective that is at once comprehensive and forward-looking, thereby fostering deep reflection on the responsible and impactful advancement of this transformative technology.

9.1 A Synthesis of the Field: Evolutionary Trajectory and Core Insights

This section systematically revisits and interconnects the core concepts presented throughout the book, constructing a coherent intellectual framework that spans from foundational techniques to frontier applications and from unimodal analysis to complex, multimodal scenarios. It synthesizes the technological evolution, consolidates the value proposition across various domains, and reexamines the persistent challenges and trade-offs inherent in the field.

9.1.1 The Technological Trajectory: From Rules to Cognitive Intelligence

The evolution of sentiment analysis is a compelling narrative of the relentless pursuit of deeper contextual understanding [1]. This trajectory, charted from Chapter 2 through Chapter 7, reveals a clear progression from simplistic keyword matching to sophisticated, near-human levels of semantic and affective comprehension.

The journey began with lexicon- and rule-based methods. These early approaches, relying on predefined dictionaries of polarized words and handcrafted grammatical rules, offered a transparent and computationally inexpensive means of gauging sentiment. However, their efficacy was fundamentally limited by their rigidity [2]. They struggled to decipher context, sarcasm, and domain-specific jargon, treating language as a static collection of words rather than a dynamic, meaning-rich system.

The advent of classic machine learning models, such as support vector machines (SVMs) and decision trees, marked the first major paradigm shift [3]. By leveraging statistical patterns from labeled data, these models moved beyond explicit keywords to learn implicit associations between features (e.g., n-grams) and sentiment categories. This statistical approach endowed systems with greater adaptability and robustness, enabling them to generalize to unseen text with significantly improved accuracy. Yet, their reliance on manual feature engineering remained a bottleneck, and their ability to capture long-range dependencies in text was constrained.

A revolutionary leap occurred with the rise of deep learning. Models like convolutional neural network (CNN), which excel at identifying local patterns (e.g., key phrases), and recurrent neural network (RNN), designed to process sequential information, fundamentally changed the game. These architectures could automatically learn hierarchical feature representations directly from raw text, effectively capturing the compositional structure of language. The introduction of mechanisms like long short-term memory (LSTM) units within RNNs specifically addressed the challenge of long-range dependencies, allowing for a more nuanced understanding of sentence-level context.

The most recent and transformative phase is defined by pretrained large language models (LLMs), epitomized by architectures like the Transformer and its prominent descendants, BERT and GPT. These models represent a paradigm shift from training task-specific models from scratch to fine-tuning massive models pretrained on vast internet-scale text corpora. Through self-supervised learning objectives like masked language modeling, LLMs acquire a profound, implicit knowledge of grammar, syntax, semantics, and even commonsense reasoning. This pretraining enables them to understand sentiment within intricate contexts, resolve ambiguities, and detect subtle emotional cues, including implicit sentiment and complex expressions across multiple modalities with unprecedented accuracy.

In essence, the core evolutionary logic of sentiment analysis technology is the escalating capacity for contextual understanding. This progression can be visualized as an ascent up a ladder of abstraction, as depicted in Figure 9.1. It begins at the word level (lexicons), advances to the statistical feature level (machine learning), then progresses to the sequential and hierarchical level (deep learning),

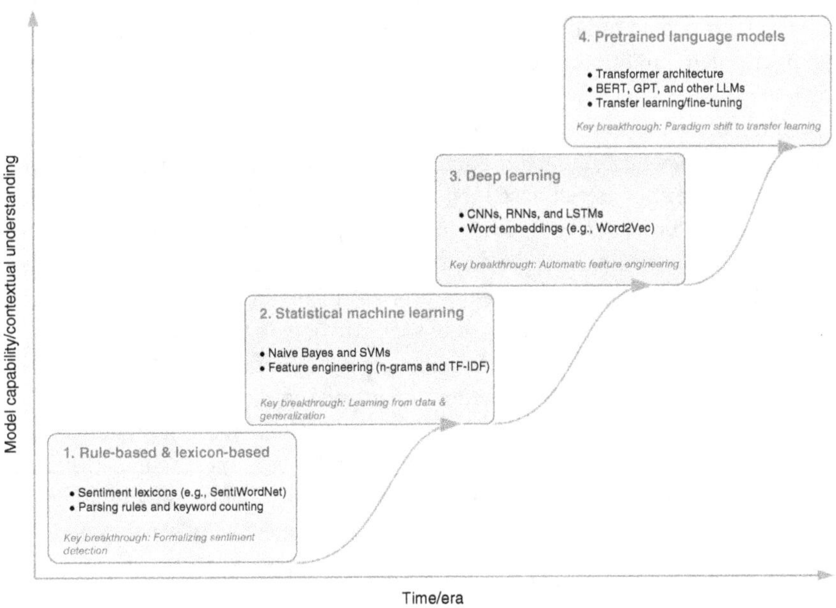

Figure 9.1 The evolutionary ladder of sentiment analysis technology. This diagram illustrates the four major stages of technological development on a timeline.

and culminates in a deep, generalized contextual intelligence (LLMs). Each stage overcame the limitations of its predecessor, pushing the frontier closer to the ultimate goal: a machine that can read between the lines.

9.1.2 The Value of Application: From Business Insight to Social Well-being

Beyond the intricacies of its technological evolution, the true measure of sentiment analysis lies in its capacity to translate unstructured human expression into actionable intelligence. As detailed in Chapter 8, its applications span a wide spectrum of domains, from the commercial imperatives of business intelligence to the critical needs of public safety and health [4]. A synthesis of these use cases reveals a consistent value chain, a four-stage framework that captures how organizations derive meaning and utility from sentiment data: listen, understand, predict, and respond.

The first and most fundamental value is the ability to listen. At this stage, sentiment analysis acts as a global-scale microphone, capturing the raw, unfiltered voice of the customer, the citizen, or the patient. For businesses, this means systematically monitoring product reviews, social media mentions, and support tickets to gauge brand perception and customer satisfaction. In the public sphere, it involves tuning into the collective conversation to gain an initial awareness of the societal mood or public pulse [5]. This stage transforms anecdotal evidence into aggregated, quantifiable data, providing a foundational awareness that was previously unattainable at scale.

Building upon this awareness, the next stage is to understand. Listening reveals what people are saying; understanding uncovers why. This is the diagnostic layer, where techniques like aspect-based sentiment analysis (ABSA) become invaluable [6]. A business, for instance, moves from knowing that a smartphone has negative reviews to understanding that the sentiment is driven specifically by poor battery life, while the screen quality is highly praised. In public safety, authorities can progress from detecting a general rise in social anxiety to understanding that it is linked to specific misinformation campaigns or policy announcements. This granular insight is the bedrock of targeted problem-solving.

The third stage elevates sentiment analysis from a reactive to a proactive tool: the ability to predict. By analyzing sentiment trends over time, organizations can forecast future outcomes and identify emerging issues before they escalate. In public health, analyzing shifts in language on social media can serve as an early warning system for deteriorating mental health trends or the outbreak of a public health crisis, as seen during the COVID-19 pandemic [7]. In finance, aggregated sentiment from news and social media can act as a leading indicator for market volatility or shifts in investor confidence. This predictive capacity enables strategic foresight and preemptive action.

Finally, the culmination of this value chain lies in the ability to respond. Actionable intelligence is the ultimate goal. In a crisis, real-time sentiment analysis can guide authorities' response, helping them allocate resources to areas where public fear is most acute or to craft public service announcements that directly address citizen concerns [8]. For a company, identifying a surge of negative sentiment around a software bug allows it to respond by prioritizing a patch and deploying customer support teams with empathic, sentiment-aware communication strategies. This final stage closes the loop, transforming passive data analysis into active, intelligent, and data-driven decision-making that can enhance commercial success, public safety, and overall societal well-being.

9.1.3 A Reassessment of Core Challenges and Trade-offs

A comprehensive review of sentiment analysis necessitates a pragmatic acknowledgment of its inherent challenges and the critical trade-offs that practitioners must navigate [9]. The preceding chapters have detailed specific technical hurdles; this section synthesizes them into a higher-level framework of persistent issues that shape the design and deployment of sentiment analysis systems.

One of the foremost challenges is data dependency and domain specificity. Models, particularly those based on deep learning, exhibit high performance when trained on large, domain-specific labeled datasets. However, they often suffer a significant performance degradation when applied to a new domain, a problem known as domain shift. The linguistic expressions of sentiment in product reviews, for example, differ substantially from those in financial news or political discourse. Addressing this requires sophisticated domain adaptation techniques or the costly process of curating new datasets for each application area.

A second major challenge lies in the complexity of linguistic phenomena. Sentiment is not always conveyed through explicit emotional words. The difficulty of identifying implicit sentiment, as explored in Chapter 4, remains a significant research frontier. Phenomena such as sarcasm, irony, and sentiment expressed through metaphors or conditional statements require a level of world knowledge and commonsense reasoning that most models still lack [10]. Similarly, the fusion of multiple modalities, text, audio, and visual data, introduces complexities in feature alignment, synchronization, and interpretation, making multimodal sentiment analysis a technically demanding task [11]. The nuances of cross-lingual and cross-cultural sentiment expression further compound this issue, as emotional cues can be culturally specific and lose their meaning in direct translation.

These technical challenges give rise to a series of fundamental practical trade-offs. The most prominent is the balance between model performance and computational cost. While LLMs offer state-of-the-art accuracy, their substantial computational requirements for training and inference can be prohibitive for many organizations, creating a barrier to adoption. This necessitates a careful evaluation of whether the marginal performance gains of a larger model justify its operational expenditure.

Another critical trade-off exists between automation efficiency and human oversight. Fully automated systems can process vast amounts of data at high speed, but they risk propagating errors or biases at scale. Incorporating a human-in-the-loop approach, such as having experts review low-confidence predictions, improves accuracy and accountability but reduces throughput and increases costs. Determining the appropriate level of human intervention is a crucial strategic decision for any real-world deployment.

Finally, all technical and practical considerations are constrained by the overarching trade-off between technological capability and ethical boundaries. The very power of sentiment analysis to infer emotional states raises profound questions about privacy, bias, and manipulation. The pursuit of more accurate and invasive models must be continually weighed against the potential for societal harm, a topic that will be examined in greater depth in the subsequent section. This tension defines the responsible frontier of the field.

9.2 The Ethical Compass: Navigating Responsibly in the Age of Affective Computing

The increasing integration of sentiment analysis into critical decision-making processes mandates a rigorous and systematic examination of its ethical implications [12]. This section moves beyond a cursory mention of ethics to provide a deep and structured analysis of the risks inherent in the technology. It serves as both a serious caution to the industry and a call to action for the development of responsible AI governance.

9.2.1 The Magnifying Glass Effect of Algorithmic Bias

Algorithmic bias in sentiment analysis is not a mere technical flaw; it is a mechanism that can systematically amplify existing societal prejudices, leading to discriminatory and inequitable outcomes. The models function as a magnifying glass, taking subtle, often implicit, biases present in human-generated data and reflecting them back with the scale and authority of an automated system.

The origins of this bias are multifaceted. The most significant source is the training data itself. Language models trained on vast swaths of internet text inevitably absorb the stereotypes and historical biases embedded within that data. For instance, models may learn to associate certain demographic groups (defined by race, gender, nationality, or disability) with more negative sentiment, not because of the intrinsic meaning of the text, but because of the prejudiced context in which these groups are often discussed. A sentiment analysis model might, therefore, incorrectly flag a neutral statement about a minority group as toxic or negative simply due to the statistical co-occurrence of that group's identifier with negative language in the training corpus.

Bias also originates from the annotation process. When human annotators are tasked with labeling data, their own subjective cultural backgrounds and personal beliefs can influence their judgments. This is particularly problematic for ambiguous or culturally nuanced text. Disagreements among annotators are often resolved by majority vote, a process that can silence minority perspectives and codify the dominant group's interpretation of sentiment as the ground truth. The model architecture can further entrench bias. Foundational components like word embeddings have been shown to learn stereotypical analogies, and when these are used, the bias propagates through the entire system.

The consequences of deploying biased sentiment models are severe and far-reaching. In recruitment, an automated resume screener might unfairly penalize applications by misinterpreting culturally specific language. In credit scoring, a model could assign a higher risk profile to individuals from certain areas by misreading the sentiment of their application text. In content moderation, a biased system could disproportionately flag content from marginalized communities as hateful, effectively silencing their voices while being more permissive toward harmful speech from dominant groups. In each case, the result is a reinforcement of existing social inequalities, cloaked in the veneer of objective, data-driven decision-making.

Addressing this challenge requires a multilayered mitigation framework. A structured overview of the primary ethical risks and their corresponding mitigation strategies is presented in Table 9.1. This framework categorizes solutions across four crucial levels: data, model, application, and governance, providing a comprehensive roadmap for responsible practice.

As outlined in the table, interventions must occur at every stage of the AI lifecycle. At the data level, this involves rigorous auditing and debiasing efforts. At the model level, techniques like adversarial training or the introduction of fairness constraints can guide the learning process away from biased outcomes. At the application level, systems must be designed with safeguards, such as robust monitoring of performance across different demographic groups. Finally, at the governance level, organizations must establish clear policies, promote diversity within their teams, and commit to external audits and transparency. By implementing such a comprehensive framework, developers and organizations can begin to counteract the magnifying effect of bias, moving toward sentiment analysis systems that are not only accurate but also equitable.

Table 9.1 Ethical risks and multi-level mitigation strategies in sentiment analysis.

Risk Type	Specific Manifestations	Data-level Mitigation	Model-level Mitigation	Application-level Mitigation	Governance-level Mitigation
Algorithmic bias	Stereotypical associations (gender, race, etc.) Silencing marginalized voices via content moderation	Dataset auditing and bias measurement Balanced data augmentation & resampling Debiasing of word embeddings	Adversarial training to remove protected attribute information Fairness constraints in the model's loss function	Disaggregated performance monitoring Transparency in model limitations	Regular third-party bias audits Establishing clear organizational fairness metrics
Emotional manipulation & social engineering	Exploiting emotional vulnerability for predatory marketing Inauthentic amplification of political narratives	Labeling and filtering known sources of disinformation Curating datasets to train detectors for manipulative language	Developing models for coordinated inauthentic behavior detection Proactive detection of synthetic/AI-generated propaganda	Clear labeling of sponsored or AI-generated content Rate-limiting and behavioral analysis of suspicious accounts	Strong industry self-regulation and codes of conduct Collaboration with researchers and fact-checkers
Invasion of emotional privacy	Inferring sensitive states (e.g., mental health) without consent De-anonymization of individuals through emotional profiles	Data anonymization and aggregation Adherence to data minimization principles (collect only what is necessary)	Federated learning: Training models without centralizing user data Differential privacy: Adding statistical noise to protect individual privacy	Granular and explicit user consent controls for emotion analysis Transparent and easy-to-understand privacy policies	Compliance with data protection regulations (e.g., GDPR) Establishing internal Data Ethics Review Boards

9.2.2 The Risk of Emotional Manipulation and Social Engineering

As sentiment analysis technology matures, its capabilities are shifting from passively interpreting emotion to actively influencing it. This transition presents a profound ethical risk, transforming the technology from a tool that reads minds to one that can potentially control hearts. The ability to understand and predict emotional states at a massive scale creates opportunities for manipulation, both for commercial and political ends.

In the commercial sphere, the line between persuasive marketing and emotional exploitation is becoming increasingly blurred. Personalized advertising has long used demographics and browsing history to target consumers. The integration of real-time sentiment analysis adds a dangerous new dimension. Systems can now identify moments of emotional vulnerability, such as stress, sadness, or insecurity, and use these windows of opportunity to push targeted advertisements for products promising relief or happiness. This practice, sometimes termed emotional hacking, moves beyond informing consumer choice and begins to prey on psychological states for profit, raising serious questions about predatory capitalism and consumer autonomy.

The risks are even more pronounced in the sociopolitical domain, where sentiment analysis becomes a tool for social engineering. Malicious actors can leverage these technologies to orchestrate large-scale disinformation campaigns with unprecedented precision. Instead of simply broadcasting a false narrative, they can craft and distribute content designed to evoke specific emotional responses, outrage, fear, or tribal affiliation, within targeted demographic groups. By monitoring the real-time emotional impact of their content via social media, they can dynamically adjust their messaging to maximize its divisive effect. This creates a feedback loop where sentiment analysis is used to identify societal fault lines, and AI-generated content is deployed to fracture them further.

The consequences of such emotional manipulation are dire. It can be used to suppress voter turnout, incite social unrest, erode trust in public institutions, and polarize public discourse to the point of paralysis. The coordinated use of bot armies and paid troll farms, guided by sophisticated sentiment analysis, can create the illusion of a widespread grassroots movement, effectively manufacturing social consensus or outrage. This undermines the very foundation of a healthy public sphere, where authentic dialogue and reasoned debate are essential.

Countering this threat requires a multipronged approach focused on detection and governance. Paralleling the development of deepfake detection, the research community must prioritize the creation of robust mechanisms for identifying emotionally inauthentic content and coordinated manipulation campaigns. This involves analyzing not just the content itself but also the behavioral patterns of its dissemination. From a governance perspective, social media platforms bear a significant responsibility. They must move beyond reactive content takedowns to proactively detecting and disrupting inauthentic behavior. Furthermore, greater transparency is needed regarding algorithmic amplification; users should have a clearer understanding of why they are being shown certain content. Industry self-regulation, coupled with clear public policy, is essential to establish and enforce standards that prevent sentiment analysis from becoming a weapon in the information ecosystem.

9.2.3 Emotional Privacy: The New Frontier of Personal Data

The evolution of data privacy concerns has historically focused on the protection of personally identifiable information, data points like names, addresses, and social security numbers that explicitly identify an individual. However, the advanced capabilities of sentiment analysis are forcing a necessary expansion of this paradigm. The technology's ability to infer an individual's inner emotional and psychological states introduce a new, deeply personal category of sensitive information, giving rise to the concept of emotional privacy.

This concept posits that an individual's emotional state is not merely another data point to be collected and analyzed; it is an intrinsic aspect of their personhood. The unauthorized inference, collection, and use of this emotional data constitute a unique and profound form of privacy invasion. Unlike personally identifiable information, which is often knowingly and voluntarily shared, emotional data can be inferred surreptitiously from text, voice, and facial expressions without an individual's explicit awareness or consent. An analysis of a person's social media posts, for example, could be used to build a detailed emotional profile, revealing patterns of anxiety, depression, or political outrage, information that the individual would likely never choose to share explicitly.

This continuous and often covert emotional surveillance has significant implications. Such data can be used to discriminate against individuals in areas like employment or insurance, where a profile suggesting emotional instability could lead to adverse decisions. It can also create a chilling effect on free expression, as individuals may become hesitant to express genuine emotions online for fear of being profiled, judged, or manipulated. The creation of persistent emotional profiles threatens individual autonomy, potentially locking people into feedback loops where platforms continually feed them content that reinforces their current emotional state, making it harder to escape cycles of negativity or outrage.

Protecting emotional privacy requires a combination of advanced technology and updated legal frameworks. From a technical standpoint, privacy-preserving machine learning (PPML) techniques are crucial. As mentioned in Chapter 7 and highlighted in Table 9.1, federated learning offers a powerful model. It allows sentiment analysis models to be trained on user data directly on their local devices (e.g., smartphones) without the raw data ever being sent to a central server. Only the aggregated model updates are shared, preserving individual privacy. Another key technology is differential privacy, which adds a mathematically calibrated amount of statistical noise to the outputs of a data analysis. This makes it possible to gather aggregate insights about a population's sentiment while making it impossible to determine with certainty whether any single individual's data was included in the analysis, thus providing a strong guarantee of personal privacy.

However, technology alone is insufficient. Legal and regulatory frameworks must evolve to recognize emotional data as a distinct and highly sensitive category of personal information. Existing regulations like the GDPR in Europe provide a strong foundation with principles like purpose limitation and data minimization, but future legislation may need to explicitly address the unique challenges of inferred data, including neurodata and emotional states. A clear legal status for emotional privacy would mandate explicit, granular consent from users before their emotional states can be inferred and used, shifting the power dynamic from data collectors back to the individual. Ultimately, safeguarding this new frontier of privacy is essential for ensuring that the benefits of sentiment analysis do not come at the cost of human dignity and autonomy.

9.3 Future Research Directions

This final section looks to the future, outlining the most promising and transformative research avenues that will shape the next generation of sentiment analysis. These directions point toward a future where models move beyond simple classification to achieve a more profound, human-like understanding of emotion and its underlying causes, all while operating transparently and collaboratively with human users.

9.3.1 Toward Deeper Understanding

A primary limitation of contemporary sentiment analysis is its reliance on correlational patterns rather than a true understanding of causal relationships. The field's next great leap will involve moving beyond pattern recognition to achieve a deeper, more robust form of comprehension, a goal that rests on three interconnected pillars: causality, commonsense, and explainability [13, 14].

The first frontier is the shift from correlation to causation. Current models excel at identifying that certain words are associated with negative sentiment, but they cannot reliably answer why a user holds a particular sentiment. This is the domain of causal inference [15]. The goal is to develop models that can distinguish true drivers of opinion from incidental features or confounding variables. For example, a customer review might state, "The setup was a nightmare, but once it was running, the performance was incredible." A correlation-based model might struggle with the conflicting signals. A causal model, however, would aim to identify that the nightmare setup is the cause of the negative sentiment regarding the setup process, while incredible performance is the cause of the positive sentiment regarding the product's function. The nascent exploration of integrating causal discovery algorithms and structural causal models into NLP pipelines will enable systems to provide more actionable insights, identifying the specific product features or service elements that truly drive customer satisfaction or dissatisfaction.

Complementary to the pursuit of causality is the infusion of commonsense reasoning. Many of the remaining errors in sentiment analysis stem from a model's lack of basic knowledge about how the world works. Sarcasm, irony, and metaphors are particularly challenging because their interpretation depends on a shared understanding of context that is often unstated. For instance, understanding the negative sentiment in "My new phone's battery life is as long as a mayfly's" requires knowing that a mayfly has a very short lifespan. The future lies in integrating large-scale commonsense knowledge graphs into sentiment models. This would equip them with a structured understanding of everyday concepts, social interactions, and physical properties, allowing them to read between the lines and more accurately interpret language that relies heavily on implicit, real-world context.

Finally, as models become more causally aware and commonsensical, their internal complexity will increase. This makes explainable AI not a luxury but a necessity. To trust and act upon a model's output, especially in high-stakes domains, users must be able to understand its decision-making process. The integration of explainable AI techniques is essential for opening this black box. Methods like LIME (Local Interpretable Model-agnostic Explanations) and SHAP (SHapley Additive exPlanations) can highlight the specific words or phrases that most influenced a particular sentiment prediction, providing localized, instance-based transparency. Furthermore, attention visualization, discussed in Chapter 6, can be extended to provide clearer insights into a model's reasoning chain. In finance, an explainable AI-enabled system could justify why a news article was flagged as having negative market sentiment. In healthcare, it could explain which aspects of a patient's feedback led to a negative satisfaction score. This transparency is indispensable for debugging models, ensuring fairness, building user trust, and enabling meaningful human oversight.

9.3.2 The Synergistic Evolution of Generative AI

The role of Generative AI in the sentiment analysis ecosystem extends far beyond its initial application in data augmentation. The future points toward a more profound, symbiotic relationship where sentiment analysis capabilities are not just enhanced by, but deeply integrated with, generative models. This synergy promises to shift the paradigm from passive analysis to active, emotionally aware creation and interaction [16].

A significant frontier in this integration is the development of empathic conversational AI. Current chatbots can process factual queries but often fail to respond appropriately to the user's emotional state. The next generation of these systems will use sentiment analysis as a core perceptual component. In this model, sentiment analysis acts as the ears of the system, discerning the user's emotional tone—such as frustration, delight, or distress—from their textual or vocal input. This emotional inference then serves as a critical condition for an LLM's generative response. The generative model is tasked not only with providing a relevant answer but with crafting it in an emotionally resonant tone. In customer service, this could mean an AI agent that responds to a frustrated customer with calming and validating language before offering a solution. In mental health and digital companionship, it could lead to empathic chatbots capable of providing accessible, nonjudgmental emotional support by mirroring and responding to a user's affective state.

Beyond interaction, this synergy is poised to revolutionize emotion-driven content creation. Here, sentiment analysis provides the creative brief, and the generative model acts as the creator. This process enables the automated generation of content designed to elicit a specific emotional response from a target audience. For instance, a marketing team could define an objective of inspiring trust or creating a sense of urgency. A generative model, guided by these emotional parameters, could then produce a range of advertisement copy, social media posts, or product descriptions. This can even form a closed-loop system, where a sentiment analysis model evaluates the generated content, provides feedback, and prompts the generative model to refine its output until it achieves the desired emotional impact. The applications of this capability are vast, from generating news headlines that accurately reflect the tone of an article to composing brand messaging aligned with a company's emotional identity. In more creative domains, it opens up possibilities for generating poetry, music, or narrative scripts that are tailored to specific emotional arcs. This evolution marks a pivotal shift, transforming sentiment analysis from a tool for understanding existing human expression to a foundational component in the creation of new, emotionally intelligent digital content and experiences.

9.3.3 A New Paradigm of Human-computer Collaboration

The pursuit of increasingly sophisticated models does not diminish the role of human expertise; on the contrary, it highlights its indispensability. The notion of fully autonomous, fire-and-forget sentiment analysis systems is receding, being replaced by a more pragmatic and powerful paradigm centered on human-computer collaboration. In many complex, ambiguous, or high-stakes scenarios, striving for 100% automation is not only unrealistic but also irresponsible. The future of applied sentiment analysis lies in designing intelligent systems that learn continuously from, and work synergistically with, human experts.

A key mechanism for enabling this collaboration is active learning. Instead of relying on a static, pre-labeled dataset, an active learning system is designed to be dynamically updated. The model can identify the data points it is most uncertain about—the edge cases, the ambiguous statements, or the novel expressions it has not seen before. It then proactively presents these specific, high-value samples to a human expert for labeling. This creates a highly efficient human-in-the-loop feedback cycle. The model performs the heavy lifting of analyzing the vast majority of data it is confident about, while human cognitive effort is reserved for the most challenging and informative cases. This approach minimizes the cost and effort of manual annotation while maximizing the velocity of model improvement.

This collaborative model redefines the role of the technology from a simple automated tool to a partner in intelligence augmentation. The sentiment analysis system acts as an "intelligent assistant" for human analysts. It can process millions of data points in real-time, perform the initial classification, identify emerging trends, and flag anomalies that would be impossible for a human to detect manually. This relieves analysts from the tedious task of sifting through raw data and allows them to focus on higher-order cognitive tasks: interpreting the model's outputs, applying domain-specific context, validating critical insights, and formulating strategic decisions. The result is a synergistic outcome where the scale and speed of the machine are combined with the depth, intuition, and ethical judgment of the human expert, leading to insights that neither could achieve alone.

Ultimately, the future of sentiment analysis is not a single, monolithic model but an integrated, intelligent ecosystem. As visualized in Figure 9.2, the core sentiment analysis engine will function as a central hub, deeply interconnected with modules for causal inference, commonsense knowledge, explainability, and generative AI. Crucially, this entire technical stack will be bridged to human experts through a dedicated human-computer collaboration platform, creating a dynamic system that is not only powerful and accurate but also transparent, adaptive, and responsibly governed.

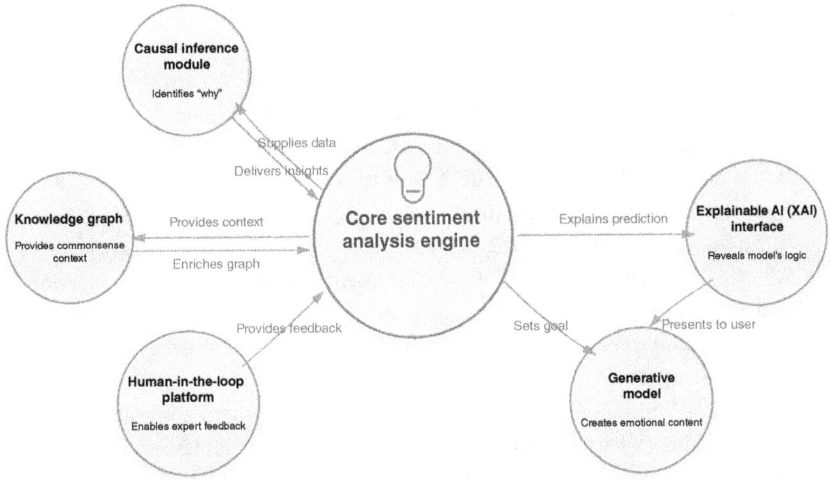

Figure 9.2 The integrated ecosystem of future sentiment analysis.

9.4 The Responsibility and Promise of Affective Intelligence

The journey through the profound capabilities of sentiment analysis chronicled in this book reveals a technology of immense power—a quintessential double-edged sword. Its capacity to decode human emotion at scale holds transformative potential for science, commerce, and society. Yet, this power demands an unwavering commitment to ethical stewardship. The central thesis that emerges is that its rapid technological advancement must be inseparably bound to a parallel maturation of our ethical frameworks and governance.

The pursuit of mere algorithmic precision is an insufficient goal. The greater, more urgent ambition must be to architect a technical ecosystem that is fundamentally fair, transparent, and respectful of human dignity. The ultimate promise of affective intelligence lies not in its capacity to predict or persuade but in its potential to foster deeper understanding, empathy, and connection. Its purpose must be to better understand and serve humanity, not to control or manipulate it. It is toward this responsible and humane future that the research and reflection within this book have been dedicated.

References

1 Cui, J., Wang, Z., Ho, S.-B., & Cambria, E. (2023). Survey on sentiment analysis: Evolution of research methods and topics. *Artificial Intelligence Review*. Advance online publication. https://doi.org/10.1007/s10462-022-10386-z

2 Bordoloi, M., & Biswas, S. K. (2023). Sentiment analysis: A survey on design framework, applications and future scopes. *Artificial Intelligence Review*. https://doi.org/10.1007/s10462-023-10442-2

3 Alharbi, A., & de la Prieta, F. (2024). Sentiment analysis methods, applications, and challenges: A systematic literature review. *Journal of King Saud University - Computer and Information Sciences*, 36(8), 102048. https://doi.org/10.1016/j.jksuci.2024.102048

4 Villanueva-Miranda, I., Xie, Y., & Xiao, G. (2025). Sentiment analysis in public health: A systematic review of the current state, challenges, and future directions. *Frontiers in Public Health*, 13, 1609749. https://doi.org/10.3389/fpubh.2025.1609749

5 Bunting, R. F., & Crane, J. (2015). A sentiment analysis of patient safety event reports. *Proceedings of the International Symposium on Human Factors and Ergonomics in Health Care*, 4(1), 140–144. https://doi.org/10.1177/2327857915041026

6 Jain, R., Kumar, A., Nayyar, A., Dewan, K., Garg, R., Raman, S., & Ganguly, S. (2023). Explaining sentiment analysis results on social media texts through visualization. *Multimedia Tools and Applications*, 82(15), 22613–22629. https://doi.org/10.1007/s11042-023-14432-y

7 Saini, M., Sharan, A., & Basu, S. (2021). Applications of sentiment analysis and machine learning techniques in disease outbreak prediction—A review. *Materials Today: Proceedings*, 81(2), 1006–1011. https://doi.org/10.1016/j.matpr.2021.04.356

8 Vázquez-Morales, I., Xu, Y., & Xu, G. (2024). Sentiment analysis in public health: A systematic review of methodologies, applications, data challenges, and evaluation practices. *Frontiers in Public Health*, 12, 1475867. https://doi.org/10.3389/fpubh.2024.1475867

9 Zhang, Y., Zhu, Y., & Liu, Q. (2025). Generalizing sentiment analysis: A review of progress, challenges, and emerging directions. *Social Network Analysis and Mining*, 15, 1461. https://doi.org/10.1007/s13278-025-01461-8

10 Gao, X., Nayak, S., & Coler, M. (2024). Spoken in jest, detected in earnest: A systematic review of sarcasm recognition—Multimodal fusion, challenges, and future prospects. arXiv preprint arXiv:2509.04605.

11 Li, Z., Liu, P., Pan, Y., Ding, W., Yu, J., Chen, H., Liu, W., Luo, Y., & Wang, H. (2025). Multimodal sentiment analysis based on disentangled representation learning and cross-modal-context association mining. *Neurocomputing*, 617, 128940. https://doi.org/10.1016/j.neucom.2024.128940

12 Mohammad, S. M. (2022). Ethics sheet for automatic emotion recognition and sentiment analysis. *Computational Linguistics*, 48(2), 239–269. https://doi.org/10.1162/coli_a_00433

13 Arrieta, A. B., Díaz-Rodríguez, N., Del Ser, J., Bennetot, A., Tabik, S., Barbado, A., Herrera, F. (2023). Computational approaches to Explainable Artificial Intelligence: Advances in theory, applications and trends. *Information Fusion*, 100, 101945. https://doi.org/10.1016/j.inffus.2023.101945

14 Carloni, L. P. (2025). The role of causality in explainable artificial intelligence. *Wiley Interdisciplinary Reviews: Data Mining and Knowledge Discovery*, 15(3), e1515. https://doi.org/10.1002/widm.1515

15 Jiao, L., Wang, Y., Liu, X., Li, L., Liu, F., Ma, W., Guo, Y., Chen, P., Yang, S., & Hou, B. (2024). Causal inference meets deep learning: A comprehensive survey. *Research*, 7, 0467. https://doi.org/10.34133/research.0467

16 Schneider, J. (2024). Explainable generative AI (GenXAI): A survey, conceptualization, and research agenda. arXiv:2404.09554v1.

Index

b

C

h

i

n

u

v

www.ingramcontent.com/pod-product-compliance
Lightning Source LLC
LaVergne TN
LVHW010606120926
847902LV00003B/28